The Complete Book of
EVERGREENS

The Complete Book of
EVERGREENS

Kenneth A. Beckett

Line drawings by Rosemary Wise

VNR **VAN NOSTRAND REINHOLD COMPANY**
NEW YORK CINCINNATI TORONTO LONDON MELBOURNE

For L. Maurice Mason, a fine plantsman,
whose gardens in Norfolk provided
specimens for study and much
inspiration.

Text Copyright © 1981 by Kenneth A. Beckett
Line drawings Copyright © 1981 by Ward Lock Limited

Library of Congress Catalog Card Number 81-1849
ISBN 0-442-28255-9

Printed in Canada

Published by Van Nostrand Reinhold Company
A division of Litton Educational Publishing, Inc.
135 West 50th Street, New York, NY 10020, U.S.A.

Van Nostrand Reinhold Limited
1410 Birchmount Road
Scarborough, Ontario M1P 2E7, Canada

Published in Great Britain by
Ward Lock Limited, London, a Pentos Company

16 15 14 13 12 11 10 9 8 7 6 5 4 3 2 1

Library of Congress Cataloging in Publication Data

Beckett, Kenneth A.
   The complete book of evergreens

   1. Ornamental evergreens. I. Title.
SB428.B42 1981   635.9'75   81-1849
ISBN 0-442-28255-9   AACR2

Contents

Acknowledgements

The publishers gratefully acknowledge Gillian Beckett for granting permission to reproduce all the colour photographs.

All line drawings are by Rosemary Wise. The drawings on p. 139 (parts 1–4) and on p. 140 (parts 1–4) are after the illustrations on pp. 68 and 69 (parts 3, 5, 8 and 9) and p. 55 (parts 2, 3, 4 and 6) respectively, in *Plant Propagation*, by Philip McMillan Browse, published by Mitchell Beazley Publishers Ltd, 1979.

Preface

If a garden is ever to acquire that mature look, then some sort of permanent planting in the form of trees and/or shrubs must be made. Such plants are very much the backbone of the garden, providing substance and form. They also provide, as climbers on the walls and shrubs at their feet, a means of marrying home to garden in a most satisfying way. In the very small garden, a foundation planting of this sort can be an end in itself. In the larger garden it can provide a focal point, linking and unifying the various features.

All too often deciduous shrubs, trees and climbers are used, but by so doing the overall effect is lost once the leaves fall in autumn. In winter when the branches are bare and the garden is open to icy winds even the most ordinary of evergreens stands out and gladdens the eye. Evergreen trees and shrubs can provide winter wind shelter and a great diversity of shape, form, texture and colour. Many have richly green and glossy leaves, in some instances large and of tropical luxuriance. Some are variegated or flushed with shades of yellow, red, copper or purple, particularly when young, while others provide a bonus of attractive or interesting flowers and colourful fruits. For these reasons it needs only half an eye to see that evergreens would serve the purpose more efficiently and effectively. Not that I am advocating the total use of evergreens in any one garden. A combination with deciduous species would be ideal, using choice evergreens to occupy the key positions.

Evergreen trees and shrubs can be classified into two groups, broad-leaved and conifers. The former have broad-bladed leaves and flowers rather like those of their deciduous counterparts and belong to the same botanical families. The conifers are very different being more primitive in an evolutionary sense of lacking true flowers. Their reproductive organs ('flowers') are called strobili and consist of single sexed spikes or clusters of tiny scale leaves upon which are borne naked ovules and pollen sacs. After the wind-blown pollen has done its work, the female strobilus becomes the familiar woody cone—from which the conifers (*Coniferae*) derive their name. In overall appearance the conifers provide great contrast to the broad-leaved group. Their leaves are frequently very small and scale- or needle-like in shape, often surfaced or lined with blue-white or grey. They are usually arranged in fern-like sprays or stiff whorls which in turn, combine to create columns, pyramids and spires of great architectural potential. Not all are of this form, others form decorative mats, hummocks and buns. There are in fact, evergreens of every shape, hue and size suitable for the tiniest backyard or the grandest garden. Among the conifers can also be found the majority of the toughest and most cold resistant evergreens, some of which thrive naturally beyond the arctic circle. The worth of conifers in the garden is seen in their overall shape, colour and texture. Fewer broad-leaved trees and shrubs have outstanding architectural shapes, but many have fine foliage. The two groups then complement each other and should be used together for the best effects.

In the chapters that follow, I have described as many as possible of the garden worthy evergreens that can be grown in the cool temperate region. This region is a wide one in terms of absolute temperature and as considered here starts near the arctic zone and makes incursions into the warm temperature region many miles south. The intended readership is the gardeners of Britain, Europe, North America and hopefully similar temperate areas of the Southern Hemisphere, particularly New Zealand and south east Australia (including Tasmania). There is, however, undoubtedly less incentive to plant evergreens in these latter countries with their predominantly evergreen floras.

I am all for experimenting with the plants of so-called borderline hardiness in one's own area and quite a few have been included that need careful siting in the colder areas or some special winter protection when young. It may be that these

Contrasting examples of a broad-leaved and a coniferous tree. The conifer, *Picea omorika* (right), is entirely dominated by its spar-like main stem, whereas the broad-leaved *Quercus ilex* (holm oak) has many spreading branches none of which truly dominates.

plants will be cut back to ground level or even killed during the exceptionally cold winters but to have enjoyed them for a few years only gives great satisfaction to one's gambling instincts. Hardiness is such a tenuous thing and so many plants that have a reputation for tenderness survive in the most unlikely places. For those prepared to take up the challenge there will be unexpected rewards and some bitter disappointments.

For the hardiness ratings of all the plants mentioned, see the Index and numbered key that prefaces it.

All but a few of the plant descriptions are based upon specimens I have grown or observed in other gardens. Nevertheless I am indebted to such standard reference works as Hillier's *Manual of Trees and Shrubs* and Bean's *Trees and Shrubs Hardy in the British Isles* for the more technical details. I am also grateful to Richard Fulcher, Head Gardener of the National Trust for Scotland's Gardens at Inverewe, Scotland, who drew my attention to several fine-foliaged rhododendrons and later supplied specimens for the drawings.

While I have endeavoured to mention all the most useful and attractive evergreens, many more could have been described. In the end, the final list of species varieties and cultivars selected was largely one of personal favourites, but with commercial availability as a final criterion for inclusion. The 'complete' of the title therefore denotes that this book is one of a series, not that it contains a definitive text on evergreens. This situation does have its compensation though. Hopefully, what I have written will stimulate a desire to grow many more evergreens of all kinds. If it does, and when all I describe are finally tried, it will be a heartening thought to realize that many more await personal discovery.

Stanhoe   K.A.B.
Norfolk,
England

1 Conifers

CEDARS, CYPRESSES, FIRS AND PINES

Under one or other of the names above are to be found most of those plants collectively known as conifers. This latter term is a popular abbreviation of the Latin scientific name *Coniferae* for that class of primitive plants which, with some exceptions, produce their seeds in woody structures known as cones. Most conifers are evergreen trees, but a few are deciduous, e.g. larch and dawn redwood, and some are of shrub-like habit. Notable exceptions to the cone bearing habit are yew, plum-fruited yew and juniper. Technically, the juniper berry is a small fleshy cone, but in yew and plum-fruited yew the seeds are surrounded by a fleshy aril or arillus, a special covering attached to the seed coat. Although not unique to conifers, an intriguing habit of some species is the production of a different sort of foliage when young. This is known as juvenile foliage and is best seen when raising the various species of *Chamaecyparis*, *Cupressus*, *Thuja*, and *Juniperus* from seed. After the seed leaves have expanded, narrow or awl-shaped leaves develop, later to be followed by the tiny overlapping scale leaves typical of adult specimens. Some of the horticultural varieties (cultivars) retain their juvenile leaves throughout life and owe their appeal to this characteristic. In retrospect, it is now amusing to recall that

an earlier generation of botanists was fooled by this same juvenile leaf character and founded the genus *Retinospora* to contain such plants. Several cultivars of *Thuja* and *Chamaecyparis* were once so classified. Conifers combine extreme utility (they provide much of the world's timber and turpentine) with great beauty of form, texture and colouring. No garden, however small, should be without a few of them. If the garden is tiny there are even miniature and dwarf sorts, some natural species, others cultivars resulting from mutation, to provide interest throughout the year.

Arbor-vitae

According to some authorities arbor-vitae is the Latinized version of the French *l'arbre de vie* (the tree of life) a name bestowed upon *Thuja occidentalis* by a king of France in the sixteenth century. Whether apocryphal or not, this little story is certainly very apt, in view of the toughness and attractiveness of this genus of conifers known as *Thuja*. In appearance these trees much resemble the very familiar false cypresses (*Chamaecyparis*) in the nature of their flattened sprays of tiny overlapping gland dotted scale leaves. If cones are present however they quickly identify the bearer. *Chamaecyparis* cones are composed of 6–12 peltate (umbrella-shaped) scales, the heads of which fit together to form an angular globe. *Thuja* cones are elongated, composed of thin tapering scales the tips of which turn outwards when mature.

Eastern arbor-vitae

Hardiest of all is the above mentioned *T. occidentalis* from eastern Canada and North America south to Virginia and Tennessee. Variously known as American or eastern arbor-vitae and confusingly as eastern or northern white cedar, it forms a conical tree, often rather sparsely branched, to 20 m (60 ft) or so tall. When bruised, the generally rather yellow-green foliage has an aromatic odour reminiscent of apples. Although it thrives well in wet soils this arbor-vitae is not much cultivated in its wild form. There are, however, numerous, mostly dwarfer cultivars of great appeal and most suitable for the smaller garden. Quite commonly seen but none the less attractive is *T. o.* 'Rheingold'. It is fairly slow growing and seldom reaches above 3 m (10 ft) and at least when young has a broadly conical outline. The ample foliage is rich amber-gold in winter, paler in summer. It contrasts boldly with rich green conifers and other plants such as heaths and heathers or small leaved hebes. Small plants of 'Rheingold' may have awl-shaped juvenile foliage but in time this will give way to adult leaves.

For this reason there has been, and sometimes still is confusion with the name *T. o.* 'Ellwangerana Aurea' which effectively is a synonym of 'Rheingold'. Very different in appearance and seldom above 1 m (3 ft) in height is *T. o.* 'Ericoides', one of those juvenile leaved oddities originally placed under *Retinospora*. It is a dense, rounded to broadly conical, rather fluffy-looking shrub which is grey-green in summer and purplish-brown in winter. One of the tiniest of all dwarf conifers is

T. o. 'Hetz Midget' which forms tiny globes a few centimetres wide and is suitable for the smallest rock or sink garden.

Chinese arbor-vitae

Probably the most distinct of all the true *Thuja* species is *T. orientalis*, the Chinese arbor-vitae. Although outstanding specimens may attain 15 m (45 ft) in height, it is uncommon to see trees much above half this. They are sometimes of shrub-like form. Conical or columnar when young, older specimens may have oval to rounded heads and a very unconifer-like stance. In old age they become gaunt and shapeless. At closer quarters it can be seen to carry its compact and flattened branchlets vertically. A further identifying characteristic is the hooked or rolled tips to the scales of the prominently displayed cones. About 60 cultivars are known, some of the dwarf ones being very garden worthy. My favourites are *T. o.* 'Aurea Nana', forming an oval bush of bright greenish yellow, and 'Rosedalis' a most decorative, small chameleon changing from summer green to winter purple, then butter yellow with the young growth in spring.

Western arbor-vitae

Confusingly also known as western red or canoe cedar, the western or giant arbor-vitae, *Thuja plicata* is the largest species, attaining 60 m (200 ft) in its homeland. Still sometimes listed under the old name *T. lobbii* this majestic tree inhabits the high rainfall areas of west North America from Alaska south to north California. The glossy foliage is amply borne and on bruising exudes a very pleasant sweetly aromatic smell likened by some authorities to that of pineapple. This is a vigorous tree ultimately too large for the smaller garden but

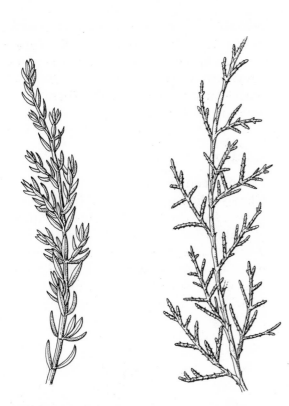
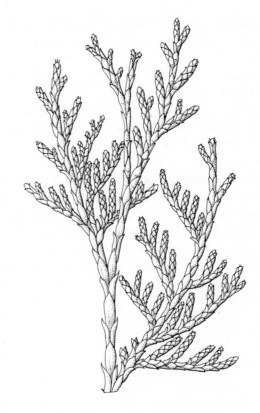

making a good wind-break or large hedge. It is also an important timber tree providing the highly rot-proof timber known as red cedar, now becoming better known in the construction of greenhouses. In the humid forests this thuja inhabits, it is quite common for seedlings to spring up in the mossy covering of wind-blown fallen trunks. The seedlings grow into trees, rooting into the soil on either side. Years of fallen leaves completely bury the original prostrate trunk. It says much for the durability of the wood that when the trees have been felled and the area cleared the original buried trunk has been sound enough to be used by carpenters. Among cultivars of full size, *T. p.* 'Zebrina' ('Aureovariegata') has foliage sprays banded with yellow providing what must surely be one of the best and most striking of variegated conifers. Among the dwarfs are the compact 'Stone-

Examples of conifer foliage: left, *Juniperus communis nana* with whorls of awl-shaped leaves; centre, *Cupressus glabra* and right, *Thuja plicata*, both with scale leaves.

ham Gold' in shades of bright golden yellow and bronze, and 'Hillieri', a rounded bush of mossy rich green foliage. The latter is reputed to have grown to 2·4 m (8 ft) in about 25 years.

Other arbor-vitae
Two other *Thuja* species are sometimes available and well worth seeking out. *T. standishii* (*T. japonica*) the Japanese arbor-vitae is a small tree with gracefully drooping loose sprays of yellow green foliage redolent of lemon verbena. Korean arbor-vitae, *T. koraiensis* is usually only of shrub size but it can be a narrowly conical small tree. The attractive foliage is carried

in large sprays, green to sea-green above, whitened beneath and rather pungently scented. The Hiba or false arbor-vitae of Japan is now classified in a genus of its own, *Thujopsis dolabrata*. It differs from the members of *Thuja* in having much larger, broader, boat-shaped scale leaves and larger, more rounded cones. The foliage is very glossy and conspicuously suffused with blue-white beneath. Although of tree size in its homeland, Hiba arbor-vitae is more often seen in western gardens as a large shrub. If a really tree-sized specimen is required, *T. dolabrata hondai* should be sought. It is the hardiest form with smaller but more boldly marked leaves. *T. d.* 'Aurea' is a much neglected gold-suffused

cultivar, and *T. d.* 'Nana' forms a dwarf bush. More often seen is *T. d.* 'Variegata', but though striking in its way, the rather irregularly-placed white shoots make each bush look as if it had been dive-bombed by an army of sparrows.

Cedars

Incense cedar

Closely allied to arbor-vitae is *Calocedrus* (*Libocedrus*) *decurrens* from the mountains of California, Oregon and Nevada. Like *Thuja plicata*, it has acquired the common name of cedar in various combinations. Incense cedar is the best known, but bastard, California post, red and white cedar

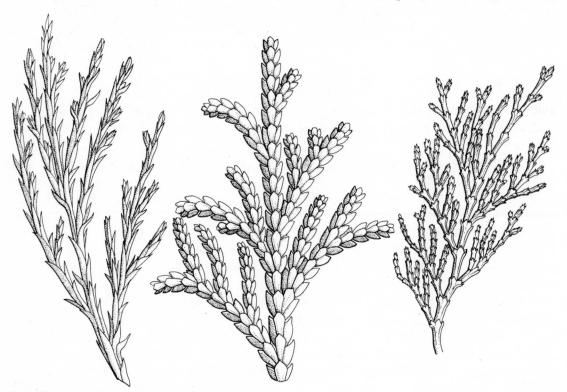

Examples of conifer foliage: right, *Calocedrus decurrens*; centre, *Thujopsis dolabrata*, both with flattened sprays of scale leaves, and left, *Sequoiadendron giganteum* with leaves that are halfway between scale and awl in form.

are listed. In foliage this hardy tree much resembles a *Thuja*, though the individual rich green scale leaves are more elongated. The cones appear to have only three long narrow scales but a closer look will reveal several more very small ones. The seeds too differ, each having a single wing after the fashion of firs and pines. (*Thuja* seeds have two smaller marginal wings or none at all.) In its homeland the incense cedar rises up to 35 m (116 ft) or more in height with spreading branches creating a broadly conical outline. Transplanted to Great Britain however, it assumes a columnar outline and has been used with great effect in the landscaping of large gardens. In most soils it grows vigorously, adding up to 60 cm (2 ft) to its height annually. The broad-based tapered trunk is clad with plates of red-brown bark that curl outwards at the edges. In common with western red cedar it yields a highly rot-resistant timber. For the smaller garden there are *C. d.* 'Compacta' and *C. d.* 'Nana', the latter growing 5–6 cm (2–2½ in) per annum and with branchlets that are curiously recurving and twisted.

The true cedars

A mention of the name cedar immediately conjures up in my mind a vision of the stately mansion surrounded by lawns from which arise strategically placed noble trees. In Britain at least, the true cedars (*Cedrus*) are often seen at their best in such situations. A maximum of four species is known and some botanists combine two of these to make only three. They are unique among the evergreen conifers in carrying most of their needle-like leaves in rings or whorls at the tips of short, slow growing spurs. Only the actively growing stem tips bear well spaced spirally borne leaves. The erect barrel-shaped cones are handsome objects taking two years to mature, then

disintegrating *in situ*, showering the ground beneath with scales and winged seeds. In all species the young trees form elegant spires but when mature (at 60–100 years old), they broaden out forming the characteristic wide crowns of plate-like branches. Best known and the hardiest—surviving −26°C (−15°F)—is *C. libani*, the cedar of Lebanon. Native to the mountains of Syria to south east Turkey it can attain 40 m (133 ft) but is usually less. It has very broad heads of the most magnificent plate-like branches clad generally in somewhat greyish green foliage, though darker and lighter tones occur. *C. l.* 'Aurea' is smaller growing with bright gold leafage. Cyprus cedar is sometimes considered to be a variety of the cedar of Lebanon and called *C. l. brevifolia* though most nurserymen still list it as a separate species, *C. brevifolia*. It is obviously much akin to *C. libani* but is smaller and much narrower in habit with leaves only about half the length. It is the best choice for the smaller garden but can still attain 18 m (60 ft) when well sited.

Although somewhat less spreading when mature, the typical Atlas or Algerian cedar, *C. atlantica*, is much like the cedar of Lebanon. In cultivation, however, it is usually represented by its superbly blue-grey form, *C. a.* 'Glauca', which immediately renders it distinct. All too often the lure of its bright foliage results in its being planted in small suburban gardens where it can soon outgrow its welcome. At this stage the indignity of lopping has to be resorted to or felling long before its stately maturity can be achieved. Where room is restricted try *C. a.* 'Pendula' or 'Pendula Glauca', both weeping trees of real distinction. When mature they produce a living curtain which shimmers in the breeze. Even so, 8–10 m (25–33 ft) in height must be allowed for development. If there is a desire to grow this tree in less expansive conditions than it really requires, then the erect, columnar form C. a. 'Fastigiata' should be chosen.

A native of the western Himalayas and the mountains of adjacent Afghanistan, the deodar, C. deodara is easily identified by its longer leaves—3–5 cm (1¼–2 in) long—and spire-like top to its crown of branches, even when old. Young trees are particularly elegant and very fast growing in fertile soils; 90 cm (3 ft) or more is possible each year. Certainly not a tree for the small garden, but where room allows, it is one of the most satisfying of all conifers.

Japanese cedar

Quite unlike the cedars and equally un-related is the Japanese red cedar, *Crypto-meria japonica*. It might well be described as Japan's answer to the American red-wood, and indeed botanically the two are fairly closely related. It is in fact native to both China and Japan but plays a greater part in the economic and aesthetic life of the people of the latter country. There, it forms a large percentage of the planted state forests and is also widely grown in temple and other gardens. Aged specimens are almost as impressive as the redwoods with their soaring red-brown fibrous boles and tapered but blunt-topped heads of bright green foliage cleaving the sky at 45 m (150 ft) or more. To see them like this, however, one must go to Japan where they frequently grace the environs of shrines and temples in a most satisfying way. I still treasure the memory of a visit to Nikko and the superb Toshogu Shrine which is set among the living columns of giant crypto-meria boles and shaded by their pendulous foliage.

The leaves of cryptomeria are awl-shaped, flattened vertically and with a winged base. Juvenile leaves are spreading and soft textured, to 2 cm (¾ in) long; adult leaves curve inwards, are firm to the touch and rarely exceed 15 mm (⅗ in) in length. In British gardens at least, the permanently juvenile form C. j. 'Elegans' is most frequently seen. It forms a soft, fluffy column or cone of bright bluish-green foliage which turns reddish-bronze in winter. Best in shelter from strong winds it is slower growing than the species and suitable for the smaller garden, but in time can achieve 10 m (30 ft) or more. 'Cristata' is more curious than beautiful, its adult foliage partly fasciated, i.e. groups of stems fused together to form cockscombs. It is sometimes sold as a dwarf conifer, but it can ultimately get quite large.

'Bandai-sugi' is a true dwarf that arose in Japan. Growing 3–4 cm (1¼–1½ in) a year it forms congested bushlets of normal shoots and mossy tufts. My own favourite is 'Vilmoriniana' which forms a neat globular shrublet of great density, expanding at only 2 cm (¾ in) per annum.

Cypresses

As with cedar, so the name cypress is sometimes applied to trees distinct from the true cypresses, botanically members of the genus *Cupressus*. They are distinguished by scale-like leaves which overlap along the stems to create a whipcord pattern. These stems freely branch to form three-dimensional sprays, quite distinct from the similar but flattened ones of the arbor-vitae and false cypress. A further point of difference is in the comparatively larger cones, though this is not a consistent characteristic among the species. There are about 20 species scattered around the northern hemisphere but only a few are in general cultivation and even fewer are hardy in continental climates. In this latter category,

C. arizonica and *C. glabra* are outstanding as decorative trees for the moderate-sized garden. Both form dense, broadly conical trees, *C. glabra* with smooth purplish bark which blisters and flakes to disclose reddish to yellowish patches. *C. arizonica* has finely fissured stringy bark and grey-green foliage, while the better known *C. glabra* varies from grey to blue-green and is generally represented in gardens by *C. g.* 'Pyramidalis' with bright blue-grey leaves. There is much confusion in gardens and in Britain at least plants which are labelled *C. arizonica* are usually *C. glabra*. Hardiest of all is the Modoc cypress, *C. bakeri* and the similar but taller Siskiyou cypress, *C. b. matthewsii*, but they are not readily available from nurserymen.

Monterey cypress

Planted as an ornamental tree around the world where winters are not severe is the Monterey cypress, *Cupressus macrocarpa*. Curiously enough this is a rare tree in the wild, occupying an area of sea coast only about two miles long at Monterey, California. There it presents a picturesque sight, particularly the gnarled and wind-blown specimens that cling tenaciously to the bare rocks just above the sea. In this last refuge and homeland, the Monterey cypress is much at variance with its descendants growing in cooler, wetter climes. Had I not been taken to see these wild trees I should have very much doubted their identity; trunks were short or almost non-existent and the branches ascended at a sharp angle. Only in later years did I see similar (planted) specimens near the coast of Chile. Obviously the long hot summers and sea winds have a profound effect upon the growth pattern of this tree. As the name *macrocarpa* suggests it has the largest cones of its genus, varying from 2·5–4 cm

(1–1½ in) long though only just beating its counterpart across the Atlantic, the Mediterranean cypress.

Monterey cypress has given rise to several cultivars, brightest and best in my opinion being the rich yellow juvenile 'Goldcrest', with the similar but adult 'Donard Gold' as a close runner-up. There are also several very dwarf cultivars, e.g. 'Globosa', 'Minima' ('Minimax') and 'Pygmaea' but they are not particularly exciting and few nurserymen stock them. *Cupressus macrocarpa* is fast growing and makes a good wind-break, particularly near the sea and in milder regions. All too frequently it is planted as a quick hedge but it does not stand close clipping well and often becomes bare at the base.

Funeral cypress

Cupressus sempervirens is the Mediterranean or funeral cypress. It is similar to the Monterey cypress in foliage and cones, though the latter are somewhat smaller and the seeds are smooth (those of *C. macrocarpa* are studded with tiny resin tubercles). In habit, however, the two species are very distinct. The differences are even more obvious to gardeners, as the Mediterranean cypress is almost entirely represented in cultivation by the columnar form sometimes listed as 'Stricta' or 'Fastigiata', but these cultivar names are superfluous as it was the columnar form that the great botanist Linnaeus first described and named. It is one of the most telling components of the landscape of southern Europe and is remarked upon even by people otherwise not interested in trees. It is certainly fair to say that many coastal areas of southern Europe owe their distinctive appearance to the groves and clumps of slim dark green columns that seem to march across the landscape. In northern climes the columns may be less slim and in severe winters the foliage browns. If the slimmest trees possible are required then the New Zealand raised *C. s.* 'Gracilis' should be chosen, while the Australian 'Swaine's Gold' is tinted with shades of bright gold. The original wild species distinguished as *C. s. horizontalis*, is rarely seen in gardens. It is a pyramidal tree at least when young, with horizontal branches and a much looser habit. There is an impressive avenue of this tree on the Jugoslav island of Lokrum in the Adriatic.

Leyland cypress

Linking the true with the false cypresses, discussed below are several hybrids between them, one of which, × *Cupressocyparis leylandii* has become extremely popular in Great Britain and is grown in other countries with a similar climate. It first arose spontaneously at Leighton Hall, Welshpool, Wales, in 1888 appearing in a batch of seedlings raised from seeds collected from a Nootka cypress growing close to a Monterey cypress. In appearance it favours the Nootka parent but is much stronger growing, with cones intermediate in size and less aromatic foliage. Its decorative appearance, speed of growth (31 m (100 ft) in 50 years is recorded) and resistance to exposure make it ideal as a quick wind-break or tall hedge. The original plants varied in relative width of columnar habit and foliage colour, and at least five clones have been named. 'Haggerston Grey' is probably the commonest clone commercially available, with 'Leighton' as a runner-up. Worth seeking is 'Naylor's Blue', the foliage of which has a decidedly blue-grey cast particularly in winter. More recently other hybrids have arisen, but still with *Chamaecyparis nootkatensis* as one parent. × *Cupressocyparis notabilis* involves

Cupressus glabra, while × *C. ovensii* has *Cupressus lusitanica* as the other parent. Both are promising new conifers and should be looked out for.

THE FALSE CYPRESSES

Closely allied to the true cypresses are those dubbed false though the term is comparatively recent and only one of convenience. At one time the false cypresses, *Chamaecyparis*, were combined with *Cupressus* but later separated on account of the flattened scale leaves arranged in frond-like two-dimensional sprays and the generally smaller cones and seeds. The species described below are hardier than the true cypresses but need shelter from severe wind frosts. They will also tolerate shadier sites. Seedlings pass through the same juvenile stage as *Cupressus* and *Thuja*; this characteristic is fixed in some cultivars.

Lawson cypress

Best known of all the *Chamaecyparis*, at least in Britain, is the Lawson cypress, *C. lawsoniana*. Rejoicing in such alterative and confusing names as Port Orford, Oregon and white cedar, spruce gum and ginger pine, this handsome columnar tree inhabits the moist oceanic climate that prevails in south west Oregon and north west California. Considering this fact, its hardiness is remarkable, temperatures of −26°C (−15°F) without damage being recorded. In the wild it can attain 60 m (200 ft) but seldom rises much above half this elsewhere. The rich green foliage has a curiously pungent aroma, by some likened to that of parsley. The male catkins are crimson in spring and though individually tiny are often borne in such profusion as to give the tree a reddish glow. The highly durable timber is fragrant and can be finished with a glossy surface. It is used for house flooring, furniture and boat building and in the construction of aircraft, etc. The rounded cones are about 7 mm ($\frac{1}{4}$ in) wide.

Lawson cypress has proved enormously variable in cultivation, and many cultivars exist (some 200 names are recorded though not all are very distinct). The most striking cultivar in my opinion is *C.l.* 'Intertexta'. In habit and from a distance it might be mistaken for a narrow deodar, such is the nature of its open habit, and with more robust down-curving foliage sprays. Vigorous in habit and ultimately large it deserves to be planted more widely where room permits. If a smaller, narrower tree with the dark green appeal of a Mediterranean cypress is required then *C.l.* 'Kilmacurragh' should be considered. Some of the yellow or golden foliaged cultivars are particularly striking, lighting up their particular garden niches on dull days. One of the best is *C.l.* 'Stewartii', but 'Hillieri', 'Lanei' and 'Winston Churchill' are close runners-up. *C.l. glauca* occurs in the wild and is variable in the intensity of its blue-grey tinted foliage, 'Blue Jacket' is a good selected form. Best of the greys, however, is 'Allumii', a dense columnar tree of great charm and excellent for providing an accent point in a bed or border or as a lawn specimen. Less intense in colour and with its foliage sprays assuming a more or less erect posture is 'Fraseri'. If a small narrowly conical cultivar is needed 'Columnaris' can be recommended. Its ascending branches bear sprays of foliage which are glaucous below and at the tips only. Cultivars with juvenile leaves look quite unlike the normal adult state but do not lack appeal, indeed *C.l.* 'Fletcheri' is commonly grown for its fluffy grey-green semi-juvenile foliage which often takes on bronze tints in winter. It can reach 6 m or more but is usually seen as a columnar bush.

Slower growing and somewhat smaller is 'Ellwoodii' with darker fully juvenile leaves. It is often sold as a dwarf conifer for the sink or rock garden but can eventually outgrow its welcome. Very distinct are the bush-like forms of moderate size, of which my favourite is *C.l.* 'Tamariscifolia'. In no way resembling tamarisk, this cultivar develops an almost umbrella-shaped form composed of arching sea-green tinted sprays. There are specimens over 5 m (16 ft) tall in existence but growth is fairly slow. 'Tabuliformis' is smaller and greener. There are many true dwarfs, from 'Nana', a globular bush capable of attaining 2 m (6 ft) in about 35 years, to such real pygmies as 'Gimbornii', 'Gnome' and 'Forsteckensis'. The latter forms a mossy ball that increases in girth about 3 cm ($1\frac{1}{4}$ in) per annum.

Nootka cypress

If we were to proceed north from the native range of Lawson cypress we would come to the home of its near ally the Nootka, Alaska or Sitka cypress, *Chamaecyparis nootkatensis*. Sometimes also known as yellow cedar, this very ornamental tree can easily be distinguished from Lawson cypress by the pendulous branchlets and larger cones, each scale of which has a pointed boss. The foliage too is usually of a darker green and has an unpleasantly aromatic smell when bruised. The timber is even more desirable and has been used as a substitute for satin wood (*Chloroxylon swietenia*). Even more than the Lawson cypress it thrives in poor soils providing they are not dry, and stands frosty winds better. It can equally well be used as a wind-break or just as a fine specimen tree. *C.n.* 'Glauca' has deep blue-grey foliage and 'Lutea' ('Aurea') is yellow, while 'Pendula' has both branchlets and smaller branches hanging vertically, though the effect is rather gaunt.

Hinoki cypress

The Hinoki cypress, *Chamaecyparis obtusa*, comes from Japan where it is sacred to members of the Shinto faith, and it provides a popular, fragrant, easily worked timber of high quality. It forms a broadly conical tree to 23 m (76 ft) in gardens, more in its homeland. The individual foliage sprays tend to be broadest towards the tips and are composed of very small, blunt-tipped scale leaves which are glossy green above and bear a waxy white pattern beneath. When bruised the foliage gives off a sweetly aromatic odour, which to many seems to have a suggestion of eucalyptus oil.

Curiously enough the original species is not commonly encountered in cultivation, at least in Britain, its place being taken by many cultivars. Of these my favourite is 'Crippsii', a comparatively small tree—to 13 m (43 ft) or so, but usually much less—with bright yellow foliage if grown in a sunny site. Also yellow leaved is the distinctive *C. o.* 'Tetragona Aurea', generally a large shrub with an open habit and more or less vertically arranged foliage sprays.

Fern spray cypress is an apt name for *C. o.* 'Filicoides', a cultivar ultimately of open and attractively irregular habit with the foliage arranged in ferny pendulous clusters. Best known are the dwarf cultivars of which *C. o.* 'Nana' is one of the best of all small conifers for the rock garden. Wider than it is high and forming a flat topped very dark green dome it grows at no more than 2 cm ($\frac{3}{4}$ in) each year. Very popular is the taller 'Nana Gracilis' with its distinctive foliage in shell-like sprays. Although slow growing it ultimately becomes a sizeable bush. From this was raised one of the smallest of all dwarf conifers, *C. o.* 'Caespitosa' ('Nana Caespitosa'), a tiny bun-shaped gem for the sink or trough garden.

Sawara cypress

Also from Japan is the Sawara cypress, *Chamaecyparis pisifera*. It can be distinguished from the allied Hinoki cypress and indeed from all other *Chamaecyparis* species by its pointed scale leaves and small cones which rarely exceed 6 mm ($\frac{1}{4}$ in) in diameter. When crushed the foliage gives off a rather acridly aromatic smell. The Sawara cypress, perhaps to an even greater extent than the true *C. obtusa*, is rarely seen in gardens in its original wild form. On the other hand, in the guise of its many cultivars it is probably one of the most commonly planted conifers, next to the Lawson cypress, at least in British gardens. Juvenile and semi-juvenile forms seem to be most popular and there is certainly no denying the feathery attraction of the best known *C. p.* 'Plumosa' and 'Squarrosa'. The latter is fully juvenile with soft blue-grey foliage and eventually forms a small to medium-sized tree. *C. p.* 'Squarrosa Sulphurea' has pale yellow leaves, while the dwarf 'Squarrosa Aurea Nana' is a darker tint and very compact and slow growing. Also derived from 'Squarrosa' is the very popular 'Boulevard' ('Cyanoviridis'), an American cultivar with appealing steely blue-grey foliage which takes on purple tints in winter. The semi-juvenile 'Plumosa' is bright green, and there are also yellow leaved and dwarf selections from it.

White cypress

For the white cypress, *Chamaecyparis thyoides*, we must return to east North America where it occurs from Florida north to Maine. Also known as coast white cedar and white cedar, this species has a narrowly conical outline and the branchlets are fan-shaped. Though of pleasing appearance it cannot compete with Lawson and Nootka cypress as a fine garden tree.

Examples of conifer foliage, all with needle-like leaves: left, *Picea pungens*, showing peg-like bases; centre, *Abies chensiensis* showing disk-like leaf bases, and right, *Pinus mugo*, a member of the two-leaved group.

However, it has valuable attributes which have not been fully exploited—it grows well in wet ground and is very hardy. In Britain at least, it is best known by two of its cultivars, *C. t.* 'Andelyensis' ('Leptoclada') and 'Ericoides'. The first mentioned slowly forms a dense columnar bush of mixed juvenile and adult blue-green leafage. Tiny red male catkins (strobili) add to its attraction in early spring; 'Andelyensis Nana' is much smaller, developing into a flat-topped bushlet of very slow growth. *C. t.* 'Ericoides' is conical and compact with sea-green juvenile foliage that takes on shades of purple in winter. It thrives best in a spot sheltered from freezing winds.

Firs and spruces

FIRS

With the familiar Christmas tree as a model, all readers of this book should be familiar with the form of the trees about to be discussed. By Christmas tree I mean of course the conifers that are decorated at Christmas time in Europe and North America. Generally they are species of spruce (*Picea*), or silver fir (*Abies*) though sometimes pines and Douglas fir (*Pseudotsuga*) are used as substitutes. Although the erect main stem and regular tiers or whorls of branches clearly distinguish the firs and spruces, separating them can present difficulties for the beginner. If erect cones are present then it is an *Abies*, if the cones are pendulous then it is a *Picea*. (It is as well to check the general description of the Cedars (p. 15), Douglas fir (p. 23) and pines (p. 26) to avoid confusion.) If foliage only is present it is still fairly easy to separate silver fir and spruce. The latter has grooved twigs and each short needle-like leaf seems to arise from a peg-like projection of the stem. In *Abies*, the stems are smooth and the slightly broader leaves have rounded, sucker-like bases that pull away cleanly if the shoot is mature. Practically all the silver firs and spruces make fine wind-breaks and splendid specimen trees. Regrettable it is then that so few are small enough for the average garden.

Small firs

Best of the smaller firs is undoubtedly *Abies koreana*. It is a comparative newcomer to western gardens, having been discovered in the mountains of Quelpaert Island in 1907 and later on, in the mountains on the adjacent South Korean mainland, by E.H. Wilson. Comparatively slow growing it can eventually exceed 10 m (33 ft) so is best not planted in a rock garden. The dark green leaves are bluewhite beneath and nicely offset the violetpurple cones which are usually freely borne even on young specimens less than 1 m (3 ft) tall.

Of equal merit but somewhat larger is Delavay's silver fir, *A. delavayi* with brighter, denser foliage and longer cones. It is a variable tree and several varieties are recognized (all at one time considered to be separate species). Trees labelled *A. delavayi* are usually *A. d. forrestii* from Yunnan and Szechuan. This variety has orange shoots and conspicuously white resinous winter buds. *A. d. fabri*, which is also sometimes grown as straight *A. delavayi*, lacks the white resinous buds. The hardiest variety is *A. d. georgei*, rather like *A. d. forrestii* but with hairy shoots. All forms of *A. delavayi* have handsome deep purple barrel-shaped cones, often borne on young trees.

All the remaining species of fir which are obtainable from nurserymen are comparatively large and not suitable for the smaller garden. Where room is available they make noble specimen trees. It is of course always worthwhile growing these large firs on a short term basis. The common ones such as *A. grandis* and *A. procera* can be obtained cheaply as one or two year old seedlings. Their subsequent speed of growth and decorative appearance can be enjoyed for 10 years, or less if its alloted space is filled up. The tree can then be cut down, the top perhaps used as a Christmas tree and another young one planted beside the stump.

Giant firs

Grand or giant fir, *Abies grandis* is indeed aptly named, for in its native west North America specimens more than 90 m (300 ft) have been recorded. It is one of the most distinctive in foliage with its mid- to yellow-green 2–5 cm ($\frac{3}{4}$–2 in) long leaves arranged in two distinct ranks on either side of the smooth olive-green shoots. Each leaf has two silvery white lines beneath and when crushed gives off an aromatic fragrance reminiscent of orange peel. It is a shade-tolerant tree but needs a moist welldrained soil to do well.

The noble, or noble red fir *A. procera* (*A. nobilis*) is also aptly named and it is a pity that its original name could not be retained. The deep greyish-green leaves spread out in two ranks but are more densely borne than in *A. grandis* and obscure the shoots from above, growing forwards with an upturned tip. Although ultimately a large tree the noble fir flowers quite early, often at about 4·5 m (15 ft) tall. The male catkins are crimson and the females yellow, the latter developing into big cones of striking appearance, barrelshaped and 15–25 cm (6–10 in) long. It needs an acid soil for healthy growth. Closely allied and also a native of west North America is the red fir *A. magnifica*. The alternative name magnificent fir is well deserved, particularly for the blue-white leaved *A. m.* 'Glauca'.

Moving to the Rocky Mountains of south Colorado we come to the northern end of the range of the Colorado White fir, *A. concolor*. It is another fir of noble proportions and tolerant of shade particularly when young. The narrow leathery leaves are borne in two ranks with a few obscuring the stem between, all curving upwards at the ends. A lemon-balm-like fragrance is given off when bruised. *A. c.* 'Violacea' has bright blue-grey leaves and is more desirable as a garden plant. *A. c. loweana* bridges the geographic gap between *A. concolor* and *A. grandis* and tends to resemble these species at either end of its range. It has leaves arranged as in *A. grandis* which vary from grey-green to almost yellow or olive green and the tree is more narrowly columnar.

Some less common firs

Balm of Gilead or balsam fir, *Abies balsamea* extends into the arctic regions of Canada and does not thrive in milder climates. Its dark green glossy foliage, smells strongly of balsam and blisters on the bark yield the resin known as Canada balsam. From a garden point of view and especially in Britain, the balsam fir is best known as the dwarf *A. b.* 'Hudsonia', a slow-growing compact bush with a flattish top which eventually reaches about 75 cm (2½ ft). *A. b.* 'Nana' is similar. *A. nordmanniana* comes from the west Caucasus and adjacent Turkey and likes cool moist conditions. It has dense shining, bright green leaves which overlap along the stems and exhale a fruity aromatic smell when bruised. The dark brown 15 cm (6 in) long cones stand up like resin covered candles. The Grecian fir, *A. cephalonica*, is one of the small group of *Abies* with leaves of equal length that radiate equally all round the stem. They are leathery, prickle-tipped, dark green above

with two narrow white bands beneath. This is a broad-headed tree and very handsome when well grown. Unfortunately it breaks into young growth early and is prone to spring frost damage.

Much hardier than its common name might suggest, the Spanish fir, *A. pinsapo*, also has the radiating leaf character. These leaves are rigidly held and dark grey-green on both sides. The most handsome form for garden ornament is *A. p.* 'Glauca' having leaves with a rich blue-grey patina. Other silver firs sometimes listed in nurserymen's or seedsmen's catalogues are *A. bracteata* a beautiful Californian with cones with long bristly bracts protruding between the scales; *A. fargesii* with large yellow-green leaves; *A. pindrow*, a handsome Himalayan with very long shining green leaves and *A. veitchii*, a fast growing fir with deep green and silver-white densely borne foliage.

Douglas fir

Several other conifers, some closely related, others not, have acquired fir as their common name. Best known of these is the Douglas fir, *Pseudotsuga menziesii*, formerly *P. douglasii* and *P. taxifolia* and the bearer of other synonyms both Latin and common. In general appearance it resembles *Picea abies* but the branchlets are more pendulous and the foliage longer and softer, fruitily aromatic when bruised. The cones are the final give-away even to the uninitiated. These are pendulous, ovoid, 5–8 cm (2–3 in) long, with trifid, tongue-like bracts protruding from between the scales. Vigorous and rapid of growth— 90 cm (3 ft) per year or more is common— this is a handsome specimen for the large garden. It is also a very important timber tree, particularly in its native west North America, the wood being marketed as Columbia and Oregon pine in addition to Douglas fir.

Less vigorous but more decorative in the garden, if one likes blue to grey-green conifers, is *P. m.* 'Glauca'. Sometimes listed as a separate species, *P. glauca*, it is a smaller, neater and more compact tree with glaucous leafage of great charm. Of similar colour but no more than a flat-topped, rounded bush eventually to 1·5 m (5 ft) or so, is *P. m.* 'Fletcheri'. Slow growing, it is well suited to the larger rock garden.

Chinese fir

In no way resembling the firs mentioned above is *Cunninghamia lanceolata*, the Chinese fir. It has narrow, lance-shaped leaves, deep green above, white banded beneath, which taper to a slender point and are 3–7 cm (1¼–3 in) long. They appear to be borne in two flattened ranks like those of yew, but a closer look reveals their spiralling origin. The ovoid to rounded cones are 3–4 cm (1¼–1½ in) long carried singly or a few together. Chinese fir is very ornamental when young, forming a pyramid of lustrous foliage. Later it may become gaunt or gappy. A sheltered site, light woodland is the ideal, should be chosen for best results. It suffers damage or may be killed once the temperature drops to about − 18°C (0°F). There is a rare form with a blue-grey patina to the leaves, *C. l.* 'Glauca'.

SPRUCES

As mentioned on p. 21, the spruces or spruce firs (*Picea*) have a similar appeal and appearance as the firs but differ notably in the way the narrower leaves are carried and in their pendulous cones. Although a very broad generalization, it is fair to say that the spruces are more tolerant of poor soils and exposed sites than the silver firs. Providing the soil is reasonably moist they will grow

well in areas where summers are dry, e.g. in the eastern counties of England.

Long-leaved spruces

Two species head the list of universal favourites, *Picea brewerana* and *Picea smithiana*. The Brewer spruce wins the grace and beauty contest by a short head. In outline it is broadly conical with the lower branches curving downwards, the middle ones about level and the top ones pointing upwards. All have long, densely carried branchlets which hang vertically and carry flattened needle leaves of a lustrous deep blue-green hue. To view a well grown, but not old tree, particularly in morning or evening light, with the curtains of foliage shimmering in a light breeze is indeed a sight to remember. It is fairly slow growing, rarely exceeding about 25 cm (10 in) a year, but ultimately it can attain 15 m (50 ft) or more. Young specimens from seed do not show the pendulous branchlet character until they are about 1·5 m (5 ft) tall. Grafted plants weep much sooner but are often lop-sided. Brewer's spruce is a rare tree in the wild, inhabiting the Siskiyou and Klamath mountains of the California–Oregon border. Regrettably it is not usually easy to find a nurseryman who stocks it, but seeds are sometimes available.

The west Himalayan spruce, *P. smithiana* has a similar overall appearance but all its branches are more or less level or curve slightly downwards with upturned tips, and the hanging curtains of foliage are generally shorter, though still very fine. In addition, the slightly longer leaves are almost cylindrical in cross section with tips that curve in towards the stem.

European Christmas tree

By comparison the remaining spruces have fairly ordinary charms and are largely variations on a theme of *Picea abies*, the original Christmas tree of central Europe. Common it may be and much used in forestry plantations, but a specimen tree on a lawn can still be an extremely telling feature with its elegantly down-swept branches and pendulous branchlets. Widespread in the wild from Scandinavia and the Alps to the USSR it has given rise to many aberrant forms or cultivars, some of the dwarf sorts being garden worthy. One of the best is *P. a.* 'Gregoryana' which forms a dense conical bush when young and then broadens out with age. It rarely exceeds 50 cm ($1\frac{1}{2}$ ft) in height. *P. a.* 'Nidiformis', the so-called bird's nest spruce is the most popular, building up in conspicuous layers into a flat-topped bush that slowly reaches 60 cm (2 ft) tall. Both are suitable for the rock garden.

Other decorative spruces

Allied to the Norway spruce is *P. omorika*, sometimes listed as the Serbian or Servian spruce, a most satisfactory tree on all counts. It forms an elegant, slender column or tapered spire of dark bluish-green which looks well in almost any setting. A small group on a spacious lawn can be most distinctive but even in cramped conditions it is sure to excite many appreciative comments. Of vigorous growth, the Serbian spruce is very adaptable as to soil and situation, thriving on chalk and acid peat, wet and dry land and even near towns where air pollution checks the growth of many conifers. Despite this adaptability it has a very restricted distribution in the wild, being native only to the Drina valley in Jugoslavia.

A splendidly showy companion for *P. omorika* is *P. pungens* 'Glauca', the blue or Colorado spruce from western central North America. It forms a conical tree, often of slightly irregular outline composed of closely-set tiers of horizontal branches. The densely borne leaves are sharply pointed and in the best forms, a vivid blue-white. In the wild, greyish green to richly glaucous trees occur and several selections have been made by nurserymen, most of them smallish trees. Two of the brightest are 'Hoopsii' and 'Koster'. For the smaller garden there is the weeping *P. p.* 'Pendula' and the mat-forming 'Procumbens', both with glaucous foliage.

A favourite of mine and a complete contrast in colour is the so-called Oriental spruce, *P. orientalis*, from the Caucasus and adjacent Turkey. It has the smallest leaves of all the spruces, 6–8 mm ($\frac{1}{4}$ in) long, dark green, densely borne and closely pressed to the slender stems. For this reason alone, once seen it is never forgotten. In habit this spruce is broadly conical and in an open site densely clothed to ground level, a fine and trouble-free conifer for the large garden.

Distinctive and worthy of being more widely planted is the Likiang spruce, *P. likiangensis*. Collected in west China by E. H. Wilson in 1910, it has proved very amenable in cultivation and already there are specimens over 20 m (65 ft) in some British gardens. The Likiang spruce forms a widely conical tree particularly when young, the long branches clothed in overlapping leaves that are bluish-green above, white or grey-banded beneath. Flowers are usually freely produced on fairly young specimens in late spring and are a feature of this tree, the red and yellow male catkins contrasting strikingly with the scarlet, erect female ones. As a garden plant, *P. l.* 'Purpurea' can be recommended. Its unique feature is the way the branch tips point upwards and even bend in towards the leader. The leaves are a darker shade of green and the smaller cones, plum-purple.

Hemlock spruces

The best known hemlocks, or hemlock spruces, *Tsuga*, come from North America but other species are found across the Pacific in Japan and Taiwan and through China to the Himalayas. Although allied to the true spruces, they are of more slender, graceful habit with small somewhat yew-like leaves and, mainly, very small cones. Frequent in cultivation is the eastern, or Canadian hemlock, *T. canadensis*, an attractive tree when young but later forming an irregular crown of wide-spreading heavy branches. If in doubt, the brief examination of a leafy twig soon identifies it. Between the two rows of dark green, white-banded leaves lies a third rank which is pressed close to the stem and points forwards. The ovoid cones usually grow only up to 1·5 cm ($\frac{3}{5}$ in) long.

Decorative at all stages of growth is the western hemlock, *T. heterophylla*, a native of that region of North America which extends from north California to south west Alaska. It forms a regular cone of level main branches, each one clad with elegantly disposed down-curving branchlets. The leaves are of mixed sizes, hence the specific name, varying from 5–18 mm ($\frac{1}{4}$–$\frac{3}{4}$ in) long, dark green and glossy when mature with white bands beneath. This fast-growing tree stands clipping well, makes a fine dense hedge and for this purpose it deserves wider recognition.

The grey-green or bluish-green mountain hemlock, *T. mertensiana* which inhabits the same wild territory as *T. heterophylla*, is slow growing when young but then gains speed. Its slow early growth and attractive foliage make it a worthwhile short-term tree if young plants can be raised from seeds or obtained fairly cheaply. It makes a pleasing lawn specimen. Of all the nine species of hemlock this one has the largest and most spruce-like cones ranging up to 7 cm (2$\frac{3}{4}$ in) long. The Asiatic hemlocks are rarely encountered in gardens and seldom available from nurserymen. Although interesting to acquire they are not superior to those already mentioned.

Pines

Of all the conifers, the pines (*Pinus*) have the most distinctive foliage. The leaves are long and truly needle-like, carried in clusters of two, three or five, depending on the species. Each cluster is in fact a tiny shoot which in turn arises in the axil of a membranous scale leaf. Seedlings have solitary, toothed leaves which densely spiral the young stem and are often grey or blue-green and quite different from the adult. Pine cones vary greatly in shape and size but are generally more woody than those of other conifers and in some species remain securely attached to the tree for several years. When young, all pines have a pyramidal habit with regular tiers of spreading branches. In maturity they lose the central leader and broaden out, some becoming quite round headed, e.g. the stone pine. Depending on the botanical authority 70–100 species of pine are recognized. These are spread around the northern temperate zone and, here and there, just across the equator, mainly in the mountains. Many of them are important timber trees and several produce resin which in turn yields turpentine and rosin. Tar and pitch are also produced and pine-leaf oil for medicinal purposes. The nut-like seeds of some species are edible and tasty.

Small pines

There are pines of all sizes and forms and no garden need be without one member of this useful and decorative genus. One of the smallest of the wild species is *Pinus mugo*, the dwarf mountain pine of central Europe. Although usually a dense but spreading shrub of 3 m (10 ft) or so it can sometimes develop into a small tree. It is a two-needled pine of rich green hue, making an interesting addition to the shrub border or large rock garden. *P. m. pumilio* is its smallest wild form, never exceeding 2 m (6 ft) and often almost prostrate. For the small rock garden the compact, rounded 'Gnom' can be recommended.

Dwarf Siberian pine *P. pumila* (*P. cembra pumila*) has a similar habit to *P. m. pumilio*, but the leaves bear blue-white lines and are borne in fives. Of small tree size but compact, vigorous and attractive is the bristlecone pine, *P. aristata* from the Rocky Mountains. It has short leaves for a pine, 2–4 cm ($\frac{3}{4}$–$1\frac{1}{2}$ in) long which are dark green with glaucous lines and spots of white resin. They are borne in clusters of five and remain on the tree 10–15 years. The 6–9 cm ($2\frac{1}{4}$–$4\frac{1}{2}$ in) long ovoid cones bear long, prickle-tipped bristles, a unique feature among the pines. Some years ago this tree hit the headlines as the oldest known living thing, a specimen estimated at 5,000 years of age being discovered. In the light of further study however, this aged specimen is now known to be an allied species, *P. longaeva*.

Regrettably, the Chinese lace bark pine, *P. bungeana*, is not easy to come by. Rarely exceeding 10 m (30 ft) in cultivation, it is a most decorative pine for the smaller garden. The dark, somewhat yellow-green leaves are in threes and have an odour suggestive of turpentine when bruised. The bark is particularly ornamental being smooth and flaking, much like a London plane in miniature. Of similar size is *P. parviflora*, the Japanese white pine, but

the deep bluish green and glaucous striped leaves are in fives. Flat topped and often of picturesque outline, this is a favourite tree in Japanese gardens and as a bonsai. Japanese red pine, *P. densiflora*, is akin to the Scots pine and has similar reddish bark, but the paired needles are a duller green. It has given rise to a garden worthy dwarf *P. d.* 'Umbraculifera', a slow-growing bush curiously like a half-opened umbrella in its branch formation.

Large pines

Among the larger pines worthy of garden space where room allows, the Bhutan pine, *Pinus wallichiana* is a personal favourite. Also known as blue or Himalayan pine, this elegant tree has several botanical synonyms and is still sometimes listed as *P. excelsa*. Attaining up to 35 m (116 ft) in height it remains conical for many years, then broadens out with massive down-curving lower limbs. The very slender blue-green leaves are carried in fives and hang down as if from a parting of hair. Banana-shaped resin-encrusted cones, 20–30 cm (8–12 in) long are borne even on young trees, often before they are 10 years old and are an attraction in themselves.

Mexican white pine (*P. ayacahuite*) has a similar impact and can be confused with *P. wallichiana* though the leaves are shorter and the cones have a 2 cm ($\frac{3}{4}$ in) long stalk. Other pines in the same group are Weymouth or white pine *P. strobus*, sugar pine (*P. lambertiana*) and Armand's pine (*P. armandii*). The latter deserves to be more widely planted being of elegant habit with white-lined needles and barrel-shaped pendent cones often in pairs or threes.

Also with five needles is the very hardy arolla pine, *P. cembra*, a native of the high Alps from France to Austria and also in the Tatras and Carpathians. This in particular is the tree that scents the mountain air with its sweetly aromatic fragrance in summer. It is pyramidal, at least when young, and is further distinguished by its thickly brownish-downy young stems. Evidence suggests it is not a long-lived tree but it is easily and quickly grown from seed and is at its most decorative when young.

From the mountains of Mexico comes *P. montezumae*, one of the most eye-catching of the round-headed pines, a well grown specimen looking like a billowing cloud, blue-grey in colour. Regrettably it is not hardy in continental climates; the hardier *P. m. hartwegii* has green leaves. Best known of the round heads is *P. pinea*, the stone or umbrella pine from the Mediterranean. It is a grey-green two-leaved species with almost globular cones up to 15 cm (6 in) long that contain large, edible nut-like seeds.

If the stone pine has the largest seeds, big cone pine, *P. coulteri* from California has the largest (but not longest) cones, good specimens weighing as much as 2 kg ($4\frac{1}{2}$ lb). The tree however is inclined to be rather gaunt even when young.

Also a Californian and limited in the wild to the Monterey area is *P. radiata*. In cooler and moister climates than its own it grows with astonishing vigour, producing billowing heads of bright green leaves. It makes a good wind-break and is a very important timber tree in the milder climates of New Zealand, Australia and South Africa.

If we move due east of Monterey and head for the Sierra Nevada, sooner or later we will encounter ponderosa or western yellow pine, *P. ponderosa*. It presents a very different picture from its coastal cousin being of comparatively spare habit with shortish, sturdy branches forming a tall columnar tree that does not lack in stateliness. Dark green of foliage and with a rugged, cinnamon-tinted trunk, it is essentially a masculine tree. By no means restricted to Californian mountains it is found wild throughout west N. America and as far east as Dakota. It is very hardy and much planted elsewhere in U.S.A.

P. resinosa, the red pine of eastern North America is another hardy and handsome pine that has found favour in the gardens and parks of its homeland. It has somewhat pendulous branches and densely borne pairs of lustrous, rich green needles that can exceed 15 cm (6 in) in length. It can be confused with its European ally, the Austrian pine, *P. nigra*, but that species has more densely set branches of somewhat shorter, stiffer leaves and the cone scales usually terminate in short prickles. There are several forms of this pine and *P. n. maritima*—the Corsican pine—is by far the most handsome, with more flexible leaves 15–17 cm (6–7 in) long and a generally less bulky appearance.

Last but by no means least in this short survey of ornamental pines is the Scots pine, *P. sylvestris*, Britain's only native pine. It has the widest range of all pines occurring through Europe, west and north Asia. Not surprisingly it is a variable species but is usually characterized by its reddish scaly trunk and thick, often twisted grey-green leaves. When mature and broad-headed it has a very picturesque appearance. Although a common timber tree in Europe it still deserves to be planted as an ornamental. If a miniature is required for the rock garden, *P. s.* 'Beauvronensis' cannot be surpassed, while *P. s.* 'Aurea' provides golden-yellow winter foliage on a small slow-growing tree.

Chile pine or monkey puzzle

Unrelated to the true pines and more often known as monkey puzzle, *Araucaria ar-*

aucana (*A. imbricata*) is one of the most improbable of all trees. Happily for the monkey tribe none of its members inhabits the mountain forests of Chile and Argentina where it grows wild. The unique character of this tree has been its undoing, at least in Britain, for the desire to own a specimen has meant its being frequently planted in the smallest gardens where it looks positively ridiculous. Having wandered through pure forests of this tree high up on the rugged slopes of the Andes—an experience never to be forgotten—I have come to the conclusion that the monkey puzzle is not a garden tree. For those with large estates, may I suggest the planting of a great drift of not less than 20–30 trees, preferably with plenty of space around. In time it will make a feature people will pay to come and see.

Japanese umbrella pine

Sciadopitys verticillata is a pine by name only. Although more nearly related to the redwood it does have a pine-like appearance and the same sort of appeal. The glossy dark green needles can attain 13 cm (5 in) in length and are in effect, two leaves fused together. They are arranged in whorls of 10–30 like the radiating ribs of an umbrella, hence its common name. Although bushy plants occur, often with several leaders, this tree is usually spire-shaped and when well grown in humus rich neutral to acid soil and sheltered from strong winds, makes a beautiful and unusual specimen tree. It is also slow growing and can be accommodated for many years in the smaller garden, though ultimately it can grow to 15 m (50 ft) or so—twice this in the wild. Smaller growing is the rare *S.v.* 'Glauca'. The foliage of this desirable form has a grey-blue patina which, in certain lights, imparts a silvery sheen to the tree.

REDWOODS: THE BIGGEST CONIFERS

Coast redwood

Tallest of all the conifers, *Sequoia sempervirens*, the redwood or coast redwood of California and south Oregon is a most spectacular tree. In the beneficent tree climate of the coastal fog belt which forms its homeland, this tree frequently achieves 90 m (300 ft) and when measured some years ago one outstanding specimen topped 100 m (357 ft). As such trees often form dense, almost pure forests, to walk among their red-brown boles makes one feel like an ant in a cornfield. Although it will not stand the severity of continental winters it is surprisingly hardy and grows vigorously in sheltered, high-rainfall areas. It makes a fine tree for parks and large gardens and can be grown as a short-term specimen where there is less room. Unlike most conifers it regenerates from the base, so if a tree gets too large it can be cut down near to ground level and will start again. The shoots that arise from the stump should be thinned to the strongest one to ensure a shapely tree. The dark green leaves are 1·5–2 cm ($\frac{3}{5}$–$\frac{3}{4}$ in) long and arranged in two ranks rather like those of yew. The globular cones are remarkably small for so large a tree, being about 2 cm ($\frac{3}{4}$ in) long. *S. s.* 'Prostrata' is more or less prostrate for a few years but then often produces one or more erect leaders. Cuttings rooted from the lower branches of mature trees often behave in this way.

Sierra redwood (Big tree)

Almost as tall and much more bulky—trees of 100 m (330 ft) tall with a girth of 27 m (90 ft) have been recorded—*Sequoiadendron giganteum* can lay good claim to being the largest tree of all. It is found only in the Sierra Nevada of California in high valleys up to 2,400 ft (800 m). The grey tinted foliage is scale-like, pressed flat to the shoots and reminiscent of cypress, though larger. The cones are ovoid and up to 7·5 cm (3 in) long. When young, the big tree, or Wellingtonia as it is still sometimes known, makes a handsome specimen tree forming a neat cone of dense foliage. It is well worth considering as a short-term tree as seeds are easily obtainable and young trees are easily raised. Of unique form and considered picturesque by some, is S. g. 'Pendulum'. Usually this cultivar forms a narrow, often leaning column clad with vertically pendulous branches but some specimens develop bizarre shapes. If a tiny form of the big tree is not too anomalous to bear thinking about, S. g. 'Pygmaeum' can be grown in the rock garden.

YEWS: CONIFERS WITHOUT CONES

It is a far cry from the redwood and big tree to the yews (Taxus), but in their way these trees can be quite majestic despite their low stature. This is particularly true of the common yew, Taxus baccata, the largest member of its genus. Round-headed and blackish-green this tree is often planted in churchyards, especially in Britain. Ancient specimens may be 1,000 years old with massive reddish fluted trunks, usually hollow within. As a garden tree the common yew is most versatile. It makes a fine specimen, particularly in one of its cultivars of erect or spreading habit or with variegated foliage. For making a hedge it has few rivals and topiary enthusiasts rank it highly. Yew leaves are flattened, narrow and dark green, 2–4 cm ($\frac{3}{4}$–$1\frac{1}{2}$ in) long and are carried in two flat ranks on its horizontal branchlets, spirally on leaders and erect tips. The fruit consists of a single ovoid nut-like seed sitting at the bottom of a red cup-like fleshy structure known as an aril. The aril is edible but all other parts of the tree are poisonous. All the yews are dioecious, that is male and female flowers are carried on separate individuals. Occasionally however, a plant arises with flowers of both sexes, as for example the Westfelton yew. Yew timber is heavy, strong and elastic but works well and makes fine furniture and panelling. Its use for bow making is well known and it is very rot resistant, making excellent fence posts. It is interesting to note that two of the oldest known wooden weapons, found in Germany and Britain are paleolithic spears made of this wood.

Best known of the many cultivars is T. b. 'Fastigiata' the erect-growing Irish yew so commonly seen in British churchyards. 'Fastigiata Aureomarginata' has leaves with golden-yellow edges, and 'Standishii' is of similar colour but smaller and slower growing, ideal for the small garden. 'Adpressa' is a large wide-spreading shrub with very much shorter and relatively broader leaves which render it most distinctive. Having even shorter, thicker, very non-yew-like leaves on a small, stiff shrub is 'Amersfoort', suitable for the small garden if only to fool one's knowledgable friends. The Westfelton yew 'Dovastoniana' has a short erect trunk and very wide spreading tiers of ascending main branches with pendent branchlets; 'Dovastoniana Aurea' has yellow-margined leaves. Both are desirable garden plants but need plenty of room.

Best known of the golden yews is T. b. 'Elegantissima' usually of large shrub size with leaves which are yellow when young and then gradually fade to green with a yellow margin. Japanese yew, T. cuspidata, is usually a large shrub in cultivation, but can attain tree stature in its homeland. It is similar to *T. baccata*, but the leaves are more leathery with a prickle point. *T. c.* 'Densa', 'Nana' and 'Minima' are dwarf hummocky bushes suitable for the rock garden, the latter being particularly small and slow growing.

Japanese yew has been crossed with common yew to create the hybrid *T. × media*. Combining the best characteristics of the parents, particularly the extreme hardiness of the Japanese parent, this American hybrid was raised at the Hunnewell Arboretum, Massachusetts by Mr T. D. Hatfield whose name is given to the best known clone. *T. × media* 'Hatfieldii' is vigorous, erect and compact and

sistently do this, as do some of the species of *Podocarpus*. In a general way all may be said to favour the true yews in their general appearance though most of the torreyas are good-sized trees as are some podocarps. Hardiest and most useful in the garden is *Cephalotaxus harringtonia drupacea* from central China and Japan. Known both as Japanese plum yew and cow's tail pine, it forms a large compact shrub with drooping branchlets clad in narrow bright yellow-green leaves which are whitish underneath. The fruits, olive-green plums 2–3 cm ($\frac{3}{4}$–$1\frac{1}{4}$ in) long, are interesting, but not particularly showy.

C. h. 'Fastigiata' has the erect habit of an Irish yew with very dark green foliage,

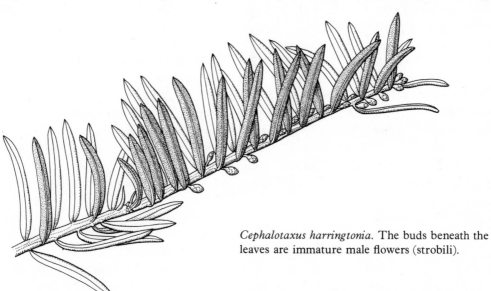

Cephalotaxus harringtonia. The buds beneath the leaves are immature male flowers (strobili).

makes an excellent hedging plant. Very similar is *T. × m.* 'Sargentii', but this is a female plant whereas 'Hatfieldii' is male.

Plum-fruited yews

Several genera of conifers go one better than the yew and completely enclose their seeds in a fleshy covering creating a plum-like fruit. *Cephalotaxus* and *Torreya* con-

while 'Prostrata' is prostrate and 'Gnome' forms a small flat-topped dome. Chinese plum yew or cow's tail pine, *C. fortunei*, is even more handsome in foliage, the longer, tapered, 5–9 cm (2–$3\frac{1}{2}$ in) long leaves being usually a deep, glossy green. The fruits are olive or brownish green. *C. f.* 'Prostrata' spreads sideways and may be used in gardens to make good ground cover.

Known as Chilean or plum-fruited yew or plum fir is *Podocarpus andinus*, formerly placed in a genus of its own as *Prumnopitys elegans*. In its south Chilean homeland it can form a tree to 15 m (50 ft) tall but only rarely attains this height in cultivation. It is not unlike the common yew in habit, but the leaves are bright green above and somewhat glaucous beneath, generally partially twisted to reveal both surfaces at once. I have not seen the fruits, but they are conflictingly described as green or blue-black, about the size of a damson.

Equally or almost as hardy is the very handsome *Podocarpus macrophyllus* from China and Japan. Aptly named it has leaves up to 13 cm (5 in) or more long, bright green above and glaucous beneath. It thrives best in humus-rich moist soils, preferably with shelter of other trees, but is fairly hardy, having withstood −20·5°C (−5°F). This is one of the podocarps with naked seeds, each one borne on a thick, fleshy, purple stalk. *P. salignus* also has long leaves though generally not more than 10 cm (4 in). It is a taller tree in its native Chile and of more elegant habit with pendent branchlets. There are several New Zealand species worth looking out for, though none are fully hardy. *P. acutifolius* with yellowish-green prickle-tipped leaves forms a shrub to 1·5 m (5 ft) or more and is garden worthy, and the somewhat hardier *P. nivalis* even more so. The latter forms a denser, smaller shrub and is particularly attractive when set with red berry-like fruiting stalks, each bearing a small polished seed at its apex.

JUNIPERS

It can fairly be said that the junipers (*Juniperus*) constitute one of the most important coniferous groups for temperate gardens. Among its 60 strong cohort of species and larger number of cultivars is something to please all tastes and situations. Despite the berry-like cones, the scales of which are fused and fleshy, *Juniperus* belongs to the same family as the true cypresses and has the same sort of foliage consisting of awl-shaped juvenile, and scale-like adult leaves.

Two American junipers

Tallest of the hardy junipers is *J. virginiana* from the eastern half of North America north to Quebec. Known variously as pencil, red, or Virginian cedar—for the uses of its fragrant wood, not its appearance—this species can achieve 30 m (100 ft) in the wild but is rarely even half this height in British gardens. Attractively pyramidal when young and inclined to be ragged when old, it has mixed juvenile and adult leaves, the latter small and pointed on slender stems. There are several cultivars, some of which are more garden worthy than the original species. *J. v.* 'Burkii' has a dense columnar habit and blue-grey leaves that take on bronzy-purple hues in winter. Dense but conical in outline is 'Canaertii' with bright green leaves and freely borne vividly blue-white fruits. 'Skyrocket' produces one of the narrowest columns of all, a specimen of say 2·5 m (8 ft) tall being about 15 cm (6 in) wide. Blue-grey in colour it is a splendid accent tree but needs to be planted in groups for the best effect. A solitary specimen looks rather like an exclamation mark with only itself to exclaim about.

'Grey Owl' is now considered to be a hybrid of *J. virginiana* with *J.* 'Pfitzerana' as the other parent. It certainly resembles the latter parent in outline but has the grey-silver foliage of *J. v.* 'Glauca', the putative seed parent. Rocky mountain juniper, *J. scopulorum* might well be described as the western version of *J. virginiana*. It is less tall however, rarely above 12 m (40 ft) in the wild and less in cultivation with slightly more robust branches. 'Hills Silver' is a real charmer, forming a narrow pillar of silvery-blue foliage; 'Pathfinder' is a similar colour but conical, while 'Repens' is a mat-former with juvenile blue-green leaves.

Asiatic junipers

Most commonly planted in gardens is *J. chinensis* a most variable species from the Himalayas, China and Japan where it can attain 18 m (60 ft). It has mixed juvenile and adult foliage, the former consisting of awl-shaped 8 mm ($\frac{1}{3}$ in) long leaves borne in whorls of three. It is represented in gardens by many cultivars of lesser stature, some of which may be of hybrid origin with *J. sabina* (see below). *J. c.* 'Aurea' is known as 'Young's Golden Juniper', a narrowly conical or columnar tree with splendid golden foliage. Ideally it should be planted out of the full mid-day sun as it can scorch. 'Kaizuka' is an erect, large bush of irregular outline and bright green foliage which can be quite picturesque in a large rock garden, or surrounded by spring-flowering heaths. One of the top five most planted junipers must be 'Pfitzerana', a wide-spreading shrub with ascending branches and down-arching branchlets densely clad with grey tinted foliage. It makes a first rate specimen plant for the edge of a lawn and also makes good ground cover though in time it can rise to a height of 1·5 m (5 ft) or more. Some authorities place this cultivar under the hybrid species *J. × media* (*J. chinensis* × *J. sabina*), but opinions vary and it is convenient to retain it here in the way most nurserymen do. 'Hetzii' is another of the 'Pfitzerana' sorts but it is a tree with a somewhat more upright habit and glaucous foliage.

Common juniper

Having the most widespread distribution of all junipers in the wild, the common juniper, *J. communis* occurs in all the mainland areas of the Northern Hemisphere. Very variable, it can be a sizeable tree or a prostrate shrub, but always with awl-shaped juvenile leaves only. Perhaps best known of the many cultivars is *J. c.* 'Depressa', a gem of a shrublet forming a slow growing pillar of congested grey-green foliage. Seldom achieving more than 45 cm (1$\frac{1}{2}$ ft) it is the ideal tree for the small rock or trough garden. Magnified to a total of 3–5 m (10–16 ft) we have the Irish juniper, *J. c.* 'Hibernica', another exclamation mark tree but having more body than *J. v.* 'Skyrocket' and again very striking as a solitary specimen surrounded by heathers.

'Oblonga Pendula' is a favourite of mine, an erect shrub eventually to 3 m (10 ft) or more with gracefully pendulous branchlets, a decidedly neglected cultivar with specimen qualities. Pleasing ground cover is provided by the dark green vigorous 'Repanda' and 'Hornibrookii', with leaves whitened beneath. The latter was collected in Ireland by Murray Hornibrook, the first authority on dwarf conifers to write a book about them. In effect 'Hornibrookii' is one of the naturally prostrate forms of *J. communis* that one can find on mountains or in the north. On the Orkney island of South Ronaldsay this prostrate form is a feature of the top of Sandy Hill. A plant raised from a cutting I collected there is now, after 15 years, a most attractive mat several feet across. Cuttings have been given to nurserymen under the name of this Orkney Island.

Other good junipers

The Japanese *J. conferta* is a naturally prostrate species, forming glaucous-tinted deep fluffy mats of juvenile foliage and provides ground cover of great charm. Also prostrate but sleek and flat by comparison is *J. horizontalis*, the creeping juniper of North America and Canada. I have seen exciting mats of it plastering cliff ledges and the natural rock gardens of the coast of Mount Desert Island, Maine, not far from the town of Bar Harbor. One of the best cultivars was in fact found in just such a site in about 1930 and bears the name of that small American town. It forms compact, steely-grey tinted foliage and is a fine ground coverer. 'Douglasii' is similar but of more spreading and open growth and of a blue tint. Both take on purple tones in winter and have mainly scale-like leaves.

In foliage, if not always in habit, *J. horizontalis* resembles the savin, *J. sabina* but the latter gives off a pungent rather unpleasant smell when crushed. The savin is a native of the mountains of Europe eastwards to the Caucasus and has long been cultivated, in earlier times for its medicinal properties. Best known of the cultivars is *J. s.* 'Tamariscifolia', a spreading form of horizontal growth that builds up gradually in layers to become a flat-topped low bush of juvenile bright green foliage. It is fine for the larger rock garden or beside steps, and looks very well among heathers. 'Rockery Gem' is similar but less vigorous.

Another of the top five most popular junipers is *J. squamata* 'Meyeri'. Bearing dense blue-green awl-shaped leaves, this Chinese cultivar has an ascending to erect habit with short spreading branchlets. In time it can get quite large but with gentle pruning will stay manageable for many years. The wild *J. squamata* grows throughout the Himalayas and varies in habit. Rarely seen in gardens, it is usually a low-growing plant sometimes under the name *J. s. pygmaea*. On the China–Tibet border grows *J. s. fargesii*, a slow-growing small tree with pendent branchlets and bright green leaves. It is not commonly met with but provides a link with the next species, *J. recurva*. Known as drooping juniper this eastern Himalayan is among the most graceful of all junipers. It forms a small tree or large shrub of broadly conical habit with weeping branchlets. *J. r. coxii* is the most desirable variety with longer pendent branchlets of loose sage-green foliage. 'Embley Park' is a bright green selection of more spreading habit and deserves to be better known. *Juniperus rigida* seems to blend the characteristics of *J. recurva* and *J. communis* but has longer leaves, 12–20 mm ($\frac{1}{2}$–$\frac{3}{4}$ in) long, and very distinctive lobed, cone-like berries. Graceful and bronze-green in winter this is another juniper that deserves to be planted more widely, though it can reach 12 m (40 ft) or so in time. It is a native of Japan inhabiting mountain slopes.

2 Broad-leaved trees

TREES WITH LARGE LEAVES

Although most evergreen trees and shrubs achieve their effect by habit of growth or texture and colouring of the foliage when seen *en masse*, there are some noteworthy exceptions. These are the plants with large leaves, often of architectural merit, so useful in providing a contrast among their lesser-leaved brethren. Regrettably, none of these large-leaved trees are fully hardy in continental climates but elsewhere they are well worth trying for the eye-catching effect they can produce.

Palms

A mention of palms inevitably conjures up a picture of a lush, tropical landscape and most of the 2,500 known species do come from warm climates. Happily there are, however, a handful of palms which can be described as reasonably hardy and a few others which tolerate low temperatures but only a minimal frost. Hardiest of all the true palms is undoubtedly the Chusan or windmill fan palm, *Trachycarpus fortunei* from China. It cannot be described as the most elegant of palms, but a well grown specimen 3–10 m (10–33 ft) in height with its black-brown fibrous trunk and a head of large 60–120 cm (2–4 ft) long green fan-shaped leaves is a handsome sight. It can sound an impressively unreal note in winter when viewed amongst leafless trees and shrubs above a coverlet of snow. Hardiness is of course a relative thing and prolonged temperatures below − 12°C (10°F) can damage or kill the Chusan palm. In catalogues it can still be found listed as *Trachycarpus excelsa* or *Chamaerops excelsa*.

Somewhat less hardy and much smaller is the European fan palm, *Chamaerops humilis*. Unlike most palms it suckers freely from the base and often forms bushy plants to 2 m (6 ft) tall and almost as wide. In gardens it can be induced to look like a more traditional fan palm by removing all suckers and the remaining stem may then achieve 4–6 m (13–20 ft) in height.

Among palms that will stand a few degrees of frost only, pride of place must go to the Canary Island date palm, *Phoenix canariensis*. Although lacking the grace of the familiar tropical coconut palm, it has the same feather-shaped pinnate leaves. These can reach 6 m (20 ft) in length and are carried in a dense but neat head atop a sturdy, grey trunk. Mature specimens bear a profusion of small, yellowish date-like fruits, each one of which is, however, little more than a hard, stony seed. In Britain it thrives outside only in the Isles of Scilly and in North America from Florida to California via the Gulf States. Of somewhat similar impact, but having more down-curving, somewhat bluish-grey leaves and a trunk often with persistent leaf bases is the

Examples of broad-leaved tree forms: left, *Cordyline australis*; centre, *Rhododendron arboreum* and right, *Trachycarpus fortunei*, the hardiest of all true palms.

jelly palm of South America, *Butia capitata*. Often grown under the erroneous names of *Cocos australis* and *C. capitata*, this is probably a little hardier than *Phoenix canariensis* and deserves to be tried more often in mild areas.

Cabbage trees

New Zealand cabbage tree
The New Zealand cabbage tree, *Cordyline australis* has a palm-like stance, particularly before it starts to branch. Familiar as a small specimen used as a dot or accent plant in beds of summer annuals, it can eventually reach a height of 6–12 m (20–40 ft), then having several upswept branches each

terminating in a dense head of leathery, grassy leaves. Formerly classified in the lily family, it is now placed with the dragon tree in the family *Agavaceae*. The cabbage tree provides a bonus of small, fragrant, whitish six-petalled flowers in large airy clusters in summer and later followed by white berries. There is also a purple-leaved cultivar which contrasts well with the lacy green mounds of spiraea and similar shrubs. It will stand short spells with temperatures down to −8°C (17°F), perhaps below, but is happier in milder winter conditions. It is however, very tolerant of cool summers and sea winds and can be used very effectively as a palm substitute as it is in Britain.

Broad-leaved cabbage tree
The allied broad-leaved cabbage tree, *C. indivisa*, is in some ways more impressive, even though ultimately of lesser stature. It has a more robust appearance and often remains unbranched for many years.

The leaves are 1–2 m (3–6 ft) long by 10–15 cm (4–6 in) wide, leathery in texture with a bluish-white suffusion beneath and prominent reddish veins. The less-freely produced flowers are carried in compact clusters and followed by bluish berries. Although almost as hardy as *C. australis*, the broad-leaved cabbage tree is less easy to please, needing a site which is ideally sheltered from strong cold winds and in an area of regular rainfall.

Magnolia

There are no reasonably hardy trees of traditional form with leaves as wide or as long as those of the palms. Nevertheless, a few evergreen trees do have sizeable simple leaves and one or two should be included in every garden large enough to take them. Readily available is the bull bay, *Magnolia grandiflora* with oval leaves to 25 cm (10 in) long. When young they are felted with red-brown hair, but soon develop their leathery texture and dark green colour with its high gloss. Despite its handsome leaves, bull bay is grown for its superb flowers, great creamy white chalices, in *M. g.* 'Goliath' to 25 cm (10 in) wide. With leaves of equal size or larger is *Magnolia delavayi*, a native of Yunnan province in China, whence it was brought as seeds in 1899 by the plant collector Ernest Wilson. It has deep, somewhat greyish-green leaves of rather sombre hue above, but shaded blue-white beneath. Fragrant, 15–20 cm (6–8 in) wide dull cream flowers open from summer to autumn, but they are rather hidden by the leaves and short lived. Despite these rather less than eulogistic words, *Magnolia delavayi* is a tree of distinction, especially when 12 m (40 ft) or more tall. It also thrives better than *Magnolia grandiflora* on chalky soils and in areas of cool summers.

Several large-leaved rhododendrons reach tree stature and are discussed in Chapter 4.

Cherry Laurel

Last, but by no means least in this brief survey of large leaves is the hardiest of all, *Prunus laurocerasus*. Better known as cherry laurel and much used and abused as a hedging plant it is a native of Eastern Europe and west Asia where it is essentially a forest dweller. When planted among other trees it grows to 6 m (20 ft) or more and then can truly be considered a tree. In gardens it is more usually seen as a large shrub. It can, however, be easily trained into a tree by restricting it to a single stem, cutting out all the basal and lower growth as it forms. Cherry laurel is very variable in leaf size and stature and the dwarf forms will be mentioned in Chapter 3. The commonly seen wild original has leaves to 15 cm (6 in) long, oblong in shape, toothed, leathery and lustrous. There is a bonus of small cream flowers in erect spikes in spring which are followed by glossy black-purple cherries. Several larger leaved cultivars are obtainable, e.g. *P. l.* 'Latifolia' ('Macrophylla'), 'Caucasica' and 'Colchica', but pride of place must go to 'Magnoliifolia'. Strong growing and eminently suitable to be trained as a tree, this fine evergreen has leaves to 30 cm (1 ft) long and a well-grown specimen makes an imposing sight.

TREES WITH SMALL LEAVES

Although there are exceptions, all the reasonably hardy broad-leaved evergreen trees have smallish leaves of generally simple outline. To make up for this however, their shades of green, textures, statures and habits vary widely, providing trees for all purposes. For convenience, the

Prunus laurocerasus 'Magnoliifolia', the most magnificent of all the cherry laurels.

species discussed here are arranged in alphabetical sequence.

Strawberry trees

Popularly and aptly known as strawberry trees from the appearance of their fruits, few evergreens have more to offer in the way of all-year-round attraction. Members of the genus *Arbutus*, they have amply-borne, rich green, glossy oval to elliptic leaves and nodding clusters of urn-shaped flowers followed by globular red fruits. An added attraction of some species is the smooth, often flaking bark, with a reddish suffusion or lustre. This bark characteristic reaches a peak of perfection in *A. menziesii*, the madrona of west North America. Lustrously smooth and cinnamon red, the branches writhe up into a broad crown which can attain 20 m (60 ft) in height in cultivation and much more in the wild. Like most members of the genus it needs to be raised from seed and planted out when young to avoid root disturbance. A moist but well-drained acid soil is essential for a good performance and some shelter when young. Once well established, this all too seldom-planted tree can increase in height at the rate of 30 cm (1 ft) per year and its bark soon becomes very beautiful.

For those who garden on a limy soil, *A. × andrachnoides* is a very worthy substitute. More open in habit and less massive, it is a natural hybrid between *A. unedo* and *A. andrachne*, both from southern Europe. An added attraction is its autumn to winter flowering habit and its more amenable nature in cultivation. Although found in the wild where the parent species grow together and introduced into cultivation from there, *A. × andrachnoides* was reputedly also produced purposely by hybridization in Britain about 1800. *A. andrachne*, the Grecian strawberry tree, is similar but less vigorous and rather tender when young. It needs a Mediterranean climate to do of its best.

The common or Killarney strawberry tree (*A. unedo*) can stand 30°F of frost under ideal conditions and is as hardy, if not more so, than *A. menziesii*. Although it can attain tree stature it is fairly slow growing and is generally seen as a large dense bush. The bark is fibrous and more brown than red, so less effective than that of the other species mentioned. The fruits, however, are the largest, up to 2 cm ($\frac{3}{4}$ in) wide and ripen in late autumn at the same time as the following season's flowers, a most effective combination. *A. unedo* 'Rubra' is a particularly desirable form with pink flowers and abundant fruits.

Two ceanothi

The praises of *Ceanothus* are sung in Chapter 10 and very few species achieve true tree status. However, where frosts are not severe and specimens can be planted away from the protection of walls, both *C. arboreus* and *C. thyrsiflorus* can attain 5–10 m (15–30 ft) in height. The glossy, boldly veined leaves of the latter make it effective at all times of the year and both can be literally smothered in pale blue flowers from late spring to early summer. 'Treasure Island' is the name given to a hybrid between these two ceanothi. It combines the best characteristics of its parents and should be sought out and given a try whenever possible.

Lily-of-the-valley tree

Engagingly known as the lily-of-the-valley tree, *Clethra arborea* has long been grown in areas where frosts are not severe. It was for long indisputably considered among the finest of Madeira's native trees, but recently a Chinese botanist has claimed it for his country and proclaimed the Madeiran population to be immigrants gone wild. Having seen this tree gracing the mountain slopes of Madeira I find it difficult to believe but have to concede that it is possible. Whatever its native provenance, the lily-of-the-valley tree has handsome, narrow, slender-pointed dark green tooth-ed leaves and terminal clusters of small, nodding, pure white cup-shaped flowers which are fragrant and open in late summer and autumn. Acid, humus-rich soil is necessary, and shelter from cold winds. It stands partial shade and thrives well in light woodland.

Winter's bark

Winter's bark (*Drimys winteri*) is of similar hardiness and in the colder areas needs the protection of a warm wall or high tree cover. It has oblong elliptic leaves up to 19 cm ($7\frac{1}{2}$ in) long which can vary from deep to palish green suffused beneath with a blue-white patina. The long-stalked, creamy-white fragrant flowers are carried in pendent umbels and but for the irregular number of rather narrow petals could be mistaken for those of a cherry. The whole plant is aromatic, particularly the bark which has medicinal properties and is still used in its native South America. Captain William Winter, after whom the tree was named, was among those who accompanied Sir Francis Drake on his voyage around the world. He believed it to alleviate the symptoms of scurvy. This drimys is variable in habit, some forms bushing out from the base and rarely developing a true central trunk. Tree-like forms are sometimes listed as *D. w. latifolia*. Both forms can, under favourable conditions, grow 10–16 m (30–50 ft) tall and when flowering freely present a striking appearance. *D. w. andina* is a hardy form of shrubby habit.

The eucalypts

Eucalyptus is a genus of more than 500 species almost all of which are native to Australia. All are evergreen and none are hardy in continental winters. Where frosts are not severe, however, quite a number of species make very decorative specimen trees and deserve to be tried more often in the home garden. There are two important points to be remembered by the would-be grower of eucalyptus: firstly they are very fast growing and can soon look awkward in the wrong site, and secondly they must be planted in their permanent sites as young as possible. If allowed to become pot bound before planting out they seldom make proper anchoring roots and are liable to blow over in a strong wind. Plants are raised from seeds and potted singly as soon as the seed leaves are fully expanded. If sown in warmth in late winter young plants are ready to put out in late May or when fear of frost is past. Alternatively, the seed can be sown in late summer and the seedlings overwintered in a frost-free greenhouse.

A curious characteristic of many *Eucalyptus* species is the production of two distinct sorts of foliage, juvenile and adult. The juvenile stage may last for months or years but gradually gives way to the adult phase. In general the adult leaves are narrowly to broadly lance-shaped and carried alternately. Juvenile leaves vary more widely and are often carried in opposite pairs. In extreme examples each pair of juvenile leaves is broader than long and fused together to form an ellipse or disk resulting in what appears to be a single leaf pierced through the centre by the twig. This arrangement is known botanically as perfoliate. In addition, juveniles are often richly grey-green to blue-white and the combination proves very decorative.

Already the growing band of flower arrangers have appreciated its value and many florists stock cut sprays of the foliage of such species as *E. gunnii*. This species is a good one to start with being readily available and reasonably hardy, in sheltered sites surviving short spells almost to $-18°C$ ($0°F$). Known as cider gum in its native Tasmania, *E. gunnii* can put on $1\cdot5$ m (5 ft) annually in a fertile soil, producing sprays of blue-white rounded juvenile leaves followed by grey-green lance-shaped ones. White multi-stamened flowers open in summer. Glaucous-leaved forms of the urn-fruited gum (*E. urnigera glauca*) are rather similar though easily distinguished by the intriguing urn-shaped seed pods. Equally decorative and almost as hardy is the Tasmanian snow gum, *E. coccifera* with broad heart-shaped to elliptical juvenile leaves and green to glaucous narrow willow-like adult ones. The bark on the trunk and main branches peels off in longitudinal strips revealing a white inner surface which later darkens to grey.

Cast in the same mould but reaching only small tree size is the spinning gum (*E. perriniana*). Its pairs of juvenile leaves form neat disks which become detached when they die but cannot fall and spin around in strong winds, hence its common name. Deserving of much greater popularity is the snow gum, (*E. niphophila* (*E. pauciflora alpina*)) from the mountains of Victoria and New South Wales where it grows at an altitude where snow lies throughout the winter. In cultivation it is somewhat hardier even than *E. gunnii* and being slower growing and ultimately a tree of lesser stature is more desirable for the smaller garden. Its juvenile leaves are silvery white and the broadly lance-shaped adult ones may be either glossy grass-green or glaucous. Of particular attraction is the

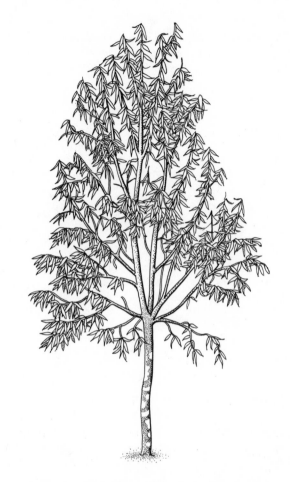

Eucalyptus niphophila, one of the hardiest species. Note the sparse habit so typical of all eucalypts.

smooth bark which is shed in strips and takes on tints of brown-gold and sienna-red. Among other eucalypts of moderate hardiness and all well worth trying are *E. glaucescens* (tingiringi gum) with brightly glaucous, rounded juvenile leaves; *E. nicholii*, very slender and elegant with linear grey leaves; *E. delegatensis*, erect and pyramidal when young with deep green lustrous adult leaves and *E. stellulata* (black sallee). The latter, which is strangely neglected, forms a small tree with sage green leaves that seem to glow in morning and evening light. In the wild it sometimes

Eucalyptus stellulata, a strangely-overlooked and decorative species of surprising hardiness.

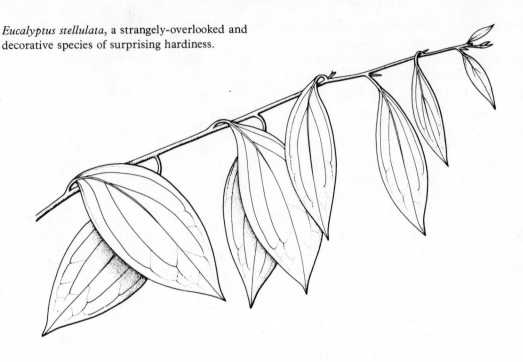

grows with the snow gum and if seeds from such a high locality can be obtained it is remarkably hardy. A three year old plant in my garden survived − 18°C (0°F) of frost during the 1978–79 winter.

Where frosts are slight and the summers sunny, eucalyptus has much to offer in the way of foliage and flowers. Planted worldwide where the climate allows and even familiar in colder climates owing to its use as a bedding plant when very young, is *E. globulus*, the blue gum of Tasmania. The broad, blue-white juvenile leaves are very striking and show off the bright colours of summer flowers. Later, long, narrow and much greener adult leaves appear and the tree very rapidly attains a large and imposing stature. It will stand a fair amount of frost if of short duration. A superb flowering tree is *E. ficifolia*, the Western Australian flowering gum. It is comparatively small and round-headed with green leaves and abundant bright vermilion blossom. It

is closely allied to the much taller and pink-flowered *E. calophylla*, the marri of its homeland. The two species have hybridized and many of the pink to red forms grown as *E. ficifolia* are of this origin. *E. sideroxylon* 'Rosea', the red ironbark or mugga, also has pink flowers but there the similarity ends.

The ironbark group of eucalypts are very distinctive by reason of their fissured, hard rough bark which is dark grey to black. In *E. sideroxylon* the bark is black and nicely contrasts with the grey leaves and white or pink flowers. The red river gum, *E. camaldulensis* is the most widespread of Australia's gum trees. It does not immediately register to the visitor as a eucalypt being sturdy of trunk with a well branched broad head of green to bluish-green leaves. A big mature tree could almost pass as an oak from a distance. The small flowers are creamy-white. In contrast the lemon-scented gum, *E. citriodora* is tall and airily graceful, with a smooth grey-white trunk and branches, sometimes pink-tinted, and willow-like leaves that are rich in oil of citronella and very fragrant of lemons when crushed. *E. viminalis*, the candlebark, is somewhat similar but with powdery-white bark and rather denser foliage that lacks the lemon aroma. All the above six species are much cultivated in California and similar climates. It is a pity that they do not thrive in frostier areas.

Silk tassel tree and bay laurel

Considering its California/Oregon homeland, *Garrya elliptica*, the silk tassel bush or tree, is a surprisingly hardy and successful evergreen. In cooler areas, notably Britain, it is often grown as a wall shrub but in sheltered sites it can soon form a small tree and ultimately quite a large one. It has abundant deep green lustrous, leathery, oval leaves with grey downy reverses and long silky silvery-grey male catkins. The latter are first observed in late summer and gradually get longer, finally to open during mild spells in winter and early spring. Female catkins are shorter and carried on separate plants which are seldom offered by nurserymen. Where there is room however, it is very worthwhile planting both sexes together and later enjoying the sight of fat chains of berry-like, silky-hairy, purple-brown fruits. If a male plant only is to be grown seek out the clone known as 'James Roof' which bears catkins up to 35 cm (14 in) long.

Bay laurel is everyone's favourite not only as a useful evergreen but for its historical association as a garland for heroes and not least for its culinary uses. *Laurus nobilis* is the common sweet or bay laurel and comes from the Mediterranean region. Although frequently seen as a clipped shrub, this aromatic evergreen will make a handsome tree eventually to 10 m (30 ft) or more tall. During its early years it has a naturally pyramidal outline and really needs no pruning at all. Grown naturally in this way the twigs of small trees become wreathed in fuzzy yellow-white flower clusters and if a female tree is nearby it will bear a crop of fruits rather like glossy oval cherries. Particularly desirable is the golden bay (*L. nobilis* 'Aurea') with yellow leaves that are particularly cheering in autumn and winter. There is also *L. nobilis* 'Angustifolia', a more curious than beautiful form with very narrow leaves.

A strangely neglected ally of the witch hazels (*Hamamelis*) is *Sycopsis sinensis*. Collected in China by E. H. Wilson as recently as 1901, this is a small tree with leathery, somewhat corrugated elliptic leaves to 10 cm (4 in) long and intriguing petalless flowers. The latter are unisexual and are borne in downy chocolate-brown buds in late winter. Male specimens are usually offered by nurserymen as they produce hanging clusters of slender yellow filaments and reddish anther lobes.

Phillyrea latifolia is more likely to be seen and grown as a large shrub, but will easily attain small tree size particularly if restricted to one main stem when young. Easily grown, densely leafy and reasonably hardy, it can provide a very satisfying background for lighter coloured choicer things. The leaves vary in shape and size, being ovate to lanceolate, 1–6·5 cm ($\frac{1}{2}$–$2\frac{1}{2}$ in) long, with or without teeth. Insignificant whitish flowers are followed by blue-black berry-like fruits. Two very distinct clones are available, 'Rotundifolia' with very broad to rounded leaves and 'Spinosa' in which they are narrow and sharply toothed.

Three Chilean Trees

White flowers and glossy deep green leaves can be a most effective combination particularly when the blooms are of good size and centred with an elegant puff of slender stamens. Such are the credentials of *Eucryphia*, an aristocratic genus which demonstrates the continental drift theory by having representatives in south east Australia including Tasmania, and southern South America. The best known and most garden worthy eucryphia is undoubtedly *E. × nymansensis*, a spontaneous hybrid between the Chilean *E. glutinosa* and *E. cordifolia* which arose in the famous garden of Nymans in Sussex in 1914 and later at Mt. Usher, Eire. It is a columnar slender tree eventually to 12 m (40 ft) or more with mostly trifoliate leaves (the deciduous *E. glutinosa* has pinnate leaves and *E. cordifolia* has simple ones). In late summer the branches become wreathed with 6 cm ($2\frac{1}{2}$ in) wide flowers composed of four pure white overlapping petals. *E. lucida* is a large Tasmanian tree with glossy, simple, oblong leaves 4–7.5 cm ($1\frac{1}{2}$–3 in) long, and pendent, fragrant white flowers up to 5 cm (2 in) wide. It is less hardy than *E. × nymansensis* but neatly columnar and elegant in bloom and well worth experimenting with as a wall shrub.

Sharing the same home country (South America), is the Chilean fire bush, *Embothrium coccineum*. In southern Chile it can attain 20 m (60 ft) or more in height and a forest largely composed of these trees, as I have seen them on the island of Chiloe, is an astonishing sight when in full bloom. Truly the whole forest seems to be ablaze. It is a variable species in both leaf size and stature. In the mountains of Chile bushy, almost deciduous forms occur and there is a range of intermediates. Of particular merit is *E. coccineum* 'Norquinco', a smallish tree of rangy habit bearing narrow dark green leaves and profuse clusters of crimson tubular flowers in early summer. In colder

areas it can be semi-deciduous and only just qualifies for a place in this book.

Staying for the moment with trees of doubtful hardiness we come to the myrtles, one of which can form a beautiful small tree. This is *Myrtus luma*, also sometimes listed under the species name *apiculata* within the genera *Eugenia*, *Myrceugenia*, *Myrceugenella* and *Luma*, such are the differences of botanical opinion on its status. A native of temperate forests in Chile and Argentina, it combines very successfully smooth, cinnamon coloured bark, which regularly flakes away to disclose creamy-white patches, ample deep green foliage and white flowers with golden anthers. The latter are about 2 cm ($\frac{3}{4}$ in) wide and open in late summer. Rather similar is the hardier *M. lechlerana*, but it lacks the attractive bark and produces its frost-tender flowers in early summer. Both species are best in light woodland; *M. luma* then shows more of its mottled bark unobscured by foliage.

Southern beeches

As garden trees the southern beeches (*Nothofagus*) are very much neglected, though sadly, none of the evergreen species are fully hardy, but where frosts are not severe or prolonged they are well worth trying. Although vigorous and generally fast growing, neutral to acid soil is preferred and a site sheltered from strong cold winds. Like the better known northern or true beeches (*Fagus*) the branchlets of nothofagi are produced in flattened, frond-like sprays, a characteristic which naturally lends an air of grace to young and old trees alike. In addition, the leaves of the species mentioned below are very much smaller than those of *Fagus* and this frequently imparts a lightness or airiness to the head of even a large tree. In the wild any given species may

The intriguing curly-tipped cones of Chinese arbor-vitae. Although usually known as *Thuja orientalis*, some botanists consider it merits special treatment and it has been named *Biota orientalis* and *Platycladus orientalis*.

The golden foliage of *Chamaecyparis lawsoniana* 'Stewartii' seems to glow with a light of its own on dull days.

Common or Killarney strawberry tree (*Arbutus unedo*) in flower. It is the hardiest species and will grow in limy soils.

Fruiting catkins of *Garrya elliptica* have a fascination all of their own but are seldom seen as both male and female bushes must be grown side by side to obtain them.

Nothofagus solandri. This tiny leaved southern beech extends to the snow line in New Zealand's Southern Alps.

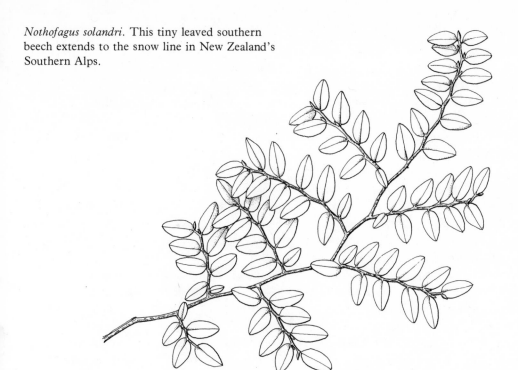

occupy a considerable range of altitude, in some cases from sea level to well up in the mountains. As with *Eucalyptus* it is important to get seeds from the upper limit of a species' range to ensure the greatest possible hardiness. This is particularly true for the potentially hardy New Zealand and southern S. American species that follow.

Although by no means the choicest species for garden decoration, *N. solandri*, the black beech is a particular favourite of mine. This is mainly because it conjures up memories of happy days plant collecting in the Southern Alps of New Zealand where it is abundant up to the limit of tree growth. Nevertheless, it does not lack charm and deserves to be grown more often. It is one of the smallest leaved species, the deep green untoothed oval blades ranging from 6–15 mm ($\frac{1}{4}$–$\frac{2}{3}$ in) in length.

N. s. cliffortioides is much the same but the leaves are pointed, with reflexed to waved margins. Silver beech, *N. menziesii*

has equally short but relatively broader leaves with a high gloss and doubly toothed margins. The trunk too is attractive, being grey-white and smooth when young, furrowing with age. Although it grows up to sub-alpine limits in the wild, my experiences suggest that in Britain at least, the early stages of growth are rather frost tender. Like the silver beech, red beech (*N. fusca*), is also a New Zealander. It differs greatly however, being more robust and ultimately taller in the wild, with zig-zag twigs and 2–4 cm ($\frac{3}{4}$–$1\frac{1}{2}$ in) long, broadly ovate leaves, coarsely and sharply toothed. On mature trees the dark bark is thick and furrowed.

Moving across the Pacific to Chile and Argentina we encounter coigue de Magellanes (*N. betuloides*) a most distinctive if somewhat sombre tree clad in an abundant canopy of deep varnished green foliage. The leaves are 10–25 mm ($\frac{1}{3}$–1 in) long, ovate and bluntly toothed, somewhat paler beneath and punctuated by dark glands. It

47

is reasonably hardy but does not appreciate cold, windy sites.

New Zealand trees

All the pittosporums are notoriously tender where winters are punctuated by longish cold spells. One tree-sized species is so decorative and fast growing, however, that it is well worth planting even if it survives only for a few years. This is *P. tenuifolium*, known in its native New Zealand as kohuhu. It is an erect slender-stemmed small tree to 10 m (30 ft) but often never gets beyond large shrub size in colder climates. The commonest form in cultivation has purple-black twigs and glossy pale green oval leaves with wavy margins. One to two year old sprays of foliage combine well with cut flowers and as a result the kohuhu is extensively grown as a stooled shrub to provide cut material for the florist. It is also a useful seaside plant either as a free-growing wind-break or a clipped hedge. The spring-borne small, chocolate-purple flowers are often overlooked but are well worth seeking out. On warm days they exude a pleasant honeyed fragrance. There are some variegated foliage forms, noteworthy among them being 'Garnettii', marked white flushed pink; 'Silver Queen', suffused grey-white; 'Purpureum', flushed purple-bronze and 'Warnham Gold', with the mature leaves golden yellow. All these coloured foliage forms tend to be more tender than the original green plant.

New Zealand has several other evergreen trees to offer, two of which have a bonus of flowers and are very garden worthy where winters are not too cold. Lacebark is a pleasing and apt name for the two most attractive evergreen members of *Hoheria*, a genus confined to New Zealand. The Latin name is adapted from the Maori *houhere*. A small tree or large shrub, *H. populnea* has the best foliage, glossy, boldly-toothed ovate leaves 7–12 cm ($2\frac{3}{4}$–$4\frac{3}{4}$ in) long. During late summer to early autumn clusters of white flowers like cherry blossom shine out from among the leaves. Curious little winged fruits follow. It is widely planted in its native country and has given rise to some interesting cultivars, notably 'Alba Variegata', with creamy-white margined leaves, often pink-tinted when young, 'Purpurea' with purple leaf undersides and 'Macrodonta', selected for its bolder more prominently toothed leaves. Marginally hardier and more graceful in habit, the branch tips of mature trees being pendulous, is *H. sexstylosa*, the long leaved lacebark. It has much narrower leaves, sometimes to 15 cm (6 in) or more long and is very free-flowering, well grown specimens presenting a foam of white blossom in late summer.

New Zealand's national flower

Possessing the charming Maori name *kowhai* are two species of *Sophora*. In Britain, and in other areas prone to hard frosty spells they are liable to shed most of their leaves before mid-winter and thus are only marginally evergreen. However, if the winter is mild, the elegant ferny leaves remain all the year and there is the added attraction of big yellow pea-shaped flowers in late spring. In Britain, *S. microphylla* is the hardiest and most commonly seen. It has leaves composed of 20–40 pairs of rounded to broadly oblong deep green leaflets, each one to 7 mm ($\frac{3}{10}$ in), very occasionally to 1 cm ($\frac{2}{5}$ in) long. The 4–4.5 cm ($1\frac{1}{2}$–$1\frac{3}{4}$ in) long flowers are carried in pendent clusters of 4–6. Although basically pea-shaped, they differ in having the broad standard petal pointing down and partially rolled around the remainder. The bulging helmet-shaped calyx adds that touch of distinction. Later, intriguing beaded, winged pods develop.

Sophora tetraptera is very similar but the leaflets number only 10–20 pairs, are relatively narrow and only 1·5–3·5 cm ($\frac{3}{4}$–$1\frac{1}{2}$ in) long. The flowers can also be longer, to 5 cm (2 in) or more, especially in the 'Grandiflora' selection. It is of interest to note that *S. microphylla* occurs wild in Chile and formerly on Easter Island. The seeds are very hard and will float in both fresh and salt water for months. They have been found in beach drift on the coast of Chile and so circumstantial evidence is strong for their transportation via the west wind drift current right across the Pacific. The seeds are often slow to germinate if sown in the traditional way and are best placed in a jar of water until they become thoroughly soaked. Once the seeds sink to the bottom they should be removed and sown at once, as germination is immediate and often happens in the water.

Evergreen oaks

Botanists estimate there to be 450 different species of oaks (*Quercus*) spread throughout the northern temperate zone and extending into south east Asia, North Africa and South America. A fair proportion of these oaks are evergreen and range from majestic trees to quite small shrubs. Among the trees, *Q. ilex*, the common evergreen, holm or holly oak, is the best known. It forms a sturdy tree 20–27 m (70–90 ft) tall with a broad dense head of leafage which appears almost black-green in winter. It is surprisingly fast-growing when young and ultimately is too big for most average gardens. It is surprisingly hardy considering its Mediterranean homeland, withstanding – 18°C (0°F) when mature provided such cold spells are not prolonged. Model-

led on a similar pattern and hailing from the west Mediterranean is the cork oak, *Q. suber*. Added attraction is provided by a trunk and main branches covered with thick rippling waves of cork. For Britain and other areas of similar climate the form known as *Q. s. occidentalis* should be sought as it is marginally hardier though having less dramatic bark characters. Generally of similar hardiness is the live oak of the south east of North America and adjacent Mexico, *Q. virginiana*. Ultimately of less stature than *Q. ilex* it rather resembles this species but is even broader in the head and has longer, narrower, elliptic leaves.

Q. agrifolia is more distinctive in mild areas reaching 24 m (80 ft) but in cooler climes rarely exceeds half this. It has leathery, dark, shining green leaves 2·5–5 cm (1–2 in) long, oval to rounded in outline and margined with narrow spiny teeth. It bears top or cone-shaped acorns about 2·5 cm (1 in) long, each one sitting in a deep stalkless cup. For the small garden there are two tailor-made evergreen oaks, *Q. myrsinifolia* and *Q. phillyreoides*. The first mentioned has willow-like glossy leaves to 13 cm (5 in) long, while *Q. phillyreoides* resembles, as its name suggests, a *Phillyrea* rather than an oak. Regrettably both these Asiatic oaks are rare in cultivation and not too easy to obtain from nurserymen. All oaks are easily raised from seeds (acorns) sown as soon as they are ripe.

Headache tree

Lastly but by no means least we come to California's answer to the sweet or bay laurel of the Mediterranean, *Umbellularia californica*. Rejoicing in such common names as California bay, California laurel, California olive, California myrtle, Oregon myrtle, headache tree and pepperwood, this aromatic tree can achieve 24 m (80 ft) in height in its homeland but seldom half this in cooler climates. Nevertheless it is surprisingly hardy, surviving short spells of near −18°C (0°F) temperatures. It has lance-shaped, pale to almost yellow-green foliage which emits a strong, sweetly pungent almost fruity aroma which can cause a headache if inhaled for too long a period. The petalless flowers appear as yellowish fluffy axillary tufts in spring, giving way to oval, dark purple fruits like small plums. In sheltered gardens this can make an excellent specimen tree for a lawn, or at the back of a wide shrub border. Like the sweet bay it stands clipping well but is best if left to achieve its pleasing outline of natural growth.

Several hollies (*Ilex*) naturally attain tree form and make very fine specimens. One of the best is common holly, *Ilex aquifolium* and some of its many cultivars, which assume a very elegant pyramidal habit. However, as the majority of hollies are rarely more than large shrubs in cultivation I have chosen to survey their charms in Chapter 3.

3 Shrubs

SHRUBS WITH LARGE LEAVES

At least a few evergreen shrubs should, in planting terms, form the backbone of every garden, and what could be better than that those in key positions should have large leaves of distinction. Common though it is as a pot plant and frequently planted outside, at least in Britain, *Fatsia japonica* is a firm favourite of mine. It has long-stalked, leathery, lustrous, fingered leaves about 30 cm (1 ft) wide which are a compelling sight in themselves, and a splendid foil for the large clusters of small, white autumn-borne flowers. Potentially a large shrub it can be easily kept within bounds by judicious pruning in spring. *F.j.* 'Variegata' has leaves with white tips but is no more attractive than its green-leaved progenitor. Still sometimes sold as *Aralia sieboldii* this Japanese plant tolerates the shade of trees and grows well by the sea if sheltered from the coldest winds. Mated with the Irish ivy *Hedera helix hibernica*, *Fatsia* has given rise to the bigeneric hybrid × *Fatshedera lizei*. It has ivy-like leaves 10–25 cm (4–10 in) wide and a loose vigorous habit of growth that needs support if allowed to grow naturally. If the stem tips are regularly pinched once they attain 20–30 cm (8–12 in) in length, a free standing shrub can be built up. It is very shade tolerant and hardier than its *Fatsia* parent. × *F.l.*

'Variegata' has leaves marbled grey-green and margined white.

Mahonia

Rivalling *Fatsia* in the architectural quality of their leaves are several species of *Mahonia* from west North America and Asia west along the Himalayas. Formerly united with the barberries (*Berberis*) *Mahonia* differs in having pinnate leaves and lacking stem spines. In the species mentioned the flower spikes are aggregated into a terminal cluster and thus rendered very conspicuous. Closely adhering to this general description is *M. lomariifolia* from west China and Burma. It is an erect, sparingly-branched shrub to 4 m (13 ft) or so, each robust stem crowned by a rosette of palm-like leaves 30–60 cm (1–2 ft) long. Each leaf has 9–18 pairs of leathery, lance-shaped, spiny-margined, lustrous, deep green leaflets. These provide a splendid foil for the fragrant, bright, deep yellow flower fountains which are borne any time between autumn and spring. Regrettably, *M. lomariifolia* is not very hardy and is only suitable for areas of mild winters, e.g. the western seaboards of Europe and North America. With the following species however, it has given rise to some hardier hybrids as fine as or finer than itself.

Mahonia japonica rarely exceeds 2–3 m (6–10 ft) and is wider spreading and more freely branched. The leaves have 6–9 pairs

Mahonia japonica, an aristocratic shrub with
sweetly fragrant winter flowers.

of broader but equally leathery and spine-toothed leaflets. Lemon yellow fragrant flowers open at the same time of the year and nothing can be more cheering on a dismal cold and misty day in mid-winter. Individual flower stems, technically racemes, can be 20–25 cm (8–10 in) long, and spread out and curve downwards. Beneath each flower there is a small awl-shaped bract. Blue-black berries follow in due course. The true homeland of this fine *Mahonia* is not known for certain. It came to Europe from Japan where it has long been grown, but is probably Chinese though some authorities state that it is a native of Taiwan. There seems no doubt that *M. bealei* is a native of China though the original plants were obtained by the collector Robert Fortune from a Chinese garden in 1848. Subsequently almost identical material was collected wild in west China and Taiwan.

M. bealei is much like *M. japonica* but the racemes are stouter and erect or ascending and each flower arises in the axil of a tiny scale-like bract. In addition there is a tendency for the terminal leaflet of each leaf to be broader than the remainder, not narrower as in *M. japonica*. *M. × media* covers the progeny of *M. japonica* crossed by *M. lomariifolia* and vice versa. Several cultivars are available, combining and recombining the best characteristics of the parents. All are garden plants of quality, boldly architectural in leaf, eye-catching in flower. 'Charity' is the best known cultivar and nicely blends the parental features. In 'Winter Sun' and 'Lionel Fortescue' the characteristics of *M. lomariifolia* are more apparent, the latter being a superior plant with flower stems to 40 cm (16 in) long. Desirable though these Asiatic mahonias are, they tend to be rather demanding in their requirements: humus rich, moist but well-drained soil and sheltered partial shade are needed for satisfying results.

Oregon grape

Much easier to please is *Mahonia aquifolium*, the Oregon grape of west North America. Although cultivated elsewhere in the USA where winters are not too severe, in Britain it has found a second home. Planted as game cover in private and state forests it has spread and naturalized itself and now claims a place in the standard *Flora of the British Isles* by Clapham, Tutin and Warburg, Cambridge University Press. It is a suckering shrub varying greatly in height, from 30 cm (1 ft) or so to 2 m (6½ ft) depending on soil, situation and the form cultivated. The lustrous pinnate leaves are 15–30 cm (6–12 in) long and composed of two to four pairs of broadly oval leaflets bearing small spine-tipped teeth. The floral racemes are densely crowded and golden yellow, starting to expand in late winter with a crescendo in spring. Blue-black berries in grape-like clusters follow. Oregon grape makes a fine ground

cover plant and would still, I feel sure, grace nurserymen's catalogues even if it never flowered. The leaves are fresh green when young, richly toned when mature and take on shades of purple in winter, particularly in exposed sites; the odd leaf may turn red at any time. *M. a.* 'Atropurpureum' consistently turns purple in winter, while 'Moseri' has matt-green foliage which is pale green flushed coppery pink or red when young. It is now generally accepted that this latter plant is a hybrid with the allied *M. repens*, a species rarely above 30 cm (1 ft) with fewer leaflets per leaf.

Finest of the *M. aquifolium* clan is undoubtedly 'Undulata' with waved leaves of superlative gloss and quality and usually very free flowering on stems that can attain 3 m (10 ft) or more. Its true origin is unknown. The original plants grew at the famous Rowallane garden in Northern Ireland and were probably of hybrid origin with *M. pinnata*, a tender ally from California and Mexico. Not quite in the big leaf class but conveniently mentioned here is *M. fremontii* from semi-desert regions of south west North America. It grows 1·5–3 m (5–10 ft) tall and has leaves with two to four pairs of small, crimped, spine-toothed leaves of a vivid blue-white hue with a matt finish. Yellow flowers are followed by spongy, more or less inflated pale yellow to red berries. It makes a good wall shrub in a sunny site with well-drained sandy soil and deserves to be planted more often.

Chilean hazel

Also with foliage of pinnate pattern is *Gevuina avellana*, sometimes known as Chilean hazel. Sad for cool temperate climate dwellers that it is so tender. It is best planted with a high tree cover where frosts are light or non-existent, and in acid to neutral soil. Fine specimens have existed in south west England, west Scotland, Ireland and west North America forming handsome pyramidal trees up to 12 m (40 ft) or so. The leaves may be simply or doubly pinnate, up to 40 cm (16 in) long, and a rich glossy green. They are carried on stout stems clad in soft rufous down. Spikes of spidery white flowers are followed by nut-like fruits which turn red, then black. *Gevuina* can be trained as a wall shrub and is then more easily protected in winter.

Chilean abutilon

In all but the most sheltered areas or sites *Abutilon vitifolium* is semi-evergreen. When not tattered by winter gales, however, the large maple-like grey-green leaves are handsome even if rather thinly disposed on the branches. The glory of this large, none too hardy Chilean shrub is undoubtedly in its flowers, 6–8 cm ($2\frac{1}{2}$–$3\frac{1}{4}$ in) wide saucers of satiny mauve usually produced in profusion in early to mid-summer. *A. v.* 'Album' is white, while 'Veronica Tennant' has larger flowers of a richer hue. *A. ochsenii* is more tender, smaller growing and of slender habit, but has lovely lavender-blue flowers. Mated with *A. vitifolium* it has given rise to *A. × suntense*, a vigorous shrub, hardier than *A. ochsenii* and bearing violet-purple flowers. All of these abutilons make good wall shrubs. These saucer-flowered Chilean abutilons are now classified by some botanists in the genus *Corynabutilon*.

Spotted laurel

Until recently, the spotted laurel, *Aucuba japonica* of Victorian shrubberries was neglected and even scorned. Firstly it made a come-back as a pot plant for unheated rooms and corridors, and now it is being planted again in gardens. There is no denying the appeal of bold, glossy, elliptic leaves, particularly when the shrub will survive in deep shade. There can also be the bonus of cherry-sized shiny red berries, providing that male and female plants are grown together. I must admit that I do not much care for the virus-induced yellow spotting, though when thickly spangled with gold as in 'Crotonifolia' (male) and 'Gold Dust' (female) it can be very showy. For those who also dislike the spotty effect attention may be drawn to the very handsome plain green cultivars, notably 'Crassifolia' (male) with broad, toothed blades; 'Longifolia' (female) having bright green leaves to 13 cm (5 in) or more in length and 'Salicifolia' (female) with willow-like foliage. *Aucuba japonica* will not stand continental winters and is best sheltered from cold winds. When obtainable, *A. j. borealis*, a much hardier dwarf form from north Japan should be tried in cold areas.

Cherry laurel

Of similar impact but of more spreading habit and very distinctive alternate leaves is the cherry laurel, *Prunus laurocerasus*. The taller-growing forms have already been mentioned in the tree chapter but all can be grown as shrubs and some are naturally so. *P. l.* 'Caucasica' can be imposing, with narrow leaves to 18 cm (7 in) long; 'Angustifolia' has narrower willow-like foliage and is not so vigorous. Not easily available but well worth looking out for is *P. l.* 'Bruantii' a large shrub with very dark polished leaves that have a somewhat convex upper surface. It seems to be very hardy, surviving temperatures of − 18°C (0°F). The wide-leaved 'Rotundifolia' is most distinctive as indeed is the horizontally growing *P. l.* 'Zabeliana', an excellent ground coverer.

Not really in the large-leaved class but conveniently mentioned here are 'Schipkaensis' and 'Otto Luyken'. Both have smallish narrow leaves but the former is very hardy and has a spreading habit and the latter is small, neat and compact. Just meriting inclusion, with leaves 6·5–13 cm (2¼–5 in) long is *Prunus lusitanica*, the Portuguese laurel from Spain and Portugal. Although occasionally of small tree size it is usually seen or grown as a shrub to 3 m (10 ft) or so. Grown in shade it has the deepest green oval leaves with an almost satiny lustre and in summer, erect white flower spikes appear, to be followed by strings of small cherries that pass through red to black as they ripen. This is a hardy plant very adaptable as to soil and situation, and forming an excellent clipped or informal hedge as a backing for a shrub border. It is also very worthy as a specimen shrub in its own right. *P. l.* 'Variegata' has white-margined leaves but it is not quite as hardy and for me, less desirable than the type species. *P. l. azorica* has larger, finer foliage but regrettably is less hardy.

Camellia

Camellias are of course grown almost entirely for their flowers, but even judged purely as evergreens they rank highly among those of laurel-like form. *C. japonica* in particular has fine, lustrous, elliptic leaves to 9 cm (3½ in) long. The leaves are tougher than the flowers which are rather prone to spring frosts. For this reason the bushes, which will eventually become quite large are best planted against west or sheltered north walls or under the dappled shade of high trees. If this splendid dual purpose shrub is to be grown, then it is worthwhile selecting those with flowers that please. Hundreds of cultivars have been raised in Japan, Europe, North America and elsewhere and the choice is wide with flowers 5–13 cm (2–5 in) across and in all shades of pink, red and white, single and double. *C. saluenensis* is rather more elegant, with slimmer twigs, smaller, narrower leaves and single blush-pink flowers having notched, tipped petals. It arrived in Britain from Yunnan in 1917 having been collected there by the redoubtable George Forrest. It is not as hardy as *C. japonica* but when mated with that species produced a race of first rate hardy garden shrubs and was given the name *C. × williamsii* after Mr J. C. Williams, one of the primary originators of the cross. They are tall, almost columnar shrubs when grown in the open garden, producing their almost rose-like flowers in great profusion.

Names to look out for are *C. × w.* 'J. C. Williams', 'Donation', 'Salutation', 'Parkside' and 'November Pink'. The latter is desirable, beginning to flower as it does in late autumn if the weather is mild. Naturally an autumn to spring flowerer is *C. sasanqua*, another native of Japan with good, dark glossy leaves and pink to deep rose blossoms. Although hardy however, its flowers are not and a mild winter is needed for its winter delights. It is a good camellia for a sunny wall.

Wheel tree

From the same countries, including also Taiwan and equally hardy is the wheel tree, *Trochodendron aralioides*. Although tree-sized in its native lands, it is slow growing and seldom seen above 3–4 m (10–13 ft). It is of spreading habit and has bright, almost yellow-green obovate leaves up to 13 cm (5 in) long with neatly scalloped margins. The small bright green flowers are wheel-shaped with many spoke-like stamens but no petals and are carried in rounded umbels several of which terminate the stems about mid-summer. For those who seek out the unusual among evergreens, this is a must. Were it seen more often there is little doubt that it would be extremely popular among flower arrangers.

Viburnum

Several members of the genus *Viburnum* have outstanding foliage of good size plus attractive flowers and fruits. Largest in terms of length is the Chinese *V. rhytidophyllum*. Well-grown leaves can reach 20 cm (8 in) but 10–15 cm (4–6 in) is more usual. Each leaf is grey-felted beneath, glossy and intriguingly finely corrugated above. In early summer, flat heads of small off-white flowers appear and in due course red berries which ripen to glossy black. This is a large shrub, when well suited exceeding 3 m (10 ft) in height which it does at a great speed. Crossed with the deciduous wayfaring tree (*V. lantana*) it has given rise to an even more vigorous and suckering shrub, *V. × rhytidophylloides*. As its name suggests, (*oides* meaning like) it much resembles its evergreen parent but has broader somewhat shorter leaves. When well grown (it thrives exceedingly well in boulder clay soils), a height of 5–6 m (15–18 ft) can be attained, usually with a lesser spread. But for its suckering habit and dense leafage to ground level it could be classified as a small tree. It provides a splendid plant for blocking out an unpleasant view.

V. × pragense is another child of *V. rhytidophyllum*, this time with the small-leaved *V. utile* as the father. Why this hardy, medium sized shrub is not seen more often is beyond comprehension. It has dark green elliptic leaves to 14 cm (5$\frac{1}{2}$ in) or so with the most intense satiny lustre that I know of. In a shady site, which is not obligatory but suits it well, and intensifies the gloss of its leaves, the foliage seems to shine with a light of its own. When the wind blows, each leaf is seen to be white-felted beneath providing a wonderful contrast. Creamy white flowers open in late spring from pink buds.

Collected in China in 1904 by Ernest Wilson, *V. cinnamomifolium* has a rather undeserved reputation for tenderness. It certainly can survive − 18°C (0°F) for short periods though may lose some leaves. It has leathery, dark, glossy, boldly-veined leaves 7·5–14 cm (3–5$\frac{1}{2}$ in) long and compact clusters of off-white flowers which are followed by intriguing, glossy blue-black berries. It thrives best in a wind-sheltered site and tolerates quite heavy shade. Another Wilson viburnum whose merit has long been recognized is *V. davidii*. Akin to *V. cinnamomifolium* is has narrow leaves and brighter blue berries though the latter are seldom carried in real abundance. It has the most admirable low hummock-like growth form, seldom above 90 cm (3 ft) tall but wider; an excellent ground cover shrub for sun or shade. It should in fact always be planted in groups, the individuals raised from seeds. In this way the flowers can be cross pollinated and a heavier crop of fruit expected. There is a tendency for some plants to be male, others female and a third category to be neuter; at least some plants seldom produce fruits. Hence the advisability of obtaining the variability that seed-raised specimens can provide.

Bamboos

Frequently overlooked as potential evergreens, the bamboos have much to offer the gardener in the way of elegance and beauty. Technically woody stemmed grasses, they range from about 60 cm (2 ft) to 6 m (20 ft) and more in height with erect to arching canes bearing short slender branches and narrow oblong to lance-shaped leaves of varying tones of green. The flowers are generally insignificant and typically grass-like. Several species have never been observed to flower in gardens; others do so regularly and unsuspectedly, e.g. *Arundinaria japonica*. It is often stated that if a bamboo flowers it dies but this is much too broad a generalization. Some species do die after flowering, others are much weakened but eventually recover, while others bloom regularly as does the above mentioned *A. japonica*. This latter species is the commonest bamboo which is hardy in the British Isles. It thrives in shade or sun and, unlike many hardy bamboos, will grow in exposed positions and even makes a good hedge and windbreak. It is by no means the most graceful species, however, and can be invasive, spreading by underground woody rhizomes. This spreading characteristic is common to many of the hardier bamboos and such species should be planted with caution in restricted areas. The best kinds of bamboo are the clump-formers which erupt from the ground like vegetable fountains of undeniable beauty. They are quite unlike any other kind of evergreen tree or shrub and for this reason alone are valuable for adding contrast to the garden scene.

Although there are at least fifty sorts of hardy bamboo, comparatively few are generally available from nurserymen. Among the taller species to look out for are the clump-forming *Arundinaria murieliae* and its close ally with purple flushed stems, *A. nitida*. Both are Chinese and grow to 3·5 m (12 ft) or more tall. Forming rather wider clumps is *A. simonii* a vigorous species from Japan, the young stems of which bear a waxy-white patina. It can reach 4·5 m (15 ft) in height and is abund-antly leafy, making an excellent screen. *Phyllostachys nigra* is not so tall and has brighter green leaves which contrast well with the dark brown to near black stems. Like *A. japonica*, the Himalayan *Arundinaria anceps* spreads widely and forms thickets, but is much more attractive and to be preferred if rampancy is required. Some of the smaller running bamboos make good ground cover and worth considering are several species of *Sasa*, notably *S. veitchii* and *S. palmata*, the latter with leaves to 30 cm (1 ft) or more long. The leaves of both species develop straw-coloured margins in autumn, creating an interesting variegated effect. Really dwarf (about 90 cm (3 ft)) tall and truly variegated is *Arundinaria variegata*, its dark green leaves bearing white stripes.

The sacred or heavenly bamboo (*Nandina domestica*) is an example of a plant long associated with Japan but not native there. It was taken to Japan from China by immigrants centuries ago and cultivated for the grace and beauty of its finely dissected leaves, carried on slim bamboo-like stems to 2 m (6½ ft) or more tall. Bronze when young, bright green when mature and often purple-tinted in autumn and winter, the leaves vary from 25–45 cm (10–18 in) in length, each composed of numerous narrow leaflets. Terminal clusters of white flowers appear in summer and may be followed by bright red, white or yellow berries. In Britain and areas of similar climate it needs a sheltered, sunny site, but in its adopted Japanese homeland it is essentially a shade plant and looks superbly at home beneath high tree cover.

Adam's needle

Just as *Cordyline* merited inclusion in the large-leaved trees on length rather than width, so does *Yucca* receive an honourable mention here. In matters of form and stance, the two genera have much in common: robust, sparingly branched stems and terminal rosetted clusters of sword-shaped leaves. *Yucca*, or Adam's needle to use the common name, goes one stage further with a group of species that are stemless or apparently so, the leaves springing from ground level. The yuccas too, have the best floral display, large waxy-white or creamy bells in spires. The genus is native to central America, north to the southern United States, and all the hardy species emanate from the latter country. Very aptly named, *Y. gloriosa* is a favourite, with stiffly erect dark green sword-shaped leaves to 60 cm (2 ft) or so long. The robust stem, which may or may not be branched, can reach to 2 m (6 ft) or more and the majestic flower spike rises to an equal height above, bearing numerous cream flowers sometimes red-tinted in bud. Equally popular and almost as fine is *Y. recurvifolia* which differs in the softer leaves that arch outwards when mature.

Y. filamentosa is one of the best known with thick grey-green leaves 35–75 cm (14–30 in) long, the tips of which widen out slightly and are often concave or spoon-shaped. The leaf margins have whitish, curly horny fibres, just as though they had been inexpertly planed.

Y. smalliana and *Y. flaccida* are similar and probably confused in cultivation. Basically they resemble *Y. filamentosa* but have tapered pointed leaf tips. As its name suggests, *Y. flaccida* is further distinguished by somewhat flabby leaves that carry straight marginal fibres. All have summer-borne white bells on stems 2–3 m (6–10 ft) tall. Smaller and more dainty is *Y. glauca* with narrow glaucous leaves that have a few marginal fibres and greenish-cream red-tinted flowers on stems about 1 m (3½ ft) tall.

SHRUBS WITH SMALL LEAVES

There is no clear cut division between shrubs with large leaves and those with smaller leaves and this section starts with several popular genera which nicely link the two. In general the smaller-leaved species and varieties make their impact in overall habit, texture and colour though many repay a closer look at individual leaves.

Elaeagnus

Elaeagnus contains deciduous and evergreen species, some of the latter in particular being very garden worthy as specimens for background planting and as wind-breaks. All those mentioned here do well by the sea and some at least grow naturally within the spray zone of a stormy ocean. The best of these is the Japanese and Korean *E. macrophylla* with broadly elliptic to rounded leaves to 10 cm (4 in) long. Each leaf is glossy above with a silvery, pearly lustre beneath. In the autumn, small, pendent silvery-white flowers open among the leaves. They are often overlooked and are more likely to be detected by their sweet fragrance. As in all the elaeagni, the flowers lack petals, the somewhat fuchsia-like form being composed of a scaly tubular calyx and four flared petal-like sepals. The scaly berry-like fruits are red. *E. macrophylla* is a big bushy shrub eventually to 3 m (10 ft) tall, though easily kept lower by judicious early-summer pruning. In the municipal nursery of the Hague, in Holland, this fine elaeagnus has been crossed with *E. pungens* to create *E. × ebbingei*. Although several seedlings were raised only one seems to be sold commercially, and is a favourite with the garden centres. Faster growing and gener-

Elaeagnus × ebbingei, a vigorous, handsome hybrid which thrives near the sea.

ally more vigorous than *E. macrophylla* and with somewhat narrower leaves this is a splendid plant to provide shelter near the sea.

E. glabra is akin to *E. macrophylla* but has narrower leaves with brown varnished undersides. It further differs in habit of growth, when well established producing long vigorous semi-climbing stems to 5 m (16 ft) or more. In Britain at least *E. pungens* is equally as popular as *E. × ebbingei* particularly in its bright yellow splashed 'Maculata' form. Another native of Japan's coastal areas it can grow as high as *E. macrophylla*, though it is usually less, and responds equally well to pruning. Its

stems are densely red-brown and scaly, and the stiff, leathery leaves are oblong-oval, 5–9 cm (2–4½ in) long. Individual leaf blades are a deep lustrous green above and densely whitish and scaly beneath enlivened with a sprinkling of red-brown scales. Fragrant white flowers open in late autumn and brown scaly red fruits may follow though usually rather sparingly in Britain.

E. p. 'Maculata' is just about the showiest of all variegated evergreens, each leaf irregularly splashed across the centre with brightest gold. On a dull day in winter it provides a cheering sight indeed. Its sterling merits have long been recognized, for the Royal Horticultural Society conferred upon it its highest award, the First Class Certificate, in 1891. 'Gilt Edge' is also good but here the yellow is confined to a wide border around each leaf. 'Dicksonii' ('Aurea') is similar.

New Zealand broadleaf

Splendid as a seaside shrub or small tree and forming a sizeable wind-break in milder climates is the New Zealand broadleaf, *Griselinia littoralis*. Of bushy, rounded habit, it has yellowish twigs and leathery, bright yellow-green broadly oval leaves 3–10 cm (1¼–4 in) long. The flowers are greenish and insignificant. Ubiquitous in its homeland from sea level to almost sub-alpine height, this is another useful New Zealander of which one feels hardier forms could be found with little difficulty. *G. l.* 'Variegata' has the leaves broadly margined creamy-yellow, while those of 'Dixon's Cream' are splashed in the same colour. Superior in foliage is the more tender *G. lucida* with lustrous leaves 7·5–20 cm (3–8 in) long with a beautifully varnished surface. Shade tolerant, it is often an epiphyte in the wild but grows well in soil and can attain large shrub to small tree size in favoured climates.

Hollies

The hollies (*Ilex*) really need a chapter to themselves. Most of the 400 known species are evergreen and among them is something to suit all tastes. Indeed, it would be very easy to plan an evergreen garden using hollies alone, such is their wealth of variety.

English holly

Handsome and highly regarded where growing conditions are suitable is the common or English holly *Ilex aquifolium*. Ultimately a sizeable tree with smooth grey bark, it is usually grown as a large free-growing shrub, or regularly clipped as a hedge or topiary. If restricted to one main stem when young it develops a pleasing and often elegant pyramidal outline, the green or purple flushed stems bearing the typical lustrous deep green wavy and spiny-margined leaves. Individual plants may be male, female or sometimes hermaphrodite and if a good crop of berries is required this must be borne in mind. Common holly is not reliably hardy in continental climates, but the hardiness factor is a variable one and some cultivars stand severe cold better than others. Much depends on when the cold strikes. If it comes early in the winter more damage can result than if a long period of gradually dropping temperatures is experienced to harden the stems and leaves. Cultivars are numerous and those originating in France and Holland tend to be hardier than those from Great Britain. Such cultivars have been further developed in the United States, notably in the Pacific Northwest where hollies are grown commercially for Christmas decoration and wreath making. At least 50 cultivars are available from nurserymen and so only a few favourites can be mentioned here. Readers wishing to increase their knowledge of hollies in general and the common holly cultivars in particular should consult *Holly, Yew and Box* by W. Dallimore and the *Handbook of Hollies*, a special issue of the American Horticultural Society.

Although red is the usual colour of common holly berries other colours exist.

Variations on a theme of holly: **1** *Ilex aquifolium*, **2** *I. a.* 'Ferox', **3** *I. a.* 'Hastata', **4** *I. a.* 'Aureomarginata', **5** *I. a.* 'Scotica', **6** *I. a.* 'Monstrosa', **7** *I. a.* 'Integrifolia', **8** *I.* × *altaclarensis* 'Lawsoniana', **9** *I. cornuta*, **10** *I. fargesii*, **11** *I. pernyi*, **12** *I. p. veitchii*.

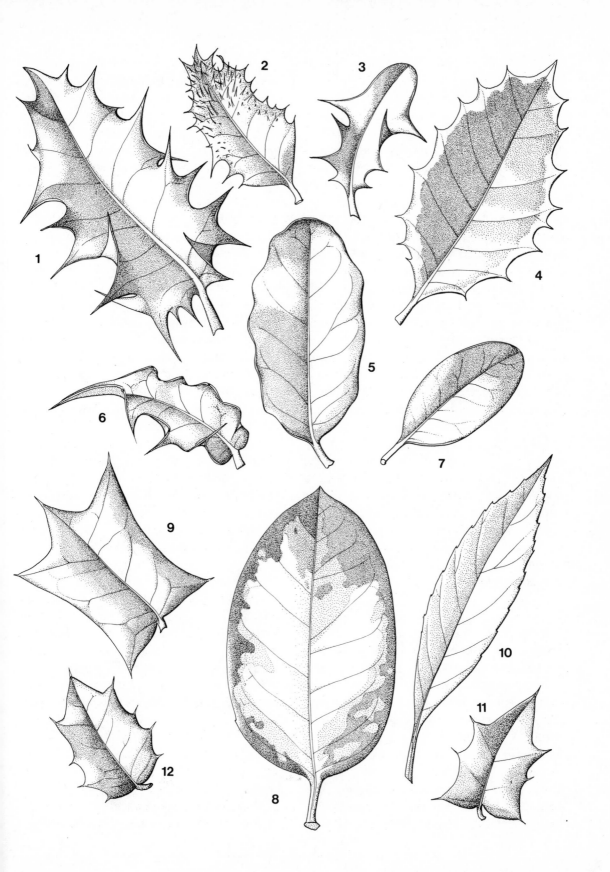

I. a. 'Bacciflava' ('Fructoluteo') bears heavy crops of yellow fruit, while 'Amber' has bronze-yellow ones. I have seen an orange-fruited form, ('Orange Gem' or 'Fructo-Aurantiaco') but can find no mention of it in nurserymen's catalogues. Various mutations have occurred to change the leaf shape, sometimes radically, and this is the origin of several cultivars. More intriguing than beautiful is the hedgehog or porcupine holly *I. a.* 'Ferox', the leaves of which have a crop of spines sticking out from the upper leaf surface particularly towards the tip. 'Ferox Argentea' has white spines and leaf margins while 'Ferox Aurea' has the centre of each leaf splashed yellow. All are males. 'Crispa' ('Tortuosa') is decidedly bizarre, the leaves appearing as if roughly twisted longitudinally to form one complete spiral; some are spiny, others have an irregular spineless margin. 'Monstrosa' ('Latispina Major') is positively horrific; no two leaves are quite alike but most are somewhat cupped with a swept-back spiny tip and lots of very long marginal spines creating the appearance of a shark's mouth; in other examples the spines appear as if stuck on at all angles by an impatient child. A talking point in the garden maybe, but not a thing of beauty.

Rather more appealing is 'Hastata', having smallish, thick-textured leaves with a few pairs of spines only, mostly restricted to the lower half, one pair much longer than the others. 'Scotica' is a spineless female cultivar with extra lustrous dark green elliptic leaves, often with a cupped tip, attractive and curiously neglected. 'Angustifolia' is very distinct, slow growing and narrowly pyramidal with rather small leaves weakly armed with small narrow spines. It is sometimes offered under such names as 'Hascombensis', 'Pernettiifolia' and 'Serratifolia' and is also confused with

'Myrtifolia' which has broader spines and a blunter apex. One of the best smooth-leaved hollies is 'Laurifolia', a male cultivar with leaves to 6·5 cm (3 in) long, dark and very glossy. Weeping holly 'Pendula' is female, with fairly normal leaves on vertically pendulous stems. It makes an interesting small specimen tree for a lawn, being grafted on to 2–2·5 m (6–8 ft) stems of common holly. Grown on its own roots it would presumably be prostrate and a good candidate for ground cover. Several showy variegated cultivars are known which have leaves either white or yellow margined (Argenteo-marginata and Aureo marginata) or bearing a yellow or white central blotch (Aureo Mediopicta and Argenteo Mediopicta). Best of the Argenteos is 'Handsworth New Silver', a female with dark purple stems and long leaves with a broad white edge. Paradoxically, 'Golden Queen' with broad yellow margins is male. 'Golden Milkboy' is male as it should be, having leaves boldly splashed golden yellow; 'Silver Milkboy', also male, does the same thing in creamy white. 'Pinto' is an American female with gold-splashed leaves and is very hardy.

Highclere hollies
From the islands of the Azores, Madeira and the Canaries come some very fine hollies, closely allied to *Ilex aquifolium* but with larger leaves and not so hardy. *I. perado*, the Azorean holly has flat broad leaves 5–10 cm (2–4 in) long, often without marginal spines and with winged stalks. *I. platyphylla* (*I. perado platyphylla*), Canary Island holly, is found also on Madeira. It has even larger leaves, often 10–15 cm (4–6 in) long with or without spines. *I. perado*, and probably *I. platyphylla* also, hybridized with the common holly has produced a race of large-

Rhododendron williamsianum has year round appeal and is, in the author's opinion, the loveliest species in the 60−90 cm (2−3 ft) height range.

Hedera colchica dentata 'Variegata' makes a perfect self-clinging cover for a dark, ugly wall.

The comparatively new, solidly
silvered *Lamium maculatum* 'Beacon
Silver'.

Ramonda myconii is grown mainly
for its floral display, but the rosettes
of deep green, wrinkled leaves have a
sombre charm all of their own.

leaved, reasonably hardy hollies of great vigour and of impressive appearance under the collective name of *I. × altaclarensis*. The species themselves are now seldom grown and even when the names are encountered in collections, hybrids often masquerade in their stead. The cultivar sold as 'Altaclarensis', the Highclere holly, greatly resembles and may be the same as 'Hodginsii'. This latter is a male tree and one of the finest, with purplish stems and large, mainly non-spiny leaves. Equally as good and female, is 'J. C. (Jan) Van Tol', producing heavy crops of dark glossy berries. Although not offered by many nurserymen in Britain, it regularly turns up in garden centres generally from Dutch stock. Also female is the aptly named 'Camelliifolia' with lustrous leaves not unlike those of *Camellia japonica* and sometimes to 13 cm (5 in) long. 'Golden King' is probably the best holly, with a yellow marginal variegation, but I prefer 'Lawsoniana', each of its handsome leaves being splashed more or less centrally with gold and yellow-green.

American holly

In the colder eastern United States at least, the native holly *Ilex opaca* is grown, much as common holly is in Britain. It is of similar habit and ultimate size to *I. aquifolium*, but the leaves often lack gloss. It is less adaptable too, needing an acid soil to thrive. There are many cultivars, including several with yellow fruits, notably 'Canary' and 'Xanthocarpa'. 'Norfolk' and 'Old Heavy Berry' are heavy-cropping females, the latter with quite good glossy leaves. 'Cobalt' is male with very dark fairly glossy leaves and is exceptionally hardy, having survived $-36°C$ ($-32°F$). Comparatively few of the North American evergreen hollies are cultivated but the ink-

berry, *I. glabra* is an exception. It is a suckering shrub 2–3 m (6–10 ft) tall, of compact habit and clad in smallish glossy-green leaves which can be light or dark and with or without a few blunt teeth. The berries are black, a radical but not unique departure from the red norm of the genus. *I. g.* 'Leucocarpa' ('Luteo-carpa') has white fruits. Yaupon, *I. vomitoria*, is native to south east North America and is grown as a hedging plant and for foundation planting. It has glossy, elliptic leaves up to 5 cm (2 in) long with neatly scalloped margins. Red is the usual fruit colour but yellow is available in the cultivar 'Yawkeyi'. The leaves have a high caffeine content and in the past were infused by the local Indians to make a self-purging vomit-inducing 'tea'. Less drastic beverages can also be made.

Oriental hollies

Among the many hollies from Asia, *Ilex cornuta*, the horned holly is surely the most intriguingly attractive. A native of eastern China and Korea it is usually seen as a compact, rounded bush 2–3 m (6½–10 ft) tall and generally of greater spread. It is slow growing, however, and can grace the smaller garden for many years without becoming awkwardly large. The 4–9 cm (1½–3½ in) long leaves are stiff, leathery, dark and shiny, and remind me of a flying squirrel in full glide. On mature specimens the upper leaves lose their distinct rectangular sharply spiny form and become broadly oval with a terminal spine only. The cultivar 'Burfordii' has all of its leaves of this form and 'Dwarf Burford' is an even slower lower-growing selection. Unfortunately the comparatively large berries are seldom freely produced but the plant is very garden worthy without them. The same can be said for *I. pernyi* a small tree of character first discovered in west China in 1858 by the Abbé Perny and collected and brought to Britain in 1900 by Ernest Wilson. Subsequently Wilson introduced it again for the Arnold Arboretum in 1908 and 1917. Next to *I. cornuta* it is among the more popular hollies for foundation planting in the USA.

When young, Perny's holly is pyramidal in outline, the slender twigs densely set with small 5-spined leaves up to 2·5 cm (1 in) long. Individual plants often produce berries so presumably this species produces a lot of hermaphrodite individuals. *I. pernyi veitchii* (*I. bioritsensis*) has larger leaves with more spines and is marginally more vigorous though no more desirable. From the Himalayas, eastwards to Yunnan, China, comes *I. dipyrena*. Sometimes known as Himalayan holly, this large shrub or small tree may best be described as falling between *I. pernyi* and *I. aquifolium*, having purple-stalked narrowly oval matt-green, slender-pointed leaves 4–13 cm (1½–5 in) long with or without marginal spines. One could wish that the comparatively large deep red berries were produced in greater profusion. The same must be said of its near ally *I. ciliospinosa*, a pleasing holly from central and west China, with smaller leaves bearing slender bristle-like spines and egg-shaped berries. Cast in a similar mould and also from central China is *I. fargesii*. Another E. H. Wilson plant of 1908, it makes a small tree to 5 m (16 ft) or so with narrowly oblanceolate leaves 5–13 cm (2–5 in) long bearing a few teeth which curve in towards the apex. If it produces its small, bright red fruits freely it can be a striking sight and makes a nice specimen tree for a sheltered site. Of similar stature is the Chinese and Japanese *I. pedunculosa*. It does not seem to have a common name as yet but if one is required,

may I suggest cherry holly? The fruits are carried on long slender stalks and much resemble small cherries dangling among the smooth un-holly like oval leaves. Not only does it make a desirable specimen but it also makes a nice talking point and is sure to surprise one's less knowledgable gardening friends.

Japanese holly

Equally un-holly-like but in a very different way is the Japanese *Ilex crenata*. A variable shrub in many ways, it can be under 1 m (3 ft) or less and 3 m (10 ft) or more. Generally it is slow growing and densely foliaged. Individual leaves range from 1 cm ($\frac{3}{8}$ in) to 2 cm ($\frac{3}{4}$ in) or more in length, elliptic to oblong-lanceolate to obovate with a few rounded teeth. Tiny whitish flowers are followed by black berries. The wild species is seldom seen and it is represented in gardens by a number of cultivars largely of Japanese origin. *I.c.* 'Convexa' is justifiably popular, forming a low, wide mound of convex shiny leaves which contrast well with the freely produced berries. Lower and denser than 'Convexa' are the American raised 'Helleri' and 'Stokes' with neat, dark green leafage. 'Longifolia' has lance-shaped leaves to 3 cm (1¼ in) long, white 'Latifolia' has box-like leaves of similar length and can in time achieve small-tree status. 'Mariesii' is a real pygmy, stiff and stunted with tiny rounded leaves and even smaller fruits; ideal for trough or sink gardens or the smaller rock garden where it provides a bonsai without all the training and root pruning. 'Golden Gem' has yellow leaves that are brightest in a sunny site and has a pleasing, low hummock-like habit. 'Aureovariegata' ('Variegata') is bright and fairly small and has its devotees, but the yellow-blotched and suffused leaves always look to me as though in the grip of a malignant virus. *I. yunnanensis* can best be described as the Chinese *crenata*, differing most significantly in its red fruits and slightly larger leaves. I like it for its dark reddish-bronze young leaves.

Osmanthus

From a foliage point of view, several members of the genus *Osmanthus* might easily be mistaken for hollies, such is their leathery nature and spiny armature. The observant gardener would of course soon notice that the leaves occur in pairs (those of *Ilex* are always alternate). The closest relation of *Osmanthus* is in fact the olive (*Olea*) and this is more readily appreciated if the fruits are seen. All the species here described have small white flowers, not very showy but delightfully fragrant. *O. delavayi* (*Siphonosmanthus delavayi*) is the exception often producing a veritable foam of white blossom in spring and well worth growing for that alone. The flowers are tubular as distinct from the tiny stars of other species. First collected in west China by the Abbé Delavay in 1890 it made its western debut in France, then crossed the channel and obtained a Royal Horticultural Society Award of Merit in 1914. It is a wide-spreading shrub taking some years to reach 2 m (6½ ft) in height though it can eventually well exceed this. The leaves are dark green, oval, toothed and up to 2·5 cm (1 in) long. Blue-black, egg-shaped fruits each with a single seed, follow the flowers but are rarely seen in gardens.

Formerly and aptly known both as *O. aquifolium* and *O. ilicifolius* is *O. heterophyllus*, in its normal spiny-leaved form, very holly-like. Not that the name *heterophyllus* is inapt (the Greek *hetero* meaning diverse or various) for this is a variable species in leaf-shape. A slow growing rounded shrub to 2 m (6½ ft) or so it has dark green oval leaves 4–6 cm (1½–2½ in) long, each one with two to four prominent spine-tipped teeth. In autumn small clusters of tiny pure white flowers emerge in clusters from the leaf axils. *O. h.* 'Myrtifolius' has spineless, rather myrtle-like leaves and is more compact in habit, while 'Rotundifolius' has rounded, spineless but blunt-toothed very dark green foliage and is even slower growing. 'Variegatus' has a quite pleasing creamy-white marginal variegation. Sombre but interesting is 'Purpureus' with glossy black-purple young growth ageing to purple-tinted dark green. Raised at Kew in 1880 it is the hardiest of all osmanthi. *O. armatus* merited inclusion in the previous chapter, having leaves 7·5–15 cm (3–6 in) long, but it is convenient to keep it with its brethren here. A species native to west China, it makes a large, handsome shrub to 3 m (10 ft) tall amply covered with narrowly oblong, coarsely spine-toothed, deep matt-green leaves. The autumn-borne, creamy white flowers are carried in axillary clusters. Growing well in sun or shade, this osmanthus deserves to be planted more often where room permits.

The dividing line between *Osmanthus* and *Phillyrea* is a slender one and recently a leading British botanist has re-classified the familiar *Phillyrea decora*, placing it in *Osmanthus*. By whatever name you choose to call it, this is a most garden worthy evergreen forming a compact, rounded bush to 2 m (6½ ft) or so and usually relatively wider. It has glossy willow-shaped leaves 5–13 cm (2–5 in) long and small white flowers which, when carried in abundance as they can be, almost rival *O. delavayi*. The flowers are borne in spring and sometimes a crop of small plum-like black-purple fruits follow.

Blending the characteristics of

O. delavayi and *O. (Phillyrea) decora* is the hybrid *O. × burkwoodii*. Good though it is, however, it is in my view no better than either parent though it does make a fine dense hedge. At present it is better known under its original bigeneric name, × *Osmarea burkwoodii* and will probably long remain so, we gardeners being die-hards where names are concerned. *Phillyrea angustifolia* is surprisingly hardy considering its Mediterranean homeland. Densely rounded and tidy of habit it has no other special merit than for use as an unusual hedge. The smooth, dark, matt-green leaves are narrow, 5–10 mm ($\frac{3}{16}$–$\frac{3}{8}$ in) wide by 2·5–6 cm (1–2$\frac{1}{2}$ in) long, with or without teeth, and the tiny flowers are yellowish-cream, fragrant and sometimes abundant. Often a coastal plant in the wild it stands sea air well.

Photinia

The bright red young leaves of *Pieris* are familiar to many gardeners, particularly those that garden on acid soils. It is not so generally realized that other shrubs produce leaves of equal brilliance and what is more important, that they will grow on a wide variety of soils including chalky ones. The desirable genus in question is *Photinia* a member of the rose family and an ally of the thorns (*Crataegus*). Depending on the botanical authority, between 40 and 60 species are known, some deciduous. Most of the evergreen sorts are tender, but two and the hybrid between them are fairly hardy. *P. glabra* comes from China and Japan and makes a large shrub with glossy, narrow, oval, shallowly toothed leaves 4–9 cm (1$\frac{1}{2}$–3$\frac{1}{2}$ in) long. Each leaf is carried on a stalk 6–12 mm ($\frac{1}{4}$–$\frac{1}{2}$ in) long and is bronze when young. The best form is *P. g.* 'Rubens' which has bright bronze-red young foliage. Clusters of white hawthorn-scented flowers open in summer. *P. serrulata* is Chinese and much more imposing, forming a tree in its homeland and other favoured areas, but seldom more than a large shrub elsewhere. It has leaves 10–20 cm (4–8 in) long on stalks 2·5–4 cm (1–1$\frac{1}{2}$ in) long and thus deserves to be placed among the large-leaved fraternity. It flowers in late spring just as the glossy copper-red young leaves expand. Crossed together, the above two species produce *P. × fraseri* which blends in various degrees the best characters of its parents. *P. × f.* 'Birmingham' favours the *P. glabra* parent but with the young leaf colour of *P. serrulata*. 'Robusta' favours *P. serrulata* with even brighter young leaves and is the hardiest of all these evergreen photinias. The best of all comes last; 'Red Robin' also tends towards *P. serrulata* but has bright red young leaves equal to *Pieris formosa forrestii*. A fine plant indeed but needing a fair amount of room to develop properly. On the other hand, all these photinias stand clipping well and make most distinctive hedges.

A hybrid is now in existence—though not, as far as I am aware commercially available—between *Photinia × fraseri* 'Robusta' and *Stranvaesia davidiana*. Christened × *Stranvinia* this bigeneric hybrid seems to blend the parental characters but has an overall *Photinia* appearance. It should be looked out for in the future.

Rhamnus

Having much the same character as *Phillyrea*, and about as hardy, is *Rhamnus alaternus* from the Mediterranean region, Portugal and Atlantic Morocco. It has dark green, toothed, oval to oblong leaves 2–5 cm (2 in) long. Sometimes unisexual, the insignificant flowers are yellow-green followed by globular berries that ripen

Rhamnus alaternus 'Variegatus', the only evergreen variegated buckthorn.

through red to black. Fairly fast growing and reaching 3 m (10 ft) or more it makes a good wind-break or background to a border. 'Argenteovariegata' has narrower leaves with white irregular margins and makes an interesting specimen.

Barberries

Asiatic barberries

About 450 species of barberries (*Berberis*) are recognized and about half of these are evergreen. Despite the prickles and spines a surprisingly high percentage are worth growing and a few are outstanding. Most barberries are suckering and clump-forming, sending up from the base each year, stronger, taller stems until full height is reached. The stems grow erect, then arch

over at the top and branch out; thus most species have a basically pleasing and compact habit of growth. The primary hallmark of *Berberis* is the way clusters or rosettes of leaves arise in the axils of the trifid spines which in turn are really modified leaves. The smallish bowl-shaped yellow or orange flowers are well worth a closer look and it is fun to trigger off the sensitive stamens by gently touching their bases with a bristle or needle. All the species described below are worthy of a place in the garden for their foliage alone, some have a bonus of flowers. In general it is only a few of the South American species that are worth growing for their flowers alone.

Collected by Frank Kingdon Ward in south east Tibet in 1924, *B. calliantha*, is one of the largest flowered Asiatic barberries. Individual flowers can be 2 cm ($\frac{3}{4}$ in) or marginally more across and light up the low growing bushes in early summer. They are carried singly or in twos or threes on long slender stalks and are followed by egg-shaped blue-black berries. The leaves are rather holly-like, deep glossy green above and blue-white beneath. It is a fine shrub for the front of a border, rarely exceeding 90 cm (3 ft) in height. Two years later, in Upper Burma, Ward discovered his 'Silver Holly', *B. hypokerina*, a shrub of similar stature and in time, forming thickets. Each dark glossy leaf can reach 10 cm (4 in) or more in length, oval-oblong in outline with prominent marginal spines and a startling blue-white beneath. The flowers are much smaller and in crowded clusters and are followed by blue-purple berries. A favourite of garden centres and mine also is *B. verruculosa*, a really dense bush of 1–2 cm ($\frac{1}{2}$–$\frac{3}{4}$ in) long, rigid glossy leaves, dark above and bright glaucous beneath. Yellow flowers open from spring to autumn but never in any great quantity. This is a

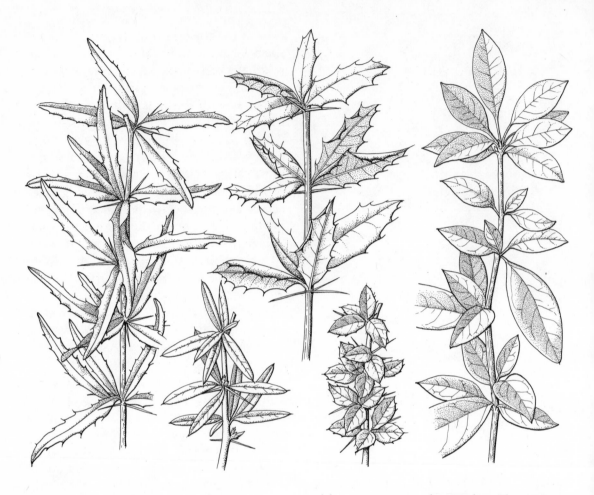

Examples of evergreen barberries: from left to right, *Berberis gagnepainii*, *B. candidula*, *B. hookeri viridis*, *B. verruculosa* and *B. valdiviana*.

first-rate shrub for foundation planting, slowly reaching 1·5 m (5 ft) or so. Crossed with *B. calliantha* it has given us *B.* × *bristolensis*, an attractive compromise but rather lacking the character of its parents. *B. verruculosa* has also combined with *B. gagnepainii* creating *B.* × *hybrido-gagnepainii* (*B.* × *chenaultii*), in effect a more compact glossy leaved *gagnepainii*. This latter species comes from west China, producing dense clusters of stems eventually to 2 m (6½ ft) or so clad

with narrow, lance-shaped, wavy-margined matt-green leaves 4–10 cm (1½–4 in) long. The bright yellow 1 cm (⅜ in) wide flowers are usually borne freely. *B. hookeri* is a similar Himalayan species but somewhat smaller and a little less graceful with broader, darker green leaves that are glaucous beneath. *B. h. viridis* from Assam and Bhutan has leaves that are green beneath and in Britain at least, is the commoner plant in cultivation. *B. julianae* and *B. sargentiana* are cast in a similar mould though the first of these can eventually reach 3 m (10 ft) in height. *B. julianae* has angled yellowish stems set with spines up to 4 cm (1½ in) long and narrowly oval spine-toothed leaves. The flowers are 6 mm

($\frac{1}{4}$in) across borne in clusters of up to fifteen. The fruits are blue-black. *B. sargentiana* has smooth reddish stems and spines rarely more than 3 cm ($1\frac{1}{4}$in), often less.

B. triacanthophora is generally considered to be the hardiest of all evergreen barberries, surviving average continental winters. It is akin to *B. gagnepainii* and has the same graceful habit and narrow leaves though the latter are smaller and have rolled-under margins. The flowers are very pale yellow. *B. pruinosa* has a rather rangy habit and can reach 3 m (10 ft) or more and as much in width. Its main attractions lies in its lemon-yellow flowers and black fruits which are so heavily coated with wax as to appear frosty white. Finally there comes what for me is the finest of the dwarf evergreen barberries, *B. candidula*. Forming a low mound of densely-arching branches to 60 cm (2 ft) or so tall but with a greater spread, it makes a superb front of the border shrub providing excellent ground cover. The leaves are darkly lustrous above and a brighter blue-white beneath than *B. verruculosa*. Narrowly oval and 1–3 cm ($\frac{1}{2}$–$1\frac{1}{4}$in) long, they have rolled-under margins and appear narrower than they really are. The solitary bright yellow flowers can be 1·5 cm ($\frac{5}{8}$in) wide and are followed by black-purple berries. This barberry was first raised in the west of France at the famous Vilmorin Nurseries from Chinese seeds collected by the Abbé Farges, one of the more noteworthy missionary naturalists.

South American barberries

In the Andes of Chile and Argentina and down to sea level at the Straits of Magellan are to be found a group of evergreen *Berberis*, some of which also rank among the finest of flowering shrubs. Pride of place for sheer exuberance of flower and general garden worthiness must go to *B. darwinii* from Chile. It was introduced to Britain in 1849 by William Lobb from the island of Chiloë but had previously been discovered by Charles Darwin during the voyage of the Beagle. Ranging in height from 2–4 m ($6\frac{1}{2}$–13 ft) or more, depending on the rainfall of the area, it has a dense habit and dark green foliage like that of a small-leaved holly. In late spring it becomes smothered with golden-orange blossom and is then a wonderful sight. Purple berries covered lightly with a white, waxy patina follow and when borne in quantity can be quietly attractive.

Inhabiting the higher but drier slopes of the Andes is *B. empetrifolia*, the most distinctive of the evergreen species on account of its almost needle-like rolled leaves. Generally of low and arching habit to about 60 cm (2 ft) or more, it has golden-yellow flowers which although sometimes produced in fair profusion cannot be described as among the finest. Mated with *B. darwinii* however, it has given rise to *B.* × *stenophylla*, in my view the finest hybrid barberry of all. Very vigorous and more graceful than *B. darwinii* it produces bamboo-like thickets of slender, arching stems bearing leaves like *empetrifolia* but darker and glossy and a profusion of golden flowers with a hint of orange. It makes a fine specimen plant and is excellent for hedging though it eventually loses much of its grace, even when pruned only once a year, just after flowering, as it should be. If plants are raised from seeds borne by this hybrid, a wide range of plants result. Several cultivars of this origin are commercially available, all fairly small and all are worth growing, from the compact 'Irwinii' to the looser 'Corallina' with coral red flower buds, and the larger rather bizarre 'Pink

Pearl', which has some of its shoots and leaves mottled or splashed creamy-white and pink and flowers that can be pink, orange, pale yellow or bicoloured.

Also from Chile and Argentina and rivalling *B. darwinii* in its profusion of darker flowers is *B. linearifolia*. No further comparisons can be made however, for *linearifolia* has a sparse, even gaunt habit especially when old, and leaves like those of *B. × stenophylla* but larger and more glossy. Nevertheless it is very well worth growing in sheltered places, thriving best beneath trees if the soil is not too dry. A better garden plant of similar appearance is found in its hybrid with *B. darwinii* called *B. × lologensis*. This is a natural hybrid first collected by Harold Comber near Lago (Lake) Lolog in Argentina where the parent plants grow together. In habit it either blends the parental characteristics or tends towards *darwinii*, and the leaves may be spine-toothed or not. Apricot-orange flowers are carried in abundance. Excellent though all these South American barberries are, they are primarily flowering shrubs and, apart from *B. darwinii* would probably seldom be grown purely as evergreens. There is one other Chilean species which adds fine foliage to beautiful flowers, *B. valdiviana*. Very different from the species described above it forms a tall almost columnar shrub to 3 m (10 ft) tall sumptuously clad with large, glossy rich green practically spineless leaves up to 7·5 cm (3 in) long. In early summer every twig is garlanded with pendent racemes of saffron-yellow flowers, a real bonus of great charm. Why this splendid barberry is not more widely grown is a mystery. It was discovered by the great Chilean botanist Philippi in 1856 and introduced into Britain in 1902 and again in 1929 by Clarence Elliott and Dr Gourlay. Like all the South American *Berberis* species it is not hardy in continental winters but will survive − 18°C (0°F) for short spells, and if cut to ground level will sprout again. Few nurseries stock it but it is well worth looking out for.

Azara

Also native to South America are the nine or ten known species of *Azara*. Although in no way related and totally spineless they do have a somewhat barberry-like appearance. They are generally more graceful however, with slender, flexible stems and abundant small leaves, each with a smaller leaf-like stipule at its base. The fragrant flowers are petalless but have numerous bright yellow stamens forming fairly conspicuous fuzzy clusters. Small berries may follow. None are fully hardy but *A. microphylla* will stand − 18°C (0°F) for short spells though some shoots may die or the leaves fall. It is a large shrub or even a small tree in mild climates. In colder areas it makes an attractive wall shrub with its arching, flattened frond-like sprays of tiny dark green, obovate, toothed leaves. There is a 'Variegata' form with the leaves edged creamy-white.

California lilac

Staying for the moment with less than hardy shrubs we move north to California, the primary home of *Ceanothus* and known there as California lilac. This is essentially a genus of evergreens grown primarily for their flowers but which are also pleasing to look upon at all times of the year. The praises of *C. arboreus* and *C. thyrsiflorus* have already been sung (see p. 39) and both can be grown as wall shrubs with some judicious annual pruning after flowering. 'Autumnal Blue' is a child of *C. thyrsiflorus*, the other parent is not known. In Britain it is considered as being 'possibly the hardiest

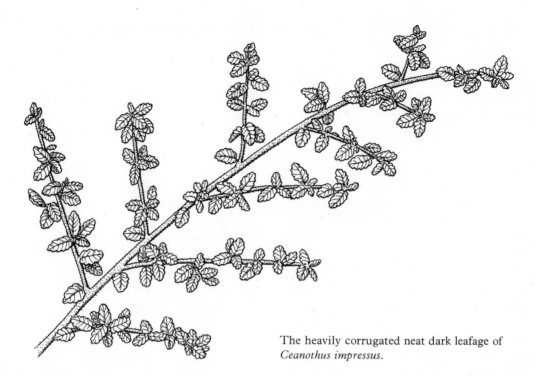

The heavily corrugated neat dark leafage of *Ceanothus impressus.*

evergreen ceanothus', but curiously, in the homeland of its parent it does not thrive well. Of lesser stature than *thyrsiflorus* it produces a profusion of blue flowers in late summer and autumn. *C. dentatus* has tiny elliptic-oblong leaves rarely more than 1 cm ($\frac{3}{8}$ in) long, with a folded-in tip, rolled margins and impressed veins. They are dark and glossy above, grey-felted beneath. In British gardens this ceanothus is confused with *C.* × *lobbianus (dentatus* × *griseus)*, a hybrid with larger leaves bearing three main veins from the base. There is also confusion with *C.* × *veitchianus* but this has flat, obovate leaves. All produce bright blue blossoms in early summer. *C. foliosus* is akin to *C. dentatus* but the leaves can reach 2 cm ($\frac{3}{4}$ in) or more in length and have wavy, not inrolled margins. It is most distinctive in its low-spreading habit, not often above 90 cm (3 ft) and often less, but at least double this in width. Occasionally it is confused in

Britain with *C. thyrsiflorus repens* but this latter plant has the typical *thyrsiflorus* leaves and a flatter, denser habit; the best of ceanothi as ground cover, it would be well worth growing even if it never produced a single flower.

Also mat-forming is *C. gloriosus*, an attractive foliage plant with thick-textured, boldly veined and toothed leaves 1.5–4 cm ($\frac{4}{5}$–1$\frac{1}{2}$ in) long. The lavender-blue flowers appear in late spring. It is a coastal plant, growing on cliffs above the sea around Point Reyes, California, but despite this it is surprisingly hardy. When happily situated it can form a mat to 3 m (10 ft) or more across. *C. g. exaltatus* grows erect and can attain 2–4 m (6$\frac{1}{2}$–13 ft) in height. Even hardier is the prostrate squaw carpet, *C. prostratus* from the higher mountains of the north coast ranges of California north to Washington State. Its leaves are similar but smaller, rarely above 3 cm (1$\frac{1}{4}$ in) and with only 4–7 teeth on each side and sometimes toothless (the leaves of *C. gloriosus* have at least twice this number). Bright blue flowers light up the dark mats in spring. In the wild, *C. rigidus* is low growing, rarely above 90 cm (3 ft) tall and often less. In British gardens it is usually grown as a wall shrub and will then reach 4 m (13 ft). It has variable leafage from narrowly elliptic to obovate, often with truncated tips, 3–12 mm ($\frac{1}{8}$–$\frac{1}{2}$ in) long. Rich purple-blue flowers open in spring. A favourite of mine and one that performs well in the British climate is *C. impressus*, the Santa Barbara ceanothus. It has an appealing fish-bone mode of branching, every slender stem densely set with tiny rounded, dark green hairy leaves. Each blade is only 6–12 mm ($\frac{1}{4}$–$\frac{1}{2}$ in) long, almost convex, with very deeply impressed veins as its name suggests. A profusion of deep blue flowers wreathe the branches in late spring and early summer. The Royal Horticultural Society has bestowed all its highest awards on this plant: Award of Merit, First Class Certificate and Award of Garden Merit, the last in 1969.

Mexican orange blossom

Very few natives of Mexico grace northern gardens but at least one shrub does it very ably and is also surprisingly hardy. This is the so-called Mexican orange blossom, *Choisya ternata*, a pungently aromatic shrub of rounded habit to 2 m (6$\frac{1}{2}$ ft) or more tall. The foliage resembles clover but is leathery and lustrously dark, providing an excellent foil for the freely-borne white flowers. Each flower is five-petalled, about 2·5 cm (1 in) wide and exhales a sweet hawthorn fragrance. The main mass of blossom of *C. ternata* is produced in early summer, but the flower sprays continue until autumn when there is often a further, but minor, display.

Carpentaria and Callistemon

Also native to California is *Carpenteria californica*, a bushy shrub 2–3 m (6$\frac{1}{2}$–10 ft) tall and hardier than the hardiest ceanothus. As an evergreen t is rather undistinguished, the 5–10 cm (2–4 in) long leaves being lance-shaped and mid-green. In summer, however, it becomes a thing of beauty when decked with 5–7·5 cm (2–3 in) pure white flowers like single roses. Across the Pacific in Australia dwell the bottle brushes, *Callistemon*, highly ornamental evergreens, but in cooler climates needing the protection of a warm wall and even then not hardy in severe winters. Like *Carpenteria* they are not particularly distinguished as evergreens though the stiff, willow-like leaves are of an unusual texture. But when in flower they are transformed and become an eye-catching sight. The individual flowers have tiny petals but it is the long red or yellow stamen filaments which provide the colour. Many flowers are densely clustered in terminal spikes forming the characteristic bottle brushes. When the flowers have finished, the tip of the spike carries on growing as a leafy shoot. Prettiest but the least hardy is the confusingly named *C. citrinus* with flowers in shades of red. Best for colour is *C. c.* 'Splendens' with glowing crimson stamens. Rather untidy in habit unless regularly trimmed after flowering, it has leaves 4–9 cm (1$\frac{1}{2}$–3$\frac{1}{2}$ in) long, coppery-tinted when young. Hardier is *C. subulatus* with very narrow leaves 2–4 cm ($\frac{3}{4}$–1$\frac{1}{2}$ in) long and crimson brushes. Similar and much confused in British gardens are *C. linearis* and *C. rigidus* but both have leaves twice as long. Not yet well known, but potentially the hardiest of all is *C. sieberi (pithyoides)* from the mountains of south east Australia. Sometimes called alpine bottlebrush, it has rigid awl-shaped leaves to 2·5 cm (1 in) long and pale yellow brushes.

A shrubby Convolvulus

The genus *Convolvulus* is best known for its elegant, tender annual twiners (morning glories) and the pernicious, perennial bindweed. Totally different and strangely neglected is the low, hummock-forming shrub *Convolvulus cneorum* from the steep rocky seaward slopes of Dalmatia in Jugoslavia. It has the silkiest silver-grey 4–6 cm ($1\frac{1}{2}$–$2\frac{1}{2}$ in) long narrow, elliptic leaves which almost glitter when ruffled by the wind on a sunny day. As a summer bonus, clusters of pointed pink-tinted buds expand to perfect funnel-shaped white convolvulus blooms. It is a fine plant for a sheltered sunny site in poor dry soil.

Box

Quite a different proposition are the various sorts of box, *Buxus*, from Europe Asia and Africa (tender species also occur in central America). More useful than beautiful they do nevertheless have a sort of cheerful charm particularly in winter. Bushy and thickly set with tiny leaves, they make excellent low wind-breaks and hedges and are splendid as a background for showier plants. The boxes are essentially foliage plants, the tiny petalless flowers being generally insignificant. When profusely flowering though, the spring-borne fuzzy masses of pale yellow stamens have a certain modest charm. The short, barrel-shaped, 3-horned seed capsules are intriguing objects, all the more so as they explode when ripe, propelling the hard seeds a considerable distance. Boxwood is famous for its hard, bony nature and was formerly much used for rulers and other precision instruments made of wood. It is still in demand and the available supply is dwindling rapidly.

Least known and not easy to come by, reputedly because it is difficult to propagate, is the Himalayan box, *B. wallichiana*. It has the longest leaves of the hardy species, 2·5–6 cm (1–$2\frac{1}{2}$ in) long, lance-shaped and glossy. About 2 m ($6\frac{1}{4}$ ft) tall in cultivation it is handsome enough to be used as a specimen and will fool your gardening friends who are conditioned to think of box or boxwood as *B. sempervirens* or *B. microphylla*. Next in leaf size comes *B. balearica* from south west Spain and the Balearic Isles, a sturdy species making a small tree in the wild but seldom more than a large shrub in gardens. Its 2–4 cm ($\frac{3}{4}$–$1\frac{1}{2}$ in) long, broadly oval leaves are moderately glossy and of a somewhat yellow-green hue, especially so if grown in an open sunny site. Like *B. wallichiana* it makes an interesting specimen tree and would make a fine hedge, though I do not know of any examples.

Best known is common box, *B. sempervirens*, a very variable species which has given rise to many horticultural varieties (cultivars). Although in general a wide, large bushy shrub, under ideal conditions it becomes a tree of small to moderate size. The leathery, notch-tipped glossy leaves vary from broadly oval to narrowly oblong and from 1–2·5 cm ($\frac{3}{8}$–1 in) in length. The most familiar cultivar in gardens is undoubtedly *B. s.* 'Suffruticosa', low growing and very twiggy. Formerly much used to edge paths and flower beds it is the essential ingredient of parterre gardening. Ideal for taller hedges and low screens are such cultivars as 'Handsworthensis', 'Latifolia' and 'Arborescens', all with larger leaves than the type species and generally more robust. Among the more distinctive foliaged sorts are 'Longifolia', having leaves up to 4 cm ($1\frac{1}{2}$ in) long; 'Myrtifolia', slow growing and with lance-shaped leaves to 2 cm ($\frac{3}{4}$ in) long; and 'Rosmarinifolia' with very narrow leaves of sage-green hue and a dwarf habit. 'Pendula' forms a large shrub of loose habit with pendulous branchlets clad in dark green foliage. Common box is native to Europe, North Africa and west Asia.

East of this range and to Japan, *B. microphylla* takes over. It is basically much like *sempervirens* but is generally lower growing, often not above 90 cm (3 ft) tall. *B. m. koreana* is even shorter with leaves to 1·5 cm ($\frac{3}{5}$ in) long. It is the hardiest of all boxes surviving severe continental cold. *B. m. sinica* is the tallest form (it occasionally reaches a height of several metres), with downy young stems and ovate to obovate leaves to 3·5 cm (1 in) long. It

may be met with in gardens as *B. harlandii*, but this name belongs rightly to a different unreliably hardy species from south China.

Sweet box

A member of the same botanical family (*Buxaceae*), but rather different in habit and overall appearance is *Sarcococca*, sometimes known as sweet or Christmas box because of its winter-borne flowers. Easy going with regard to soil, and very shade tolerant they are ideal for planting under trees where they will eventually form pleasing ground cover. In their mode of growth they resemble *Berberis*, sending up a succession of stems from ground level. The tiny flowers are petalless, separate males and females being carried in the same cluster. Each male flower has four stamens, the filaments of which are thick and usually

Three distinctive species of Buxus: left, *B. balearica*; centre, *B. sempervirens* and right, the rare *B. wallichiana*.

Two species of sweet box, ideal dwarf shrubs for a shady site: left, *Sarcococca confusa*; right, *S. hookerana digyna*.

white. Small berry fruits follow. All those mentioned are Chinese and though reasonably hardy will not stand severe cold. *S. confusa* and *S. ruscifolia chinensis* have the same impact in the garden, with glossy, deep green ovate to elliptic leaves which taper to a point. Both rarely exceed 1·5 m (5 ft) though *ruscifolia chinensis* is slower growing. The easiest way to differentiate between them is the fruit: *confusa* has black and *ruscifolia* red berries. *S. hookerana digyna* has narrow, less glossy leaves on slender erect stems and cream coloured stamens, while *S. h. humilis* has pink anthers and forms a suckering shrub to 60 cm (2 ft) tall.

The skimmias from east Asia also thrive beneath the shade of trees, and bear small, fragrant flowers. They are laurel-like in general appearance but low growing, rarely above 90–120 cm (3–4 ft) tall with a rounded or dome-like habit. All the species are dioecious, that is male and female flowers are borne on separate plants. Individual blossoms are tiny but many are carried in dense terminal clusters. They are cream or white, open in spring and are followed by conspicuous crimson berries which are usually left alone by the birds. Hardiest and best known is *S. japonica*, in one form or another a common constituent of Japanese forests. It has agreeably aromatic, oblong to

orous but worth growing for the surprise of white berries if such are appreciated. *S. laureola* is Himalayan and superficially resembles *Daphne laureola*, its dark green leaves aggregate towards the ends of each season's shoots. When crushed they are not exactly agreeably aromatic. The flowers are tinted greenish-yellow and very sweetly scented.

Cotoneaster

Showy red berries are very much the attraction of many species of *Cotoneaster*, but at the same time there may be good evergreen foliage and even a bonus of flowers. A member of the rose family (*Rosaceae*) and allied to the thorns (*Crataegus*) and less directly to apple and pear, *Cotoneaster* covers about 50 species, less than half of which are evergreen. All prefer a sunny site but tolerate light shade, and will grow in all kinds of soil except those that are waterlogged. Clusters of small pink or white flowers are borne in late spring or summer and are followed by red or orange, rarely yellow berry-like fruits. (Some of the deciduous species have dark purple or black fruits.) Ground hugging and fast growing and providing first-rate ground cover is *C. dammeri*, with lustrous oval leaves 2–3 cm ($\frac{3}{4}$–$1\frac{1}{4}$ in) long. Found by Ernest Wilson in 1900 on the open rocky mountain slopes in central China, it is one of the most distinct of all cotoneasters and has been widely planted. The small white flowers are solitary and the berries bright red, though never produced in any abundance. *C. d. radicans* and *C. d.* 'Major' are listed in catalogues and are sometimes confused with each other and the type species. True 'Major' has leaves 2·5–4 cm (1–$1\frac{1}{2}$ in) long, while *radicans* has leaves with longer stalks to 6 mm ($\frac{1}{4}$ in) with flowers often in pairs. *C.* 'Skogholm' is a form or hybrid of great

Skimmia japonica in late winter; a good all-rounder with pleasing foliage, fragrant flowers and colourful fruits.

elliptic leaves which may be dark to almost yellow-green, depending on soil, site and the form grown. *S. j.* 'Foremanii' is the most vigorous cultivar, with broader, obovate leaves. It is female and when planted alongside a male produces large clusters of berries. A highly suitable mate is 'Fragrans' with extra sweetly scented flowers usually in profusion. An equally, if not more attractive male is 'Rubella', having dark foliage and flowers with conspicuous red buds. Suitable for the larger rock garden is 'Rogersii', being slow growing and forming low mounds of waved leaves. Slightly smaller and slow growing and the only suitable mate, is the male 'Rogersii Nana'. Also dwarf is 'Fructo-albo', not particularly vig-

vigour which forms low arching branches to 30 cm (1 ft) or more high. *C. microphyllus* also has a spreading and arching habit but the stems are profusely set with tiny, dark green polished leaves rarely more than 1 cm (⅜ in) long. Small white flowers light up the dark foliage in summer and are followed by comparatively large matt scarlet berries. This is another fine ground coverer particularly for cascading down a bank. It can also be very effective used as a wall shrub when it will easily reach 2–3 m (6½–10 ft) in height. *C. m. thymifolius* is a very desirable half-sized version with smaller and narrower leaves. *C. m. cochleatus* is almost distinctive enough to be considered a separate species, having a mat-forming habit and almost glossy, much broader leaves. Essentially a small, neat compact version of *cochleatus* is *C. congestus*, one of the few cotoneasters well-suited to the rock garden. It was formerly known as *C. microphyllus glacialis* and why botanists raised it to specific rank is one of those things that puzzle mere gardeners.

Varying in habit in much the same way as *C. microphyllus* is *C. conspicuus*, one of the finest cotoneasters of its sort and valuable as a combined evergreen, flowering and fruiting shrub. Collected by the Tsangpo River in south east Tibet in 1925 by Frank Kingdon Ward, it has already gained the Royal Horticultural Society's First Class Certificate and Award of Garden Merit, and has secured a permanent place in nurserymen's catalogues. These awards went to *C. c.* 'Decorus', a low-growing form which produces a profusion of white flowers with dark anthers and bright scarlet fruits of good size. A taller growing form named 'Highlight' is equally profuse in flowers and fruits, the latter of an orange-red shade. The foliage of *C. conspicuus* is shorter, broader and less polished than that

of *microphyllus* but the dense arching habit still makes it an interesting shrub at all times of the year. Among the larger leaved, taller cotoneasters, one species stands out as an evergreen shrub, *C. lacteus* from Yunnan. Collected by George Forrest in 1913 it has steadily proved its worth in the shrub border as a specimen for a lawn, or as a large hedge and gained the R.H.S. Award of Garden Merit in 1969. Eventually reaching 3–4 m (10–13 ft) in height and as much across, it has a pleasing arching mode of growth and deep matt-green leaves of broadly oval to obovate outline and up to 5·5 cm (2¼ in) long. In late summer, dense, flattened heads of white flowers open, giving way to red berries which only attain full colour in late autumn and persist cheerfully through the winter, birds permitting.

C. salicifolius has, as its name suggests, willow-shaped leaves, otherwise it is very similar to *C. lacteus*. The leaves are a brighter green however and the flowers and fruits develop earlier. *C. s. floccosus* has the leaf undersides covered with silky down, a graceful habit and more showy fruits, while *C. s. rugosus* is more vigorous, less graceful and has larger berries. Several prostrate or wide-spreading forms have arisen in cultivation and are particularly useful as ground cover. The best of these is 'Repens' ('Avondrood') with flat growth and very slim leaves. 'Parkteppich' is a sprawler and only suitable for ground cover in the larger garden or park. Similar and not always easy to distinguish from *C. salicifolius* is *C. henryanus*. Usually however it has larger leaves—to 9 cm (4½ in) whereas those of *C. salicifolius rugosus* never exceed 7·5 cm (3 in)—and has a more open habit with pendulous tipped branches. The leaves are grey and woolly beneath and the crimson fruits tend to be egg-shaped. It is a handsome species when well grown but needs plenty of room. Both *salicifolius* and *henryanus* have combined with the deciduous tree-sized *C. frigidus* to give several first-rate berrying shrubs, notably the popular 'Cornubia' and 'John Waterer', both regrettably only semi-evergreen unless the winter is very mild. On the other hand, some hybrids are more completely evergreen, notably the pale yellow-fruited 'Exburiensis' and the deeper yellow 'Rothschildianus'.

The firethorns (Pyracantha)

Related and sometimes confused with the cotoneaster are the various species and cultivars of firethorn, *Pyracantha*. Two small but certain points of difference are the thorny stems and serrated leaves of *Pyracantha*, characteristics never found in cotoneaster. Although pleasing at all times of the year the firethorns are best thought of and used as combined fruiting, flowering and evergreen shrubs. They have several roles in the garden, as wall shrubs, to enliven shrub borders and as hedging. All are vigorous, quick growing and not fussy as to soil providing the site is not wet. Best known in Britain and, despite the fact that it is rather frequently encountered, undeniably garden worthy is *P. coccinea* 'Lalandei'. The profusion of its mid-summer creamy white flowers and bright orange-red fruits in autumn is phenomenal. Best for foliage however is *P. atalantoides* (*P. gibbsii*), having darkly lustrous oval blades to 7·5 cm (3 in) long. Another fine shrub from China and collected by Ernest Wilson in 1907, it combines good leaves with early summer flowers and long-persisting scarlet berries. It has received the R.H.S. First Class Certificate (1918) and Award of Garden Merit (1922). *P. a.* 'Aurea' ('Flava') has fruits of rich yellow.

Very shade tolerant, *P. atalantoides* brightens up a sunless wall in the most satisfying way. The remaining pyracanthas, in particular *P. crenatoserrata*, *P. crenulata* and *P. rogersiana* are all good variations on a theme and well worth growing. There are also several fairly recent hybrid cultivars raised primarily for their fruits but which also have quite good leaves, notably 'Buttercup' (yellow fruits), 'Orange Glow' (bright orange fruits) and 'Shawnee' (light orange fruits on a disease-resistant bushy shrub).

Stranvaesia

Not unlike a blend of pyracantha and one of the tall, narrow-leaved cotoneasters is *Stranvaesia davidiana* from west China. Curiously enough it is named after the English botanist Fox-Strangways (1795–1865), such are the pedantic whims of botanists when creating a Latin plant name from a surname. Tall-growing and with narrowly oblong to lance-shaped leaves 6–11 cm ($2\frac{1}{2}$–$4\frac{1}{2}$ in) long, it has flattish clusters of white flowers about mid-summer and bright but matt-red berries in autumn and winter. *S. d. salicifolia* is the form usually cultivated and has narrowly lanceolate leaves. *S. d. undulata* is the most decorative, with wavy-margined leaves and a lower, more spreading habit. 'Fructuluteo' and 'Prostrata' are forms of *undulata*, the first with bright yellow berries, the latter of more or less prostrate growth and useful for filling in around its taller brethren or for covering banks.

Staying with members of the rose family (*Rosaceae*) we come to the handsome but less than hardy *Raphiolepis × delacourii*. It combines good-sized leathery, lustrous, obovate leaves with clusters of pink flowers in spring and summer. A nice foundation plant for a sheltered site. Somewhat hardier is one of its parents, *R. umbellata*, which forms slow-growing dense hummocks eventually to 1·2 m (4 ft) tall or more against a wall. Its oval leaves are 3–8 cm (1¼–3¼ in) long, dark green above, pale and woolly beneath when young. Individual flowers are white, expanding to 1·5–2 cm (⅝–¾ in) across and are followed by blue-black fruits 1 cm (⅜ in) wide. A distinctive shrub that deserves to be more widely planted.

Shrubby hare's ear

It is an irrelevant but interesting botanical fact that the carrot family (*Umbelliferae*) has produced few woody-stemmed members. One useful exception is the shrubby hare's ear, *Bupleurum fruticosum* from southern Europe and the Mediterranean area. It can reach 3 m (10 ft) on a wall, but in exposed maritime places where it is in its element, often not above 1–1·2 m (2–3 ft) and is then of fairly compact growth. The smooth sea-green leaves are narrowly obovate, 5–9 cm (2–3½ in) long and combine well with the umbels of the summer- to autumn-borne yellow flowers.

Jerusalem sage

Of similar hardiness and equally useful by the sea are several sorts of Jerusalem sage, *Phlomis*. All have densely woolly, rough, sage-like leaves in pairs and curiously attractive, conspicuous tubular, hooded flowers in summer. Sharply drained soil and a sunny sheltered site are essential for success but given these requirements they are easily grown. Best known is *P. fruticosa*, the only one that rightfully bears the name Jerusalem sage. Vigorous of growth and 1–1·2 m (3–4 ft) tall, it has grey-green leaves which on young plants can attain 10–13 cm (4–5 in) in length and nicely set off the bright yellow flowers. The latter are 3 cm (1¼ in) long and carried in whorls in the topmost leaf axils. They open in late summer and sometimes again in late autumn. *P. f.* 'Edward Bowles' is a fine foliage plant with leaves to 15 cm (6 in) long, and paler yellow flowers. Shorter and sturdier in growth is *P. chrysophylla* with gold-tinted leaves and rich yellow flowers. Taller and of rather untidy habit is *P. purpurea* bearing lance-shaped leaves only thinly coated with white wool above, and producing lilac to lilac-purple flowers. *P. italica* is very similar but has more oblong leaves that are more thickly woolly above.

Sage, germander and rue

Common sage, *Salvia officinalis* and its variously coloured leaf forms provides us with not only flavouring for stuffings and sauces but a group of very decorative shrubs. Seldom above 45–60 cm (1½–2 ft) and at least twice as broad, they provide splendid ground cover for dry sunny borders and banks, the variegated kinds adding colour to the more sombre evergreens. Wild sage tends to have narrow leaves and plenty of spikes of blue-purple hooded flowers. It is less effective as an evergreen however and one of the broad-leaved, shyer flowering culinary selections should be obtained. Particularly effective is *S. o.* 'Purpurascens', the purple-leaved sage which has young leaves suffused red-purple. 'Icterina' has paler grey-green leaves with yellow variegation while 'Tricolor' is basically similar but with the yellow areas suffused red-purple and pink. All may lose some leaves in a hard winter but usually enough remain to be appreciated.

Like *Phlomis* and *Salvia*, *Teucrium* is a member of the dead-nettle family though the flowers lack the conspicuous hood and instead have prominent lower lips. Providing useful but undistinguished dark green ground cover is *T. chamaedrys*, the wall germander of central and southern Europe. A dense and spreading shrublet about 20–30 cm (8–12 in) tall it has neatly toothed oval leaves to 2·5 cm (1 in) long and in late summer a profusion of reddish-purple flowers. Technically it is a subshrub, the flowering stems dying back each winter. The same is true of *T. polium* a rather tufted plant of somewhat lesser stature with narrow woolly, grey or grey-white leaves. Although the purple or yellow flowers are carried abundantly they are tiny and make little impact. *T. fruticans* is the handsomest of all but not very hardy and no good for areas of persistent hard winters. Free-standing it makes a small shrub, but trained on a wall it can reach 2–3 m (6½–10 ft) and then looks most effective with its white downy stems and leaf undersides and spikes of lavender-blue flowers during summer and early autumn.

Pungently aromatic, rue (*Ruta graveolens*) is now little used as a herb but remains ever popular as a decorative evergreen shrub for poor dry soils with a fair amount of sun. Compact of habit its deeply dissected slightly fleshy-textured leaves are a charming shade of blue-grey which is much intensified in the best form, 'Jackman's Blue'. 'Variegata' is prized by some, but for me, the spotty cream effect spoils the perfection of its glaucousness. In summer, stiff erect stems rise above the leaves bearing small mustard-yellow flowers. The individual flowers are well worth close appraisal but the overall effect is not very elegant and the stems should be either pinched out as soon as seen, or immediately the flowers fade.

Viburnum

Handsome leaves, a beautiful floral display and eye-catching fruits can all be found in the genus *Viburnum*. The best of the larger leaved ones have been mentioned already (p. 56). The following lack truly handsome leaves but are no less garden worthy in their various ways. Outstanding for the lustre of its darkest green leaves is *V. utile*, a neat, graceful and comparatively quick growing shrub which is sadly neglected in gardens. As a modest bonus, rounded heads of small, white, fragrant flowers open in early summer and are followed by blue-black fruits. Mated with the deciduous and very sweetly scented *V. carlesii*, it has given rise to the semi- or almost evergreen *V. × burkwoodii* and its named clones 'Anne Russell', 'Park Farm Hybrid' and 'Chenaultii'. The last mentioned is the least evergreen but makes up for it with good red-yellow autumn colour. All have large, fragrant flower clusters and a lot of the *utile* gloss in their broader leaves. Best known of all viburnums in Britain, where winter temperatures seldom drop to continental lows, is *V. tinus*, colloquially known as laurustinus. A bushy shrub, rarely above 2–3 m (6½–10 ft), it has glossy ovate leaves 4–9 cm (1½–3½ in) long and flat heads of white flowers which are variably pink in bud. Ovoid steely-blue fruits develop which regrettably are rather hidden by the leaves. In mild winters it blooms off and on from late autumn to spring. *V. t. lucidum* has more lustrous foliage; *V. t. hirtulum* is hairier; both are marginally less hardy. 'Eve Price' has carmine flower buds and smaller leaves; 'Pyramidale' is more erect; 'Purpureum' has darker foliage purple-flushed when young and 'Variegatum' (also more tender) has its leaves marked creamy-yellow. *V. henryi* is most distinctive in its open habit and the way the branches grow out almost at right angles. It has leathery, glossy, narrowly oval, shallowly toothed leaves and fragrant cream flowers in panicles, a departure from the flattened clusters (corymbs) so characteristic of most viburnums. The fruits ripen through bright red to black and can be very colourful. It was given an R.H.S. Award of Garden Merit in 1936 and earlier (1910) a First Class Certificate as a fruiting shrub. Since *V. henryi* was only collected by Ernest Wilson in central China in 1901 this is high confirmation of its garden-worthiness.

Privet

To most gardeners, privet (*Ligustrum*) means the ubiquitous hedging plant *L. ovalifolium* known as common privet in Britain, and California privet in the USA; it is a native of Japan. In severe winters it can lose some or even all its leaves; in a mild climate it is virtually evergreen. When allowed to grow unclipped it is not unhandsome, both in leaf and profuse creamy flower trusses and grows well by the sea. The genus *Ligustrum* however has better things to offer the evergreen gardener. Also from Japan is the superior *L. japonicum*, a less vigorous shrub of slower growth with fine, dark, olive-green, polished ovate leaves 4–9 cm ($1\frac{1}{2}$–$3\frac{1}{2}$ in) long. In late summer or autumn there is the added attraction of panicles of small, white tubular flowers which contrast well with the dark foliage. Even finer is *L. j.* 'Macrophyllum' with black-green broader leaves; 'Rotundifolium' is of similar hue, the blades being broadly oval to rounded on a slow-growing bush seldom above 2 m ($6\frac{1}{2}$ ft) high. *L. lucidum* is in effect a Chinese version of *japonicum* but more robust and eventually achieving small tree size. Its leaves are less dark in hue and often longer. The sharp-eyed gardener will observe that the young stems are perfectly smooth, whereas in *japonicum* they are finely downy. *L. henryi* is not as fine as the two previous privets but

it is nevertheless a much neglected species deserving to be seen more often. Neat and compact in habit, eventually to about 3 m (10 ft) or more it has black-green, lustrous leaves to 4 cm ($1\frac{1}{2}$ in) long and fragrant white flowers in late summer. It has the same potential as *japonicum* and *lucidum* and would make a fine hedge.

Spindles

Though lacking the floral display of the privets, the various evergreen spindle bushes or trees (*Euonymus*) are equally valuable as evergreens, perhaps more so with their greater range of habits. Enjoying a well deserved popularity today as a ground cover plant is the very variable *E. fortunei*. Formerly considered a variant of *E. japonicus*, it has a wide distribution in east Asia, though it is the Japanese forms of *E. f. radicans* that largely represent it in western gardens. *E. f. radicans* has the growth form of ivy producing running and rooting so-called juvenile growth which will climb up tree trunks and walls. Later, lateral non-climbing, freely-branching adult stems arise which bear the small greenish flowers. As also with ivy, plants propagated from the adult growth retain that habit and form low-spreading bushes. 'Silver Queen' is of this origin, providing one of the brightest and most appealing of variegated plants, each oval leaf being boldly edged with creamy-yellow. 'Silver Pillar' is similar, but the leaves are narrower with whiter margins and the habit more erect. 'Carrierei' is the name given to the original green-leaved adult form with leaves to 5 cm (2 in) long and of a pleasing glossy green. 'Vegetus' is an 'improved' form, often with creeping and erect stems and broad, almost rounded leaves, half matt, half glossy, of great appeal; a first rate evergreen for planting under trees though to create the best visual appeal it is worthwhile pinching out the longer stems that overtop the main bush. *E. f.* 'Kewensis' is totally unlike any other form and makes an interesting talking point in the garden. It forms mats or low hummocks of very slender stems clad with tiny oblong-oval leaves seldom more than 1 cm ($\frac{3}{8}$ in) long. Each blade is shallowly toothed and dark olive green, with a semi-matt finish and contrasting pale veins. Some of the older leaves turn dull crimson in autumn. If planted near some form of support it will begin to climb and gradually assume the normal juvenile form of *E. fortunei radicans*. An account of this curious behaviour by Mr Ernest Brown can be found in *Gardener's Chronicle*, Vol 108, p. 146 (1940), and is repeated in Vol 2 of the Eighth Edition of *Trees and Shrubs Hardy in the British Isles*, by W. J. Bean. A somewhat larger form of 'Kewensis' is sometimes offered as 'Minimus'.

Despite its jaw-breaking name, *E. kiautschovicus* deserves greater recognition. It has much in common with the adult phase of *E. fortunei* but has a more vigorous and spreading habit, eventually building up to 2–3 m (6$\frac{1}{2}$–10 ft) in height. It has cheerful, fairly bright green, oval to obovate leaves 4–7 cm (1$\frac{1}{2}$–2$\frac{3}{4}$ in) long. Quite often it produces 8 mm ($\frac{1}{3}$ in) wide greenish-white flowers in some abundance with an aftermath of globular, pink fruits which split to reveal orange-red coated seeds. This is the hardiest of the larger evergreen euonymi and can be grown where the next species fails. *E. japonicus* is a familiar evergreen hedging plant in much of the British Isles and southern and western USA. More erect and with broader, darker leaves than *E. kiautschovicus* it can eventually well exceed 3 m (10 ft) though it is easily kept at half this by pruning or clipping. Often a coastal plant in the wild, it is excellent for seaside gardens either as a hedge, wind-break, or in less formal and more prominent places. Flowering and fruiting can be unreliable but when prolific, rivals that of *kiautschovicus*. Most handsome in foliage is *E. j.* 'Macrophyllus' ('Latifolius'), having larger, more elliptic leaves. 'Macrophyllus Albus' has broad white margins to its leaves. 'Aureopictus' ('Aureus') is most distinctive, each dark green leaf bearing a central blotch of bright yellow. Reversing this arrangement is the popular 'Ovatus Aureus' with creamy-yellow leaf margins. 'Microphyllus' ('Myrtifolius') is a real pygmy version with narrow leaves 1–2·5 cm ($\frac{3}{8}$–1 in) long on a bushy, slow-growing shrublet to 90 cm (3 ft) or so; gold and white variegated forms are available. Hardiest of the different forms of *E. japonicus* is *E. j. robustus*, a striking geographical variety of compact habit and with thick-textured broadly oval leaves that deserves to be grown more often.

Allies of witch hazel and tea

Although a member of the witch hazel family, *Hamamelidaceae*, and related to *Sycopsis* (see p. 43), *Distylium racemosum* superficially resembles the Japanese privet (*Ligustrum japonicum*). The almost black-green lustrous leaves are arranged alternately on the stems however, not in pairs like the privets. To the casual beholder a bush in flower in spring makes no impact at all. True the tiny flowers in short erect spikes are in no way showy but they well repay a closer inspection, as indeed so many tiny flowers do. Each petalless bloom has a rusty hairy stalk and a five-lobed downy red calyx from which project bright purple-red stamens. In cultivation *Distylium* slowly makes a spreading shrub to about 2 m (6$\frac{1}{2}$ ft) tall. In its native south Japan it can attain medium tree size, the dark, very hard wood of which is much prized. It thrives best in a neutral to acid soil and is very shade-tolerant, making a fine foundation shrub for a sheltered north wall.

Daphne

As evergreen shrubs the daphnes are unremarkable, though many are pleasing enough and a few might well be grown without the bonus of flowers, although they are of course widely grown as flowering shrubs and need no recommendation in that direction from me. The following are species with good foliage or which combine the best of leaf and flower. Daphnes have a rather undeserved reputation of being short lived. It is true that some species—mainly deciduous ones—are liable to collapse and die rather suddenly, more frequently than other shrub genera. Records show, however, that given well-drained fertile soil and a reasonably sunny site (except the shade lovers mentioned below), daphnes can be expected to live anything from 10 to 40 years. Even if they last for 10 years or less they are still well worth growing for their fragrance, delightful little flowers and generally neat and tidy appearance—in that order. Woodland dwellers in the wild and thus very shade-tolerant are *D. laureola* and *D. pontica*. Both have leathery, lustrously deep green leaves which give life to a deciduous wood or shrubbery in winter. *D. laureola*, inaptly called the spurge laurel, has narrowly obovate to oblanceolate leaves 3–5 cm ($1\frac{1}{4}$–2 in) or more long; those of *D. pontica* are always obovate and 4–9 cm ($1\frac{1}{2}$–$3\frac{1}{2}$ in) long. In both cases the leaves tend to cluster towards the tips of each season's growths. Both have yellow-green flowers which peep out modestly from among the leaves exhaling a sweet fragrance on quiet, mild,

humid evenings, *laureola* in late winter, *pontica* in spring. Poisonous black berry-like fruits follow and provide a ready means of increase if sown as soon as ripe. Although valuable for shade, these two daphnes have a much denser habit in fuller light and are then more effective purely as evergreens. *D. laureola* is one of the few members of the genus that thrives in wet clay soils.

As a combined foliage and flowering shrub, *D. odora* takes some beating. A native of China and Taiwan and long and widely cultivated in Japan, it is not unlike *D. pontica* but has longer leaves and terminal clusters of red-purple buds which open to paler, or almost white flowers. They emit one of the strongest, sweetest perfumes of any plant and one spray will scent a room. Hardiest and most frequently grown is *D. o.* 'Aureomarginata' which has leaves with narrow yellow margins. It will certainly stand short periods at −18°C (0°F) without much, or any harm. Other more tender forms are sometimes available with or without variegated leaves; 'Alba' has plain green leaves and white flowers. Flowering from mid-winter to spring, *D. odora* deserves a sheltered site. It thrives in partial shade and does well under high tree cover.

Smaller, neater, sun-loving and surprisingly hardy despite its south Italian homeland is *D. collina*. Slowly forming a dense bush to 45–60 cm ($1\frac{1}{2}$–2 ft) high and relatively wider it is clad in obovate leaves 2–4 cm ($\frac{3}{4}$–$1\frac{1}{2}$ in) long which are dark and glossy above, paler and silky-hairy beneath. In late spring the shoot tips become crowned with clusters of fragrant purple-red flowers and sometimes again in autumn, though not quite so spectacularly; a splendid shrub for the rock garden or for foundation planting preferably where it can easily be seen and smelt. *D. retusa* and *D. tangutica* can be considered as Asiatic versions of *D. collina*. *D. retusa* is superficially rather like *D. collina* but the leaves are a shade darker and have inrolled margins, and the flowers open almost white from rose-purple buds. *D. tangutica* is taller, to 1·5 m (5 ft) or so, less branched and more erect, with duller less rolled leaves which are generally longer. Both produce red, berry-like fruits fairly readily, and self-sown seedlings may occur. The garland flower, *D. cneorum*, is not so satisfying purely as an evergreen, though the mats of dark leafage are pleasing enough in winter. In early summer, every stem-tip bursts into a tiny posy of rich rose-pink flowers and the plant is transformed into a thing of beauty. Happy on limy or acid soils providing they are freely drained but moisture retentive, well grown specimens can attain 2 m (6½ ft) in width and about 30 cm (1 ft) in height and make spectacular ground-cover. I refer here primarily to *D. c.* 'Eximia', the commonest form in cultivation. Less commonly available are 'Pygmaea', more compact and quite prostrate, and 'Variegata', with leaves that are narrowly margined creamy-white. There are also white-flowered forms variously known as 'Alba', 'Albiflora' and 'Flore-Albo' the priorities of which have yet to be worked out. Brief mention must be made of the partially evergreen hybrid between *D. cneorum* and the deciduous *D. caucasica* listed and sold as *D.* × *burkwoodii*. This is essentially a first rate flowering shrub intermediate in character between its parents. Two clones are sold commercially 'Somerset', an erect vigorous shrub eventually to 1·5 m (5 ft), and 'Albert Burkwood', (often grown simply as *D.* × *burkwoodii*), of lower stature rarely above 90 cm (3 ft) tall, and usually broader than it is tall. Less commonly seen is *D.* × *b.* 'Lavenirii' ('Laveniriensis') which, from what I have heard, falls between 'Albert Burkwood' and 'Somerset' in height and habit. 'Lavenirii' arose naturally at the Nursery of Morel and Lavenir in France, selected from seedlings of *D. caucasica*, the parent plant growing close to *D. cneorum*. *D.* × *burkwoodii* was purposely created by the brothers Albert and Arthur Burkwood, British nurserymen, the parent plant being *D. cneorum*.

Feijoa

As might be expected of a shrub native to south Brazil, north Argentina and Uruguay, *Feijoa sellowiana* is not very hardy; it requires a sheltered sunny wall in all but the mildest areas. Quite closely related to the guavas (*Psidium*) it eventually becomes a large bushy shrub with white felted stems. The undersides of the leaves are also white, and dark glossy green above, making a fine contrast. The oval leaf blades are 3–7·5 cm (1¼–3 in) long and carried in opposite pairs. Providing the weather is reasonably warm, in summer intriguing fleshy, petalled white and crimson flowers appear from the leaf axils. Each flower is about 4 cm (1½ in) wide and has a central crown of numerous deep crimson stamens surrounded by four reflexed and curiously concave petals. In areas of warm summers, ovoid, red-tinged, green, sweetly aromatic fruits 5–7·5 cm (2–3 in) long follow the flowers. In the USA there are several cultivars with finer fruits. The latter are eaten raw or used to make jellies.

Escallonia

Also South American are the various sorts of *Escallonia*. Although grown primarily as flowering shrubs, some species and hybrids have very handsome foliage. Regretfully the best foliaged ones are not too hardy and need a sheltered wall except where winters

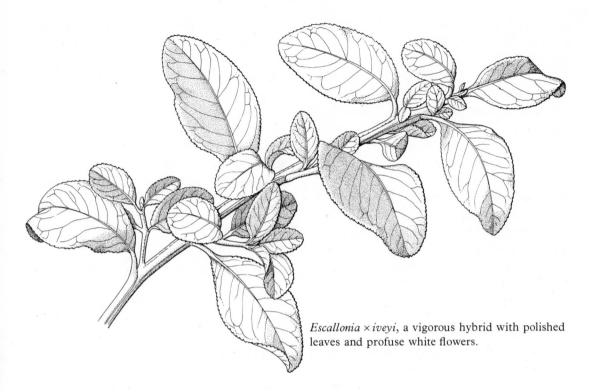

Escallonia × iveyi, a vigorous hybrid with polished leaves and profuse white flowers.

are mild. However, like all the escallonias in cultivation they are vigorous, quick growing and root readily so can easily be replaced if killed during hard winters. Finest of all in my opinion is *E.* × 'Iveyi' with deep and beautifully lustrous oval leaves and a profusion of pure white flowers in terminal pyramidal panicles in late summer. It is cut back to ground level when temperatures reach around − 18°C (0°F) but usually springs up again strongly from the base. The exact parentage of this plant is in some doubt. It was discovered as a self-grown seedling at Caerhays Castle, Cornwall, England, close to a planting of *E. bifida* and *E.* × *exoniensis* and these are its presumed parents. *E. bifida* (*E. montevidiensis*) is also a good evergreen with somewhat larger, less lustrous leaves and white flowers. *E. rosea* from south Chile is hardier. Despite its name it also has racemes

of white flowers, plus good lustrous leaves. Crossed with the pink to red flowered *E. rubra* from southern South America it produced *E.* × *exoniensis*, another glossy-leaved shrub of high speed growth and graceful habit and white, pink-flushed flowers. *E. rubra* is not to be sniffed at as an evergreen shrub, particularly its larger form *E. r. macrantha* with bright rose-red flowers. Most escallonias do well near the sea and this one in particular is in its element within sight and sound of the waves. Crosses between the deciduous *E. virgata*, *E. rubra* and *E. r. macrantha* have produced *E.* × *rigida*, an umbrella name for many popular cultivars. Most of these are not outstanding as regards their foliage but are excellent dual purpose shrubs, usually of arching habit and bearing a profusion of small flowers in shades of red, pink and white. Most of them were raised at the now defunct Slieve Donard Nursery in Northern Ireland's County Down. Still one of the best is 'Donard Beauty' with rose-carmine flowers; 'Donard Gem' has scented pink flowers and 'Donard Radiance' is rose-red with good dark, polished foliage. 'Apple Blossom' is slower and lower growing with pink and white flowers, a real beauty.

Crinodendron, Mitraria, Philesia and Desfontainia

Embothrium and *Escallonia* have already been mentioned; *Berberidopsis*, *Lapageria* and *Asteranthera* are discussed in Chapter 5. In between, come what for me at least are the best of all in the shrub category, *Crinodendron*, *Mitraria*, *Philesia* and *Desfontainia*. Regrettably none are very hardy, but where winters are mild and the soil acid they are worth every effort to grow. Still often called *Tricuspidaria lanceolata*, *Crinodendron hookeranum* is the tallest of this quartet attaining 3 m (10 ft) or more when well suited. It has dark green lance-shaped leaves and glowing crimson urn-shaped flowers which hang elegantly from long pendent stalks in early summer. Each flower is about 2·5 cm (1 in) long and when produced in quantity creates a spectacular sight; a lovely plant for a sheltered shady site, though the foliage is a little sombre. Requiring similar conditions is *Mitraria coccinea*, a member of the tropical gesneriad family from the temperate rain forests of south Chile. One of my most persistent memories of the rain forests of the island of Chiloë is this plant loosely scrambling in climber-like fashion up the trunks of trees. It had also been seen as a rather thin free-standing shrub. In cultivation it forms a low spreading shrub unless in a mild area of high rainfall where it will climb if given the opportunity. The small glossy, toothed oval leaves make a pleasing foil for the pendent, scarlet, bottle-shaped flowers which appear during summer and autumn. The Chilean common name of 'botellita' is very apt.

Philesia magellanica (*buxifolia*) is a real gem and has been described quite rightly as one of the most beautiful of all dwarf shrubs. When happily established it forms a mound of suckering stems clad in small, narrowly oblong leaves which are convex in cross section, dark green above and blue-white beneath with an intriguing ladder-like pattern of prominent veins. From mid-summer to autumn solitary rose-crimson flowers nod from the stem tips. Very much like those of its very near ally *Lapageria*, each 5–6 cm (2–2½ in) long bloom is composed of three petals which overlap and form a tube, then flare out to a bell-like mouth; a real picture of elegance. *Philesia* is not easy to please, needing cool, moist shade but minimal frost and a peaty soil. Given these conditions it will even colonize upwards as it does in its native cool temperate rain forests, strong stems growing up and rooting into mossy trunks. There is a bigeneric hybrid between *Philesia* and *Lapageria*, called × *Philageria*. Rare and interesting, as a plant it fails to unite satisfactorily the best qualities of its parents. It is worth recording that these three shrubs were all part of the booty that the English plant hunter William Lobb collected during his second expedition to South America (1845–8). During his first expedition (1840–44) he had collected the Chile pine (*Araucaria araucana*) (see p. 00), and the last member of our present quartet *Desfontainia spinosa*. Somewhat hardier than the other three it is basically a holly-like shrub eventually reaching a height of 2–3 m (6½–10 ft) and sometimes very much more across. The dark glossy leaves are carried in pairs, each one 2·5–6 cm (1–2½ in) long, oval and edged with triangular spine-tipped teeth. From summer to autumn, pendent, slender, trumpet-shaped flowers appear. They are about 4–5 cm (1½–2 in) long, scarlet with a contrasting yellow mouth and combine beautifully with the dark foliage. In Britain at least this plant varies in hardiness and although conclusive evidence is not available, this would appear to be so, as a result of its homeland habitat. At least two main introductions of desfontainia are known, the one mentioned by Lobb and another by Harold Comber, 1925–6. In Chile it grows at sea level in the equable humid climate of the Straits of Magellan but farther north it inhabits cloud forests in the Andes with a vast range extending north into Colombia. Lobb's original collections probably came from a sea-level locality, whereas those of Comber would have come from a mountain locality as he was primarily concerned with hardiness for British gardens. Comber also collected a fine self-coloured form of this shrub with flowers of vermilion to orient red. Subsequently named 'Harold Comber' it eventually gained the R.H.S. Award of Merit in 1955.

Chinese Itea and Pittosporum

Holly-like leaves are the tenuous link between *Desfontainia* and *Itea*, enabling us to span the Pacific and return to west China where Augustine Henry discovered *I. ilicifolia* prior to 1895. It is a handsome, large bushy shrub with glossy rich green leaves flatter than those of holly and with smaller, softer spines. In late summer every twig is hung with slender catkin-like racemes 15–30 cm (6–12½ in) long composed of tiny greenish-white flowers, a much more effective and eye-catching sight than it sounds. *I. yunnanensis* is only to be dis-

tinguished from it by its somewhat longer, less spiny leaves and marginally earlier flowers. Although most of the 150 known species of *Pittosporum* are found in New Zealand and Australia, it is a widespread genus with members as far away as Africa, the Canaries and Madeira. Hardiest of the Asiatic species is *P. tobira* from China, Korea, Taiwan and Japan. Slow growing in cooler climates it can eventually make a large rounded shrub. Where summers are warm and winters mild it can even become a small tree to 7 m (23 ft) tall. It has leathery, polished, bright green obovate leaves 4–9 cm (1½–3½ in) long, which are carried in rosette-like clusters towards the ends of the twigs. From early summer onwards clusters of creamy-white flowers with the scent of orange blossom open at the centre of each rosette. Like all the pittosporums, *P. tobira* is not hardy in areas of severe frost. It is variable in its hardiness and there is still scope for finding plants in the coldest parts of their homelands. For example, plants raised from seeds which I collected in Japan some years ago grew for several years at the foot of a south wall in eastern England.

Pepper tree

Having a certain resemblance to the pittosporums is *Pseudowintera colorata*, the pepper tree or horopito, a widespread shrub in the forests of New Zealand. Still often known under its former name *Drimys colorata*, it is a smallish shrub rarely more than 1 m (3 ft) tall, though it has been known to reach twice this height. It is one of the very few temperate evergreens with naturally variegated or coloured leaves. In good light, each elliptic to broadly obovate leaf is yellow-green above, margined or blotched crimson and sometimes almost entirely suffused that colour. The undersides have a bright blue-white patina and the contrast is wonderfully effective when ruffled by the wind. Insignificant yellow-green flowers are followed by dark red to black fruits. Given high tree cover or a sheltered, partially shaded site it is reasonably hardy and combines well with such woodland shrubs as *Ruscus, Sarcococca, Buxus, Skimmia* and *Rhododendron*. Of similar hardiness, perhaps even more so and deserving of greater recognition is the aromatic *Drimys lanceolata*. Its narrow, dark lustrous leaves and dull crimson stalks and stems go well together, making a pleasing foil for the usually freely-borne small white flowers. A native of south east Australia it is another useful plant for growing beneath trees where the soil is not limy.

The daisy bushes

Between 100 and 130 species of daisy bushes, *Olearia*, are recognized, much depending on the views of the botanist consulted. All are evergreen and native to Australasia, although the greater number are to be found in Australia. It is among the 32 New Zealand species however, that we find the hardiest of the more decorative members. All are bushy shrubs of rounded habit, at least in their earlier years, with alternate leathery-textured leaves and clusters, sometimes large, sometimes small of mainly tiny, daisy-like flowers, the ray florets (petals) of which are white. What is usually considered to be the pride of the genus, *O. semidentata* from the Chatham Islands, is an exception to the generalizations above, being rather tender and with large solitary flower heads the rays of which are pale purple. Its stems and lower leaf surfaces are clad in snowy-white felt and the upper leaf surfaces are dark green. Each narrow leaf is toothed and 4–6 cm ($1\frac{1}{2}$–$2\frac{1}{2}$ in)

long. In a mild climate a well grown specimen of 2 m ($6\frac{1}{2}$ ft) or more is a sight to behold in summer when covered with 5 cm (2 in) wide flowers. *O. chatamica* is similar but usually with white ray florets and has longer, broader leaves. The two species cross readily and it is likely that many plants in cultivation are of hybrid origin.

For me, one of the finest foliage olearias is *O. macrodonta*, eventually a large wide-spreading shrub or even a small rugged tree in its homeland or in mild areas. Superficially, the ovate, dark olive-green leaves are rather holly-like, but the spine-like teeth are soft and the leaf undersides are whitened with a thin felty layer. They have a musk-like scent when crushed. In summer, fragrant, flattened flower clusters up to 15 cm wide (6 in) terminate most of the stems and make the bush a handsome sight. Although reasonably hardy one could wish it were more so. As it grows from near sea level to 1,200 m (4,000 ft) in the mountains and throughout most of the length of New Zealand one feels that there is a chance to find a hardier clone.

Closely allied and marginally hardier is *O. ilicifolia*. Generally only half the size of *O. macrodonta* in British gardens it can, when happily situated, attain 3 m (10 ft) in height. The leaves are a greyer-green and much narrower, with strongly waved margins and harder teeth. The flower clusters are similar, up to 10 cm (4 in) across. Often growing in the wild in the same areas as the preceeding two species is *O. arborescens*, a large shrub or small tree reminiscent of *O. macrodonta* but with entire or distantly-toothed leaves that are more glossy above. Once again one feels that a hardier form could be found, if collections were made as high up in the mountains as possible.

It has been suggested that crossing *O. arborescens* with *O. ilicifolia* produces

O. macrodonta, an intriguing and possible theory at present unresolved. Very similar are *O. albida* and *O. avicenniifolia*, shrubs to 2 m (6½ ft) or more with narrowly oval to lance-shaped leaves dark to greyish green above, whitened beneath. The margins of those of *O. albida* are usually waved whereas those of *avicenniifolia* are flat. Both have large clusters of white blossom in late summer, *O. albida* having 1–5 ray florets to each tiny flower head, *O. avicenniifolia* with only 1–3. In Britain there is much confusion between the two and *O. albida* is usually considered to be more tender and less common. My own observations do not bear this out. To baffle further both expert and novice alike there are hybrids between the two and with other species. It is likely that the *O. albida*, of British gardens at least, is a hybrid. Such plants have 3–6 ray florets to each flower, and blunter leaves. For this plant the cultivar name 'Talbot de Malahide' has been proposed to honour the memory of a modest but very knowledgable plantsman with a keen interest in olearias. It is comparatively hardy and stands exposed seaside conditions very well. *O. moschata* forms grey globes of oval leaves 1–2 cm (½–¾ in) long, set with small clusters of white flowers in late summer. Although sub-alpine in the wild, it is not particularly hardy in cultivation. Crossed with *O. ilicifolia* it has given rise to the plant called "*O. × mollis*", a delightful silver-grey shrub with longer, strongly waved, felted leaves. The name "mollis" does not rightfully belong to this plant having earlier been used for the cross *O. ilicifolia × O. lacunosa*. The latter species is a shrub of distinction which deserves to be grown more often. It has narrow, rolled leaves to 9 cm (3½ in) or more long with a conspicuous ladder-like network of veins, impressed above, embossed

Olearia × mollis, one of the hardier daisy bushes and worth growing for its grey foliage alone.

beneath and forming small, box-like partitions. The flowers are in terminal panicles but rarely produced in cultivation.

Von Haast's daisy bush
Most frequently seen in British gardens and there considered hardy is *O. × haastii*, a pleasing but not very exciting bush with the rounded habit of one of its parents, *O. moschata*, but larger leaves, dark and matt-glossy above, a characteristic acquired from its other parent, *O. avicenniifolia*. In late summer it becomes smothered in small, white, fragrant flower clusters and then comes into its own. Equally as hardy, if not more so, is *O. nummulariifolia*, a mountain species as-

cending to sub-alpine exposures. Very different from those considered above, it forms an erect bush often less than 90 cm (3 ft) tall in cool climates but capable of attaining two to three times this. The small leaves are oval to rounded but appear narrower, being bent up at the ends and down on the sides to form a saddle-shape. They are glossy above and clad in a thin layer of yellowish, buff or white felt beneath. The flower heads are solitary and have white to cream ray florets.

Several other New Zealand olearias are well worth growing for their foliage, but the above selection gives some idea of their versatility of form and general appeal. Before we leave the genus however, a few south east Australian/Tasmanian species are well worth mentioning. All are primarily flowering shrubs but are not unattractive from a purely foliage point of view. Hardiest of these is *O. stellulata*, a rather loose, erect shrub with narrow dark grey-olive leaves 4–7·5 cm (1½–3 in) or more long, covered beneath with a yellowish-white down. In early summer, pure white daisy flowers are freely borne. Most plants grown under this name are really *O. phlogopappa* (*gunniana*), a taller, more bushy plant with white-felted stems and leaf undersides, the latter also aromatic, smaller, 1·5–5·5 cm (⅜–2¼ in) obovate or oblong (those of *stellulata* are elliptic to oblong) and grey-green above. The flowers are carried in great profusion often obscuring the leaves. There are also coloured forms, pink, mauve, purple-blue, originally collected in Tasmania by Harold Comber during his 1929–30 expedition. Known as the Splendens Group, these coloured sorts are sadly less hardy and generally not as vigorous. *O. lirata* is closely allied but has longer leaves, paler and shiny above. Crossed with *phlogopappa* it has given rise to the superior

O. × scilloniensis, a vigorous fast-growing shrub to 1·5 m (5 ft) or more which regularly smothers itself with white blossom year after year providing the flowering stems are cut out soon after the last bloom fades.

Shrubby veronicas (Hebe)

During the past quarter of a century or more the shrubby veronicas (*Hebe*) have steadily gained in popularity. In their New Zealand homeland they are frequently cultivated as ornamentals and in Britain even more so. They are also being planted in western Europe and the milder parts of the USA. Almost a hundred species are known plus numerous hybrids and cultivars. In gardens at least, their naming is in utter confusion. Similar species often masquerade under each other's names or are represented by hybrids. Unfortunately, all hebes that flower at the same time as each other will hybridize freely. The seed produced will sow itself, or is purposefully sown, and the seedlings distributed under the name of the seed parent or made into fancy cultivars. Botanists too have added to the confusion of the gardeners by re-classifying the genus at intervals, so that any one plant might be grown under its modern name and one or more older synonyms. Be all this as it may, the genus *Hebe* has a lot to offer the gardeners in the way of attractive foliage and flowers and a variety of useful and pleasing habits. A bed or border near the house closely planted with a selection of the hardier small-leaved species can give endless pleasure with a minimum of maintenance. They also provide excellent foundation planting material and make pleasing and informal hedges, particularly near the sea.

Hebe divides itself very neatly into two groups, leafy and whipcord. The first group has distinct leaf-blades which stand out from the stem in four ranks. The whipcords have minute, scale-like leaves tightly pressed to the stem and resemble conifers. In most species the flowers are white though some are mauve-tinted in bud. A few species have mauve, purple or near-red flowers and in some of the hybrids these colours are intensified. The whipcords are mostly sub-alpine in the wild and comprise the hardiest group, many tolerating temperatures to $-18°$C ($0°$F) or below.

Large-leaved hebes
Among the larger leaf group it is a fair generalization to say that the smaller the leaf the hardier the plant. Showiest from a floral point of view and also among the tenderest is *H. speciosa* with broadly elliptic leaves and beetroot to red-purple flowers. The true species is seldom seen, hybrid cultivars taking its place, e.g. 'La Seduisante' (crimson) and 'Alicia Amherst' (deep purple). Also with fairly large leaves but in the narrow willow-like sense is the hardier *H. salicifolia*. This can get quite large, eventually to 3 m (10 ft) or more in favoured sites, but is easily kept lower by pruning. Its generally bright green leaves often have finely, irregularly toothed margins, a characteristic fairly rare in the genus. The white flowers are carried in wand-like spikes. These two species have united to give us *H. × andersonii*, a fine vigorous shrub which nicely blends the parent characters but has violet flowers. It is probably the first recorded purposely formed hybrid between two hebes, being created before 1849 in Scotland by Isaac Anderson-Henry. *H. × a.* 'Variegata' is one of the most appealing of variegated shrubs, each rich-green leaf overlaid and patterned grey-green and boldly margined creamy-white. Very popular for seaside planting in

Britain is *H. × franciscana* 'Blue Gem' (*H. lobelioides*) a hybrid between *H. speciosa* and *H. elliptica*. Neat and dense in habit with silky-leathery, shiny elliptic leaves about 4–6 cm ($1\frac{1}{2}$–$2\frac{1}{2}$ in) long, it provides a long succession of blue-violet flowers in shortish, dense spikes.

Much planted in Britain under the name *H. traversii* is *H. brachysiphon*, eventually a rounded bush to 1·5 m (5 ft) or more with crowded, narrowly oblong leaves 1–2·5 cm ($\frac{1}{2}$–1 in) long and shortish spikes of purple-stamened white flowers. True *H. traversii* is seldom seen in gardens, being smaller, with narrower, pointed, greyish leaves. Also popular and wrongly named in the same way is *H. rakaiensis* still often listed and sold as *H. subalpina*. It is a beautifully dense, rounded shrub 60–90 cm (2–3 ft) with bright pale green but only slightly glossy elliptic leaves up to 2 cm ($\frac{3}{4}$ in) long by 8 mm ($\frac{3}{10}$ in) wide. The profusely-borne flowers are white. True *H. subalpina* is in cultivation in Britain, some, if not all the commercial sources being derived from cuttings I collected in Arthur's Pass, South Island in 1972. *H. subalpina* has more spreading, longer, darker glossier leaves up to 3 cm ($1\frac{1}{4}$ in) by 6 mm ($\frac{1}{4}$ in). In addition, the stems are green and the extreme base of the leaf stalks are blackish. Also growing at sub-alpine elevations, often in company with *H. subalpina* is *H. albicans*, a flat-topped bush with crowded, stalkless leaves of a charming greenish-grey. The white flowers are carried in very dense short spikes.

Of a similar grey tone are the narrow, wide-spreading leaves of *H. recurva*, an equally hardy and free-flowering species. The plant in cultivation is often named *H. r.* 'Aoira' though it is doubtful if this is really necessary. Aoira is a corruption of the Maori Aorere, the name of a river in the

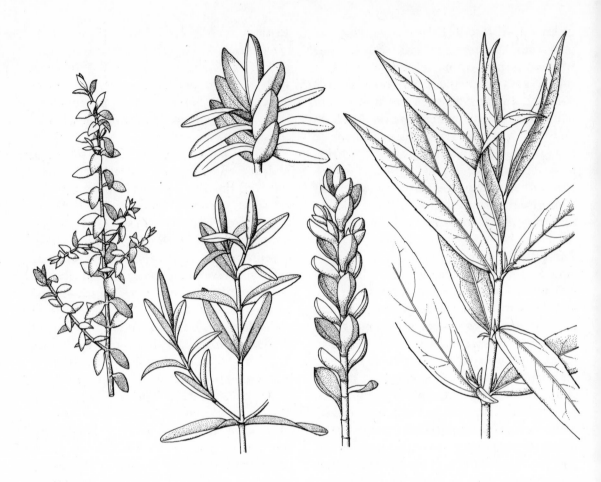

Five of the hardier shrubby veronicas. Top, *Hebe albicans*; left to right, *H. pimelioides*, *H. subalpina*, *H. pinguifolia*, *H. salicifolia*.

north west of Nelson Province where this species was first found. More intensely coloured are the tiny blue-grey leaves of *H. pimeleoides*, a very slender, purplish stemmed, almost prostrate shrub with blue-purple flowers. This charming mountain species is variable and the brightest-leaved form to look for is *H. p.* 'Glaucocaerulea'. It seems very likely that the more compact larger-leaved white flowered and popular *H.* 'Pagei' (*H. pinguifolia* 'Pagei', *H. pageana*) is a hybrid between this species and a form of *H. pinguifolia*. *H.* 'Pagei' is a first-rate ground cover shrub and surprisingly hardy. *H. pinguifolia* also makes good but rather deeper ground cover with a mixture of semi-prostrate and erect stems. The overlapping leaves are grey-green and strongly cupped. *H. buchananii* is rather like a diminutive *H. pinguifolia* with somewhat greyer more spreading leaves 3–6 mm ($\frac{1}{8}$–$\frac{1}{4}$ in) long. *H. b.* 'Minor' is even smaller, seldom above 10–15 cm (4–6 in) tall and makes a fine rock garden plant. More flatly mat-forming is *H. allanii*, one of the most distinctive of all the leafy species in its finely downy, grey-green, oblong leaves. Profusely borne white flowers add to its charms making it a first-rate plant for the front of a small shrub border or in the larger rock garden.

Also very suitable for the not too small rock garden is *H. vernicosa* a slow-growing hummock 45–60 cm (1½–2 ft) tall in time and generally wider. It has small box-like leaves with yellowish margins and a profusion of white or lavender-tinted flowers. Somewhat similar but much taller and with darker, glossier leaves is the variable *H. odora* (*H. buxifolia*). It makes a handsome ball-shaped shrub 1–1·5 m (3–5 ft) and if collected from high in the mountains is very hardy. It does not usually produce its pure white flowers with any great freedom. It is known as boxwood in its homeland and its former Latin name, *H. buxifolia* was thus very apt. *H. odora anomala* (*H. anomala*) is now recognized as a small, narrow-leaved form of *H. odora* and can be used for the same purposes in the garden. Looser in habit and with equally narrow but longer, more spreading grey-green leaves is *H. glaucophylla* (*H. darwiniana*). It is generally represented in gardens by its variegated form *H. g.* 'Variegata' which has leaves with broad creamy margins. Owing to the stance of the leaves, it is the margins that face outwards, giving the whole bush a creamy-white glow, both unique and beautiful. Unlike most small-leaved species it is not particularly hardy and is browned in severe weather.

For floral spectacle, *H. hulkeana*, the New Zealand lilac is hard to beat and can justly lay claim to being the most beautiful of all hebes. It is a loosely branched 30–90 cm (1–3 ft) tall shrub with glossy, oval, round-toothed and red-edged leaves. In early summer every stem tip produces a tall panicle of numerous lilac-lavender flowers and the *en masse* effect on a well-grown plant can be striking. *H. lavaudiana* is closely allied but dwarfer and *H. × fairfieldensis* (*H. × fairfieldii*) is a midway hybrid. Largest flowered of all hebes is *H. macrantha*, a rather straggling, low shrub with thick, oval, toothed leaves which is transformed in summer when covered with glistening white 2 cm (¾ in) wide flowers.

Whipcord species

Largest of the whipcord group is *H. cupressoides*, a most aptly named species resembling from a distance a globular grey-green dwarf cypress to 90 cm (3 ft) or more tall. Flowering is erratic and not necessary for its success as a garden plant. On occasions however, an individual plant will

Hebe imbricata, one of the curiously conifer-like whipcord species.

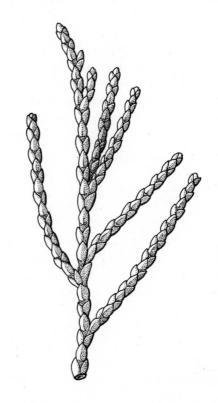

bloom well and then appear to be surrounded by a lavender-tinted haze. *H. propinqua* is similar but more bun-shaped in outline, only half the height and with green foliage and white flowers. It contrasts well with the uniquely attractive *H. ochracea*, a spreading flat-topped shrub 45–60 cm (1½–2 ft) tall which looks as if it has been lacquered in old gold. White flowers enhance the effect in summer. In British gardens it is confused with *H. armstrongii*, but in fact the rich yellow-green hue and more rounded outline of the latter species clearly distinguishes it from *H. ochracea*.

'Shrubby ragworts'

Depending on the botanical authority there are 2,000–3,000 species in the genus *Senecio*, its best known members being ragwort and groundsel. Most of the species are annuals or perennials, though climbers, shrubs, trees and succulents are included. As with *Olearia* and *Hebe*, New Zealand has the monopoly of the hardiest shrubby species, some of which are very decorative and garden worthy evergreens. *S. ×* Dunedin Hybrids 'Sunshine' will be a name unfamiliar to most gardeners but that is what we must now call the popular and much planted shrub listed as *S. greyi* or *S. laxifolius*. These two are now considered to be forms of one species, though 'true' *S. laxifolius* is hardier and more densely leafy, each leaf to 6 cm long by up to 2 cm wide (2½ × ¾ in) as against the maximum of 10 × 4·5 cm (4 × 2¾ in) for *S. greyi*. 'Sunshine' has leaf blades 3–6 cm (1¼ × 2½ in) long by 1·5–3 cm (¾ × 1¼ in) wide, sometimes a little more on young vigorous plants. They are green above, densely white felted beneath when mature and carried on similarly felted stems. The overall effect is of a bright grey shrub, compact

in habit and not often above 90 cm (3 ft) in height with a greater spread. The compact habit comes from the other parent of 'Sunshine', *S. compactus*. This species is rare in the wild and confined to limestone cliffs around Castle Point, Wellington Province. It has oblong to obovate leaves 2–4 cm (¾–1¼ in) long, the margins of which are waved and faintly round-toothed, the undersides white-felted.

Allied and similar to *compactus* is *S. monroi*, a hardier sub-alpine species with narrower leaves less white beneath and with strongly crinkled, upturned margins. All the senecios mentioned to date have a bonus of showy, bright yellow daisy-like flowers in summer. Much neglected is the

The neatly crimped and waved leathery leaves of *Senecio monroi*.

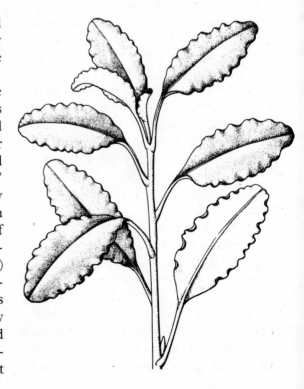

Even in cool temperate climates the flowers of *Feijoa sellowiana* can be abundantly borne during warm summers and may be followed by oval, sweetly aromatic fruits.

Senecio Dunedin Hybrids 'Sunshine' usually parades in cultivation under the names *S.greyi* and *S.laxifolius*. It is a fine plant for windy sites near the sea.

Santolina chamaecyparissus 'Sulphurea' is a highly distinctive form of the common cotton lavender which deserves to be grown more often.

The waxy bells and lustrous foliage of *Rhododendron thomsonii* combine with attractively peeling bark to make this one of the finest species in the genus.

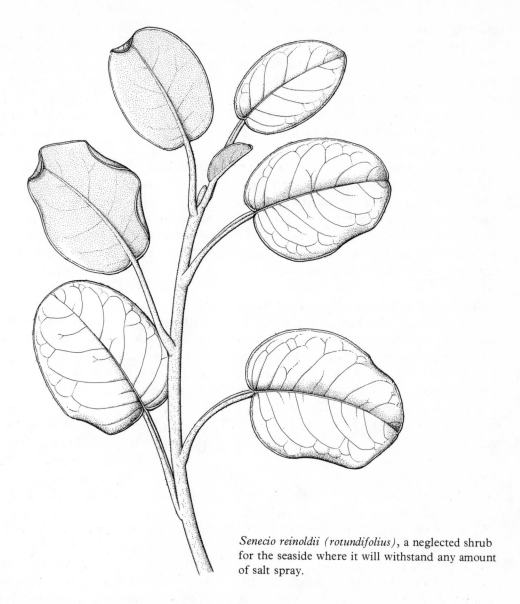

Senecio reinoldii (rotundifolius), a neglected shrub for the seaside where it will withstand any amount of salt spray.

dwarf *S. bidwillii*, another sub-alpine species rarely above 60 cm (2 ft) tall but more wide and very neat and compact. The rigidly leathery leaves are dark and glossy above, white-felted beneath, as are the stems. The flower heads lack ray florets and are relatively inconspicuous.

S. bidwillii is sometimes considered to be the smallest member of a related group of four species all with fine foliage. *S. bennettii*

and *S. elaeagnifolius* are much akin and were formerly classified together under the latter name. Both grow to 1·2–3 m (4–10 ft) tall and have leaves to 7·5 cm (3 in) long, those of *elaeagnifolius* being relatively narrower and thicker. My favourite is *S. reinoldii* (*rotundifolius*) which should really be among the larger-leaved shrubs but is conveniently mentioned here. It is without doubt the most imposing of all the

99

shrubby senecios with, in the wild at least, rounded paddle-shaped leaves to 15 cm (6 in) or more in length. Of extraordinary thick and leathery texture, each blade is shiny green above and buff felted beneath as are the stalks and stems that bear them. It is abundant around the coastline of Stewart Island and on the adjacent South Island mainland, sometimes forming a pure shrubby forest, the stems of almost tree-like proportions. In its native country it is known as mutton bird scrub, presumably being preferred by that bird for nesting. In former times on Stewart Island the large leaves were used as postcards, it being possible to write on the felted surface with a pointed stick or pencil. I remember being greatly impressed on first seeing this senecio framed against the sea and wondering why it was not more frequently grown. Unfortunately it is not fully hardy and in drier climates produces smaller, though still handsome leaves. It is *par excellence* a seaside plant, taking any amount of wind and salt spray.

Sun roses
It is a far cry indeed from the cool, wet, windy, rocky shores of Stewart Island to the sun-drenched but equally rocky Mediterranean, home of the sun roses, *Cistus*. But one thing the plants from these areas do have in common is lack of hardiness, the winters in each case being relatively mild. Where winters are not severe though, one or two *cistus* species or hybrids are a must, not only for their gorgeous single rose-like flowers, but for their varied evergreen leaves. Hardiest in my experience is *Cistus laurifolius*, some forms of which will stand − 18°C (0°F). Native to south western Europe, eastwards to central Italy, it is an erect shrub to 2 m (6½ ft) or more, with dark matt-green, leathery, lance-shaped leaves

and pure white flowers 5–7.5 cm (2–3 in) wide. Almost as hardy and also from south western Europe is *C. populifolius*, aptly named poplar-leaved sun rose, a vigorous species of equal or greater height with similar flowers. The sage-leaved sun rose, *C. salviifolius* is low, compact and desirable, but not very hardy. Mated with *populifolius* however, we get almost the best of both worlds in *C. × corbariensis*. As hardy as its poplar-leaved parent but with the compactness of *salviifolius*, it grows 60–90 cm (2–3 ft) tall, usually more in width, with dark sage-green ovate leaves 2–5 cm (¾–2 in) long and white yellow-centred flowers that expand from crimson buds. Gum cistus, *C. ladanifer* is about as hardy. It much resembles *C. laurifolius* but has aromatic, much narrower leaves and larger flowers. The latter are among the most spectacular in the genus, 7.5–10 cm (3–4 in) wide, glistening white, with each of the five petals bearing a basal blood-crimson blotch. A bush in full bloom is a spectacle worth going out of one's way to see. As one might expect, the mating of *C. ladanifer* and *C. laurifolius* has produced something good, in effect, a hardier, slightly smaller flowered *ladanifer*, (*C. × cyprius*). In addition and rather strangely it has a somewhat more graceful habit than either parent. If pure grey leaves and rosy-lilac flowers are preferred then *C. albidus* can be recommended. It provides one of the sights of the Mediterranean *maquis* and is easily identified by its totally stalkless leaves and succession of yellow-centred flowers to 5 cm (2 in) or so wide. The plant is not particularly hardy.

Rose of Sharon (Hypericum calycinum)
Although rose of Sharon or Aaron's beard is almost ubiquitous in temperate gardens,

spine-tipped cladodes. The tiny greenish-white unisexual flowers are carried on separate plants and if both sexes are planted together there is a bonus of comparatively large, bright red berries. *R. hypoglossum* is quite different, with flexible stems to 45 cm ($1\frac{1}{2}$ ft) and much larger, brighter green, elliptic cladodes.

Alexandrian laurel, *Danae racemosa* was formerly included in *Ruscus* and rather resembles a taller, more bushy *R. hypoglossum*, but the glossy cladodes are obliquely oblong-lanceolate and the flowers are borne in separate, small terminal spikes. They are also bi-sexual and solitary plants can be expected to produce clusters of attractive red berries.

SHRUBS WITH TINY OR VERY NARROW LEAVES

Tiny or very narrow leaves *en masse* can often create interesting textures which contrast well with those of bolder mien.

Lonicera nitida
A good example can be seen in the popular hedging plant *Lonicera nitida*. Used as a more informal background to a border, its tiny oval leaves produce dark billows against which the larger, brighter greens of say, *Fatsia japonica*, are highlighted most effectively. *L. nitida* also has a certain quiet charm of its own, all too often overlooked in its generally over-clipped hedge state. The leaves are thick and glossy and in early summer they shelter pairs of fragrant, white, elfin honeysuckle flowers which are followed by translucent berries, the colour of amethysts. It is a variable plant, the most robust and largest leaved being 'Yunnan' (*L. yunnanensis*), while 'Ernest Wilson' is the one commonly used for hedging.

'Fertilis' flowers and fruits freely and 'Baggessen's Gold' has yellow leaves in summer, yellow-green in winter. The allied *L. pileata* cannot always be relied upon to be fully evergreen, but is worth mentioning as a very shade-tolerant ground cover plant seldom above 60 cm (2 ft) and having an interesting horizontal habit of growth.

Pachistima canbyi
Often overlooked in much the same way as *L. nitida* is *Pachistima canbyi*, a low-growing North American shrub useful as ground cover and for foundation planting. A member of the same family as *Euonymus* (*Celastraceae*), it has opposite pairs of narrowly oblong leaves and tiny greenish flowers that may be followed by small fruits which split to disclose white seeds. *P. myrsinites* is the only other species in the genus and is native to west North America where it is known as myrtle boxwood. Although not spectacular in any way, this is a remarkably pleasing little shrub to 60 cm (2 ft) or more, with toothed, glossy leaves in dense sprays and a more bushily erect habit than *P. canbyi*.

There is really no need for me to recommend lavender and rosemary, which are well known for their narrow, aromatic leaves, but there are less common species of both these Mediterranean shrubs which are worth trying.

Woolly lavender
Lavandula lanata is a Spanish lavender and if collected from the mountains is almost as hardy as common lavender, *L. spica*. Its leaves are broader and are thick, woolly and most distinctive. Small spikes of fragrant, bright violet flowers appear in late summer and autumn. *L. lanata* usually grows to a height of about 45–90 cm ($1\frac{1}{2}$–3 ft).

Cotton lavender

Cotton lavender or lavender cotton (*Santolina*) is also a well known cottage garden plant. *S. chamaecyparissus* (*S. incana*) is one of the greyest of all plants and has lemon-yellow button-shaped flowers in summer, similar to those of tansy. Its feathery leaves are worthy of close scrutiny. Each one is very slender and pinnate with tiny, bluntly cylindrical leaflets which are arranged in four ranks at right angles to the mid-rib, a very unusual sight. *S. c.* 'Sulphurea' has primrose-yellow flowers and less intensely grey-white leaves, while *S. rosmarinifolia* (*S. pectinata*, *S. virens*) has even narrower bright green leaves.

Helichrysum splendidum

Helichrysum splendidum has a similar impact in the garden as the woolly lavender described above; it is a shrub from the mountains of Africa from the Cape north to Ethiopia. Also known as *H. trilineatum*, from the three parallel veins in each leaf, this surprisingly hardy plant rarely exceeds 60–90 cm (2–3 ft) in gardens though it is capable of doubling this in the wild. It can get rather leggy in time and is best pruned fairly hard annually in spring. During the summer and autumn a succession of small yellow, everlasting flowers appear in clusters at the stem tips. Both foliage and blossoms are useful for the smaller cut-flower arrangement.

Cassinia

Closely related to *Helichrysum* is *Cassinia*, a genus of somewhat heath-like shrubs from South Africa, Australia and New Zealand. The hardiest members come from the latter country and two species are decidedly garden worthy where winters are not continentally severe. Golden cottonwood or tauhinu, *C. fulvida* is the best known, a

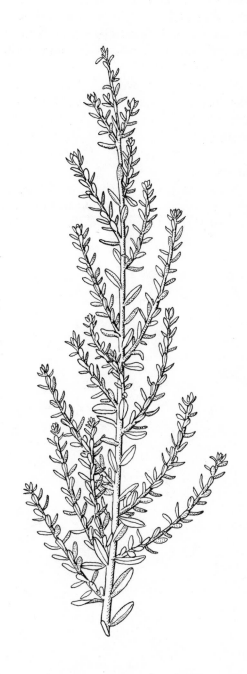

Cassinia vauvilliersii albida, a charming feathery grey shrub from New Zealand.

slender, erect shrub 60–180 cm (2–6 ft) tall. Its primary charms are the tawny-gold stems and leaf undersides, and contrasting dark varnished green upper leaf surfaces. Tiny, creamy groundsel-like flowers in terminal clusters do not greatly add to the overall effect.

Mountain cottonwood, *C. vauvilliersii albida* has the same basic structure but is charmingly silvery-grey and downy throughout.

Tea tree

Tea tree or Manuka, *Leptospermum scoparium* is a compatriot of *Cassinia* and also has tiny leaves in feathery sprays, but here the analogy ends for it is a large shrub or sometimes a small tree, grown more for its flowers than for its foliage. Nevertheless, the tiny, pointed, dark leaves *en masse* make a pleasing background for its own white or pink-flushed wide open flowers. The latter have five round petals and can be up to 1·5 cm ($\frac{5}{8}$ in) wide. Several fine cultivars are available in singles and doubles, white, pink or red. *L.s.* 'Nichollsii' has chrysanthemum-crimson single flowers; 'Red Damask' is charmingly double. My favourite is *L.s.* 'Nanum', a very compact shrub to 1 m (3 ft) or more with red-purple stems and flowers that open white and flush rose-purple as they age.

4 The heather family

Looking at the tiny scale leaves and diminutive bells of heather, then at a large shrub of *Rhododendron grande* with leaves up to 30 cm (1 ft) long and trusses of 5–7.5 cm (2–4 in) wide flowers it is difficult to appreciate that they both belong to the same botanical family—*Ericaceae*. Despite differences in size, the structure of the flowers—by which botanists classify plants—is much the same and there are other common characteristics. A large proportion of the species live in association with the thread-like bodies of a fungus (mycorrhiza), the relationship being known as symbiosis. This is particularly true of heaths and heathers and other members which live in acid, peaty, nitrogen-deficient soil. There the fungus derives essential sugars from the plant in return for equally essential nitrogen. Most members of the *Ericaceae* are adapted to acid or neutral soils and will not thrive where lime is present. For this reason they are not ubiquitous but where they do thrive they can provide some of the most rewarding displays both of evergreen foliage and showy blossom.

Heathers and heaths

Heather (Calluna)

Heather, or ling (*Calluna vulgaris*), despite its almost non-existent leaves can create some very attractive foliage effects. Of recent years several cultivars have been raised with yellow, gold, bronze, orange and red-tinted shoots, the colours of which are darker in winter. Cultivars to look out for are 'Blazeaway' (red), 'Gold Haze' (bright gold), 'Orange Queen' (gold to deep orange), 'Penhale' (dark green and bronze), and 'Ruth Sparkes' (bright yellow-green). Other cultivars are silvery grey and hairy, such as 'Silver Queen' and 'Sister Anne'. The latter forms low, compact mounds, and this brings in another aspect of the useful variability of heather, its range of ultimate size—from under 10 cm (4 in) to 2 m (6½ ft). Flower-spike size also varies and the colour of the individual bells ranges from white and palest mauve to crimson, single and double. Any heather specialist will list dozens of all sorts.

Heaths (Erica)

The heaths, *Erica*, do not vary much within each species, except in flower colour, but taking the genus as a whole there is a wide selection of statures, forms and flower size. All are typified by having small, needle-like leaves and obvious bell or urn-shaped flowers with tiny sepals. (The flowers of *Calluna* have four coloured sepals which cover the flower within.) Heathers and the smaller heaths provide splendid ground cover for peaty or sandy soil in a sunny site and beds or whole gardens devoted to them, have steadily gained in popularity. As long as a pleasing mosaic of species and cultivars is chosen, and a few other *Ericaceae* and conifers are added for contrast, this idea has much to commend it, providing all-year-round interest and very little maintenance. Even if the soil is alkaline, it is still possible to create a 'heather' garden by planting the low-growing winter heath, *E. carnea*, the bushier hybrid *E. × darleyensis*, the taller Irish heath, *E. erigena* (*E. mediterranea*) and *E. terminalis* (*E. stricta*), sometimes called the Corsican heath. The winter heath is particularly valuable where there are mild spells to open its flowers. By choosing the right cultivars it is possible to have flowers from late autumn to late spring, in shades of pink, carmine, red and white. Some cultivars have very dark green foliage, 'Loughrigg' for example, while 'Aurea' has bright gold young foliage.

Among the low-growing summer heaths, the so-called bell heather, *E. cinerea* is one of the most useful. Its dark green foliage provides the right background for the freely carried flower sprays, in shades of purple, red, pink and white, plus the pale mauve of 'Sea Foam' and black-purple of 'Velvet Night'. 'Golden Drop' has coppery-yellow foliage in summer which takes on red tints in winter. Cross-leaved heath (*E. tetralix*) is very hardy and distinct with its four-ranked leaves and globular heads of pink, crimson or white flowers. Several have very hairy foliage which gives the plants a grey or silvery appearance as in 'Alba Mollis' (white flowers) and 'L. E. Underwood' (pink, darker in bud). This species will also tolerate wet soil conditions. Vigorous plants of *E. vagans*, the Cornish heath, can be really spectacular when smothered with long, dense spikes of small pink to cerise or white flowers in late summer. 'Lyonesse' is a good white with brown anthers and 'Mrs D. F. Maxwell' is

still the best of the deep cerise cultivars having been honoured with the Award of Merit, First Class Certificate and Award of Garden Merit by the R.H.S. Among the taller species, *E. erigena* (*E. mediterranea*) is very garden worthy, forming a dense, erect shrub 1–2 m (3–6½ ft) and sometimes more in height and flowering from late winter to early summer. *E. e.* 'Superba' is tall and pink; 'Brightness' rarely exceeds 90 cm (3 ft) and has bronze-red buds and pink flowers, while 'W. T. Rackliff' is its counterpart in white.

There are several tree heaths but the only reasonably hardy one is *E. arborea*, particularly in its *E. a.* 'Alpina' form. This Spanish mountain form grows erectly to 3 m (10 ft) and older specimens much exceed this in width. The leaves are very slim and short, 3–6 mm ($\frac{1}{8}$–$\frac{1}{4}$ in) long, creating a fuzz of bright green. Tiny honey-scented white flowers appear in profusion in spring. *E. arborea* grows widely around the Mediterranean and on the mountains of central Africa and Atlantic islands. Its wood provided the French bruyère for making tobacco pipes, a name corrupted in English to briar, although nothing to do with roses. There are several other heaths worth investigating and those wishing to obtain as much variety as possible should consult a good specialist catalogue. The following are in particular worth looking out for: *E. australis*, *E. canaliculata*, *E. ciliaris*, *E. lusitanica*, *E. mackaiana*, *E. terminalis* and *E. × williamsii*.

Cassiope

Like the common heather, *Cassiope* has scale-like, though somewhat larger leaves arranged in four overlapping ranks along the stems. There are several species, some erect, others prostrate or almost so. When in flower they present a charming sight, being

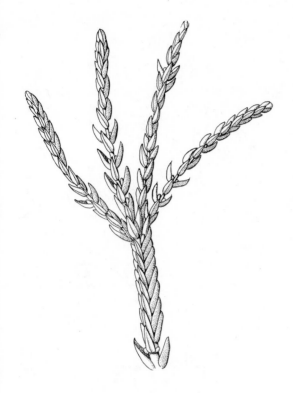

Cassiope × 'Edinburgh', tall and vigorous and one of the few easily grown members of its genus.

reminiscent of elegant dwarf conifers spangled with lily-of-the-valley like flowers. Most distinctive in habit is the prostrate *C. lycopodioides* from Arctic regions, its cord-like stems forming interwoven mats. The tightly overlapping dark olive-green leaves have papery white margins. Very erect in habit is *C. fastigiata* with keeled leaves creating almost square-sectioned 'stems' set with bell-shaped flowers 1 cm ($\frac{3}{8}$ in) wide. *C. tetragona* is similar but the leaves are furrowed down the back and the flowers are a little smaller. Like *fastigiata* it is a native of the Himalayas; the two species combined spontaneously in the Edinburgh Botanic Garden, creating a vigorous free-flowering plant known as 'Edinburgh'. Growing to

30 cm (1 ft) or more, it is the best cassiope for the beginner to try. There are several other cassiopes sometimes offered by nurserymen and all are to be recommended. All species need acid, peaty soil and a cool position to thrive. Without these conditions, they are hardly worth attempting.

Phyllodoce

Erica-like in foliage, but with terminal clusters of longer stalked, urn-shaped flowers are the various species of *Phyllodoce*. Easier to please than the cassiopes they are hummock-forming shrublets to 15 cm (6 in) or more tall. *P. aleutica*, from north Japan to the Aleutian Islands, has white to palest yellow-green blooms. *P. empetriformis* is red-purple; *P. caerulea* is purple and *P. glanduliflora* pale yellow, rather like a more robust *P. aleutica*. One of the most garden worthy is *P.* × *intermedia* (*empetriformis* × *glanduliflora*) 'Fred Stoker', a more vigorous plant with plenty of light purple flowers in early summer, then an intermittent display until late autumn. It is often confused with *P. empetriformis*, but that west North American species has wide open bells, not constricted mouthed urns as in the other species and this hybrid.

Bog rosemary

Not unlike *Phyllodoce*, but with narrowly oblong or elliptic leaves is *Andromeda polifolia*, the bog rosemary. Circumpolar in distribution and extending southwards in the mountains, it is a plant of bogs and moist peaty soil but is of fairly easy cultivation. In the more typical forms the plants grow 15–30 cm (6–12 in) tall, slowly suckering to form wider patches. The 2·5–4 cm (1–1½ in) long leaves have rolled-under margins and are blue-white beneath. In early summer, small, globular, pale-pink

Three members of the heather family: top, *Andromeda polifolia macrophylla*, left, *Gaultheria procumbens*, right, *G. cuneata*.

flowers grace every stem-tip and present an enchanting sight. For combined flower and foliage attraction the broad-leaved *A. p.* 'Macrophylla' can be recommended.

Arcterica and Pernettya

Smaller still in stature is *Arcterica nana*, a miniature shrub from Japan, with semi-lustrous elliptic concave leaves in whorls of three and fragrant white urn-shaped flowers in late spring. Some botanists make this very charming little plant into *Pieris nana* but the comparisons seem so ridiculous I prefer to keep it distinct. Superficially at least, some of the smaller sorts of *Pernet-*

tya and *Vaccinium* look more akin. *Pernettya prostrata* for example provides attractive mats or low mounds of glossy, bright green leaves each up to 2 cm ($\frac{3}{4}$ in) long and white flowers followed by purple-black berries. *P. tasmanica* is also mat-forming with very slender stems and even smaller leaves and flowers, and comparatively large red or white berries. Most popular and showy of all is the South American *P. mucronata*, a dense suckering shrub to 60 or 90 cm (2–3 ft) tall, clad in small, deep green leaves. A fine ground cover plant when not in flower, it becomes an eye-catching sight when spangled with numerous short spikes of pure white bells. Later it becomes hung with a profusion of globular berries which vary from white and lilac-pink through shades of red and purple. For a really good crop of berries more than one cultivar should be grown or a batch of seedlings planted out together for inter-pollination to be effected. *P. m.* 'Bell's Seedling' has dark red fruits; 'Lilacina', lilac pink; 'Mulberry Wine', magenta; 'Rosie', pink with dark flush, and 'White Pearl', glistening white—all these are to be recommended.

Vaccinium and St. Dabeoc's heath

Depending on the botanical authority there are 150–400 species of *Vaccinium*, some deciduous, some evergreen, and it is only possible to mention a few of the latter here. All are desirable evergreens. Not unlike a larger *Arcterica* is the cowberry from North America, Europe and Asia, *Vaccinium vitis-idaea*. It has glossier and more oblong leaves and pink-tinted white flowers which give way to edible red berries. Where something taller is required *V. bracteatum* deserves to be grown more often. Eventually to 2 m (6½ ft) it has narrow oval, smooth leaves, coppery-red when young, and scented white flowers in summer. The fruits are red. *V. glaucoalbum* is a winner, with quite large oval leaves greyish-green above and startlingly blue-white beneath. Almost cylindrical pink flowers arise from the bases of white bracts in early summer and are followed by blue-black berries with a white waxy patina.

Formerly classified under both *Vaccinium* and *Erica* is St. Dabeoc's heath, *Daboecia cantabrica* which can fairly be said to blend characteristics from both genera. A small bushy shrub 30–60 cm (1–2 ft) tall, it has dark green, elliptic, glossy leaves to 1·5 cm (⅝ in) long and terminal racemes of egg-shaped rose-purple bells to 12 mm (½ in) long. *D. c.* 'Alba Globosa' has more rounded white flowers on a dwarfer plant. Less hardy, more or less prostrate and with more rounded, purple-red flowers is

D. azorica from the Azores. Spontaneous mating with *D. cantabrica* in the Scottish garden of William Buchanan, has led to a fine compact cultivar with garnet-red flowers named after the garden owner.

Gaultheria and Arctostaphylos

In effect, the various sorts of *Gaultheria* and *Arctostaphylos* can be planted for much the same reasons as *Vaccinium* and *Pernettya*. They all closely resemble each other with their urn-shaped, mainly white flowers. Making a cheerful and almost indestructible ground cover around shrubs and under high tree cover is the east North American creeping wintergreen, *Gaultheria procumbens*. Fast-growing red rhizomes thrust out in all directions and send up at intervals tufts of stems 7·5–15 cm (3–6 in) high, bearing at their tips about three to five aromatic, leathery, glossy, dark green oval leaves. Pink-tinted white flowers appear in their axils and are followed by bright red berries. *G. cuneata* has snowy white berries and the plant does not form rhizomes, making attractive, dense low mounds 30–45 cm (1–1½ ft) tall and more in spread. The narrow, shallowly toothed leaves have an attractive vein pattern and moderate lustre. This is another good ground coverer but not for really shady sites though Ernest Wilson collected it 'on humus clad rocks in moist woods' in West China during 1909. *G. itoana* is a similar plant from Taiwan, somewhat less in stature and with narrower leaves (no more than 1·5 cm (⅝ in) long and 6 mm (¼ in) wide). Very different in every respect is the west North American shallon or salal, *G. shallon*. Extensively suckering and thicket forming it varies from 60–180 cm (2–6 ft) in height, depending on soil and situation. It is fine for large scale ground covering beneath trees especially where the soil is moist, but should not be admitted to the small garden. The leathery leaves are large, 4–10 cm ($1\frac{1}{2}$–4 in) long, broadly ovate and bristle-toothed. White, pink-flushed flowers are followed by hairy, deep purple berries. Bearberry (*Arctostaphylos uva-ursi*) is a tolerant member of the *Ericaceae* given the essential neutral to acid soil. It makes a most satisfying and very hardy mat of dark red stems and bright green obovate leaves to 3 cm ($1\frac{1}{4}$ in) long. Pitcher-shaped pinkish or white flowers appear in terminal clusters in spring and are succeeded by shining red berries. It makes the sort of ground cover that one likes to stop and admire on dull winter days.

Leucothoe and Kalmia

Where the shade of trees is a problem, the rather neglected species of *Leucothoe* should be considered. Most vigorous and satisfying for the purpose providing the soil is reasonably moist is *L. fontanesiana* (*L. catesbaei*) from the mountains of south east North America. It has an arching mode of growth usually to about 90 cm (3 ft) but occasionally to almost twice this. The leathery, lance-shaped leaves are dark and glossy, 7.5–13 cm (3–5 in) long and are arranged in two parallel ranks. Pendent pitcher-shaped white flowers open in racemes from the axils of all the upper leaves and but for the arching habit of the stems would provide a lovely sight. It is sometimes recommended that a few branches are held up on forked sticks during the flowering period so that the display can be more easily enjoyed.

Also from North America is the so-called calico bush or mountain laurel, *Kalmia latifolia*. Of large size, eventually to 3 m (10 ft) or more tall and of greater width, it makes a wall of rich greenery in winter. Although an excellent evergreen, it only

really comes into its own when the exquisitely-shaped pure pink flowers open in early summer. Borne in clusters each flower is about 2.5 cm (1 in) wide, shallowly bowl-shaped with a ring of very short spurs at the base. The buds are unique and look as though designed by a master pastry cook as decoration for a royal wedding cake.

Pieris

As fine foliage and flowering shrubs, the three hardiest species of *Pieris* take some beating. Hardiest of all and surprisingly neglected is *P. floribunda*, the fetter bush of moist hillsides in south east North America. Of bushy habit and 1.5–2 m ($4\frac{1}{2}$–$6\frac{1}{2}$ ft) tall it has bristly, hairy stems and lance-shaped to oblong leaves 4–6 cm ($1\frac{1}{2}$–$2\frac{1}{2}$ in) long, dark and somewhat lustrous above, gland-dotted beneath. By early autumn the floral display of next year can be nicely judged because the erect sprays of immature flower buds form as the current season's growth terminates. The following spring every bud expands to a pure white urn-shaped bloom about 6 mm ($\frac{1}{4}$ in) long and carried in such profusion as to give the impression of snow. If possible, obtain *P. f.* 'Elongata' ('Grandiflora') with much longer trusses of flowers up to 20 cm (8 in) long. Next in order of hardiness comes *P. japonica*, a smooth stemmed species eventually to 3 m (10 ft) high and wide but slow growing. The leaves are narrowly oval and more tapered and usually a darker green. The floral sprays arch down and are freely produced. *P. j.* 'Blush' and 'Daisen' have pink-tinted flowers, the latter the deeper colour, while 'Purity' has larger snow-white flowers; 'Variegata' has the leaves margined creamy-white, flushed pink when young. The young leaves of *P. japonica* are usually bronze or reddish-bronze and those of 'Bert Chandler' are

salmon-pink gradually changing through cream to green. This bright young leaf colour goes a stage farther in *P. formosa* from the eastern Himalayas. It resembles a more robust *P. japonica*, with leaves to 7·5 cm (3 in) or more long and an equally profuse display of white flowers. The young leaves are bronze to brownish-red or red and this is a variable feature in the wild. *P. f. forrestii* is an entity with a somewhat pendent habit of growth and longer flowers. *P. f. f.* 'Wakehurst' has bright red young leaves, fading through pink to pale mottled cream and then deep green. A shrub in young leaf is a striking and beautiful sight and from a distance is frequently taken to be some exotic shrub in gorgeous bloom. There are other good red-leaved clones including the 'vinous red' 'Jermyns' raised at the internationally famous Hilliers Nursery, Hampshire, England, and 'Forest Flame'. The latter is of compact growth

Pieris formosa showing the dormant reddish-tinted flower buds in their winter state. Left, *Daphne collina*, a charming neat dwarf profusely flowering shrub in its winter state.

and breaks into young leaf earlier. Originally a self-sown seedling it is now known to be a hybrid between *P. japonica* and *P. formosa* 'Wakehurst'.

Rhododendrons

Evergreens *par excellence*, it would have been easy indeed to have filled the whole of this book with some of the 800 species and many more cultivars of *Rhododendron*. Like camellias, however, they are grown primarily as flowering shrubs with the emphasis on the flowers. It must also be admitted that the finest foliaged species are not too hardy and need shade, humidity and shelter to thrive. Then of course there are the limitations of soil. For these reasons I have selected just a few of the most attractive-leaved species only, though many more are very handsome and garden worthy. Many of the hybrids are duller from the foliage point of view, however superb the flowers. Would that the many breeders of rhododendrons had paid attention to beautiful leaves as well as flowers.

Truly spectacular are *R. grande* and its allies, their leaves are like great ornate paddles, beautifully veined and polished. *R. grande* itself, a dweller in Himalayan rain forests, has leaves to 37 cm (15 in) long by up to 15 cm (6 in) wide, silvery or tawny beneath. *R. sinogrande* can be even larger. Both have big, broad bell-shaped flowers in the cream to pale yellow category, red-blotched at the base. Almost as big are the dark leaves of *R. falconeri* which are rufous and woolly beneath. It can eventually attain 9 m (30 ft) in height. *R. fictolacteum* can grow even taller but the glossier leaves rarely exceed 25 cm (10 in). *R. calophytum* has leaves as long as those of *grande* but they are very much narrower and a lustrous matt mid-green, pointing downwards at an oblique angle. In spring, the pyramids of leaves at each stem-tip are capped by a large truss of crimson-blotched white to pink bell-shaped flowers. *R. campanulatum* has oval leaves about 13 cm (5 in) long, the undersides of which appear as if covered with the finest quality suede. The flowers may be rose-purple or almost white and open in spring. Viewed from beneath one might suppose the leaves of *R. insigne* to be cut from pearly fawn tin-foil, such is the metallic lustre. Rigid and leathery, each pointed-tipped blade can attain 15 cm (6 in) in length and is dark and glossy above, a pleasing foil for the pink flowers.

About the same length but much broader and very round-tipped are the leafy paddles of *R. mallotum*, dark above and rufous and downy beneath. These combine well with the scarlet to deep crimson tubular bell-shaped flowers, though the latter open in early spring and may get frosted. *R. bureavii* has leaves noteworthy for their dense, soft brown woolly undersides which present an intriguing sight on a windy day.

Most rhododendron leaves are oval or more or less so, though there are several divergences. *R. degronianum* (*R. metternichii*) from Japan has narrow leaves to 15 cm (6 in) or more long, with slightly in-rolled margins. The buff suede undersides have a contrasting dull-red midrib. It grows to about 2 m (6½ ft) tall and bears pale, rose-pink flowers which may be five or seven-lobed.

Closely allied and at one time considered a variety of this species is *R. yakushimanum*, an admirable low, dense shrub of hummock-like outline and very hardy. The dark green leaves have strongly rolled margins and are thickly felted beneath. The widely bell-shaped flowers are a delightful shade of apple blossom-pink on opening but soon age to white. During the past 30 years the plant breeder has used the Yakushima rhododendron to good effect, producing a race of dwarf hardy cultivars in a wide range of colours and shades.

Narrow, but not particularly distinguished leaves are possessed by *R. arboreum*, a variable species of tree size and a noble sight when covered with its blood-red bells. In the wild it can attain 12 m (40 ft) and

Examples of the diversity of leaf form and size in *Rhododendron*: 1 *R. williamsianum*, 2 *R. mallotum*, 3 *R. oreotrephes*, 4 *R. calophytum*, 5 *R. campanulatum*, 6 *R. orbiculare*, 7 *R. sinogrande*, 8 *R. metternichii hondoense*, 9 *R. bureavii*, 10 *R. lepidostylum*.

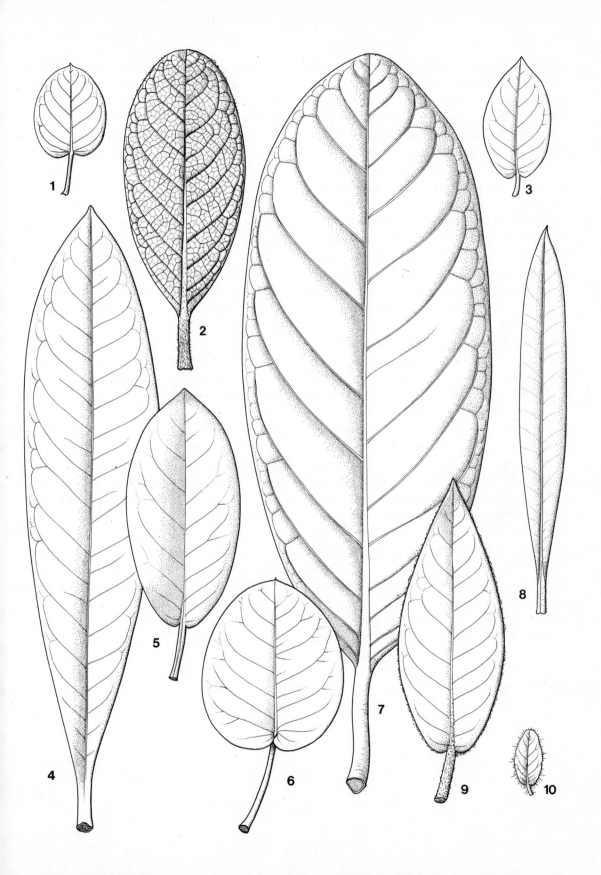

is one of the sights of its Himalayan home-land. Among the many forms are those with pink or white flowers and leaves that may be silvery-white or cinnamon downy beneath. Crossed with the rock hardy, lilac-purple flowered east North American *R. catawbiense*, it has given rise to some fine and varied coloured cultivars that withstand severe Continental winters.

Totally different are the almost round 10 cm (4 in) long leaves of the aptly named *orbiculare* with their overlapping basal lobes. Bright and semi-matt-green above they are almost white beneath with a fine intricate network of grey-green veins. The flowers are wide and bell-shaped, pink with a flush of magenta. A little smaller, lacking the basal lobes, darker and glossier above and greyer beneath are those of *R. thomsonii*, noteworthy also for its beautiful waxy blood-red nodding bells. Somewhat glaucous, particularly beneath, are the similar leaves of *R. oreotrephes*. This is a variable species from the sino-Himalayan region and has been found by several of the well known plant collectors including George Forrest, Joseph Rock and Frank Kingdon Ward. The various forms have been given such names as *artosquameum*, *exquisetum*, *timeteum*, etc. but all are now under the *oreotrephes* umbrella. The attractive funnel-shaped flowers vary from pale rose to deeper purplish-pink. Very much smaller, 4 cm ($1\frac{1}{2}$ in) long and widely heart-shaped at the base are the leaves of *R. williamsianum* which contrast so well in winter with red stalks and buds. Later, in spring, exquisite pink bells larger than the leaves, expand and make this low compact species one of the very finest of its kind. Also small-leaved and rarely above 90 cm (3 ft) tall is the Chinese *R. lepidostylum*. It is one of the very few species of rhododendron to stand on the merits of its foliage alone, this, in the best forms, being intensely blue-white above, paler and scaly beneath. Viewed in the half-light the bush seems to glow with a cold luminosity. The stems bear long, bristly hairs and the flowers are pale to greenish-yellow.

R. calostrotum is also fairly dwarf, about 90 cm (3 ft) or so with aromatic oval leaves, sage-green above and white to buff beneath. The distinctively wide-open flowers are about 4 cm ($1\frac{1}{2}$ in) across and magenta-red. *R. c.* 'Gigha' is superior, with claret-red blossoms. Not only does the genus *Rhododendron* contain trees and shrubs of all statures, but prostrate mat-formers as well. There are a number to choose from, some with tiny leaves, e.g. *R. keleticum* and *R. radicans*, others larger, as with *R. forrestii* (*R. repens*). The latter is particularly desirable though rather slow growing, with deep lustrous leaves up to 4 cm ($1\frac{1}{2}$ in) long and narrow bell-shaped flowers of glowing crimson.

The familiar *Fatsia japonica* has imposing, large leaves and makes a fine specimen shrub. It is very shade tolerant and thrives near the sea in sheltered sites.

The foliage of *Prunus lusitanica* at its peak of perfection in a sheltered, partially shaded site.

Ilex aquifolium 'Handsworth New Silver' is perhaps best of the variegated group (Argenteo-marginata) having white margined leaves.

The painted leaves of *Ilex* × *altaclarensis* 'Lawsoniana' render it one of the most conspicuous evergreens of the winter garden.

5 Climbers

Climbing plants can provide a linking element in the garden and nowhere better demonstrated than when growing up a house wall from among the shrubs of a foundation planting. Smaller climbers scrambling through shrubs or larger ones over trees perform a similar function. More artificially but no less effectively, climbers are used to clothe pergolas and free-standing pillars, summer houses and gazebos. In addition they can cover an old shed, transforming it from an eyesore into a feature of beauty. Some climbers will also grow flat on the soil and become efficient ground coverers, as ivy does in the wild woods. One of the most rewarding features of climbing plants is their speed of growth. No matter how patient a gardener may be there is always the greatest satisfaction when a plant can actually be seen to extend its growth daily and after one season look as though it had been in position for several years. This chapter is primarily concerned with true evergreen climbers, that is, those slender woody stemmed plants which grow up by twining, tendrils, or by aerial roots. Scramblers, e.g. many roses and brambles, characterized by their hooked prickles or thorns, may also be regarded as climbers.

Self-clinging climbers

Evergreens which cling to walls without additional support are a boon, and like all such are few and far between. Judged purely as foliage plants, the ivies must be considered the finest of all the hardy self-clingers. *Hedera colchica dentata*, the Persian ivy is quite the finest of all if bold, glossy, heart-shaped leaves 15–20 cm (6–8 in) long are appreciated. It can clothe a totally shaded wall to perfection and its 'Variegata' form, with creamy-yellow to white bordered leaves, will even give the impression of reflected sunlight. This latter plant is sometimes confused with *Hedera canariensis* 'Variegata' ('Gloire de Marengo') a less hardy plant with white margined foliage, most commonly seen as a house plant.

Irish ivy, *Hedera helix hibernica* has lustrous, waxy-textured five-lobed leaves 7·5–15 cm (3–6 in) wide and makes an effective cover for a wall or an old tree. Like all the ivies, when it reaches the top of its support, non-climbing branches with unlobed leaves grow out, and rounded heads of yellow-green flowers appear in autumn. Despite their colour the flowers are not unattractive and the nectar they produce is a great attraction for butterflies and other insects. Hundreds of cultivars of common ivy, *H. helix*, are listed and all those with distinctive leaf shapes are worthy of consideration. 'Deltoidea' ('Hastata') has an oval leaf with two overlapping basal lobes only, creating in outline a short, blunt arrow head. In winter the dark green be-

particularly as a ground cover plant, it gives us a pleasant blanket of winter green providing winters are not too hard. From summer to autumn it really comes into its own with fresher green leaves and a succession of bright yellow flowers about 7·5 cm (3 in) wide, each nicely centred with a boss of long, slender stamens. It is a very invasive plant and should be used only for rough banks and beneath trees and large shrubs. An annual clipping in early spring will ensure a more satisfying winter carpet, and a neater summer one.

A trio of brambles

Rubus to most gardeners means blackberries or brambles, raspberries, loganberries and perhaps the Japanese wineberry, all deciduous, sprawling shrubs grown for their fruits. Some species of *Rubus*, however, provide ornamental shrubs grown for their blossom or bright glaucous winter stems and for their attractive evergreen leaves. The three which follow are all more or less prostrate or creeping and can be usefully and effectively employed as ground cover, particularly in shade. Particularly handsome is the vigorous Chinese *Rubus tricolor* with far-spreading reddish, bristly stems and toothed heart-shaped leaves 7·5 cm (3 in) or more long, of a lustrous deep green above, thinly white-felted beneath. When well established, 2·5 cm (1 in) wide white flowers may be produced and even edible red 'blackberries'. Although a splendid ground cover plant it should be watched when grown in moist, fertile soils. It can send arching stems which grow through shrubs and form an untidy wild tangle.

Very much smaller, providing ground cover for the larger rock garden or small shrub border is *R. calycinoides* (*R. fockeanus* of gardens), an alpine mat-former

from Taiwan, with small, lobed, maple-like leaves, finely wrinkled and glossy above, grey and hairy beneath. White flowers may appear in summer but are not very conspicuous. To complete the trio is a New Zealander, *R. parvus*, a rather unbramble-like plant except for the characteristic (red) fruits. The leaves are simple, in effect having one large leaflet only, 2·5–9 cm (1–3½ in) long, narrowly lance-shaped with a squared off base and fine, neat, prickle-toothed margins. They are variable in colour, from yellowish to deep or bronze-green. Although a woodland plant in the wild, the best leaf colour develops in a sunny site and more of the small white flowers are produced. It is not as hardy as most brambles and in colder areas needs the shelter of trees. As ground cover it is distinctive and unusual.

Butcher's broom and Alexandrian laurel

Very shade-tolerant and very useful for planting under large trees is the butcher's broom and its relatives. Curiously enough they do not have true leaves but small flattened stems known as cladodes or cladophylls, which mimic them exactly in form and function. A close look at *Ruscus aculeatus*, the common butcher's broom, particularly when in bloom will reveal that each flower appears to sit in the centre of a leaf and arises in the axil of a tiny bract. The neat, small, six-petalled flowers themselves are well worth examining, being virtually invisible at a distance. It is always difficult for gardeners to equate these tiny blooms with the gorgeous lilies, although both are members of the same family, *Liliaceae*. *Ruscus aculeatus* is a clump-forming shrub usually about 60 cm (2 ft) tall, dark green throughout with stiffly erect stems and densely borne ovate, 2–4 cm (¾–1½ in) long,

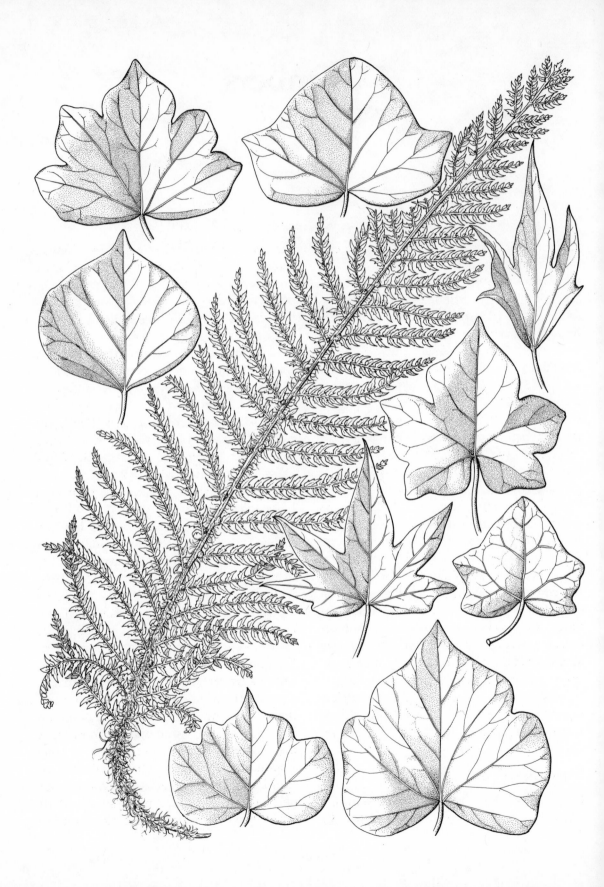

Above: *Decumaria sinensis*, a rarely seen self-clinging ally of the hydrangea.

Left: A range of leaf shapes of common ivy, *Hedera helix*, combine pleasingly with the fern *Polystichum setiferum* 'Acutilobum'.

comes flushed with bronze, presenting a pretty picture when growing up a smooth tree trunk. 'Digitata' is equally distinctive with its wide five to seven-lobed leaves, each lobe tapered to a slender point. Among smaller variegated cultivars 'Goldheart' is my favourite. For a long time wrongly known as 'Jubilee' this cheerful-looking ivy has a bold yellow splash in the centre of each small three-lobed leaf. It does not lack vigour and reaches up to 5 m (16 ft) or more. Less vigorous and equally effective on a tree trunk or wall is 'Glacier', a favourite pot-plant that is neglected in the garden. Each five-lobed leaf has a silvery-grey patina and irregular white margins. Very rare in cultivation but worth seeking out is *H. h. poetica* (*H. chrysocarpa*), the yellow berried ivy, (all the others have black fruits). It has bright green, shallowly-lobed leaves that take on bright coppery hues in winter.

Rare Hydrangea allies

Also rather rare and neglected is the Chinese *Decumaria sinensis*, a member of the same family as *Hydrangea* with narrow, shining green leaves 3–9 cm ($1\frac{1}{4}$–$3\frac{1}{2}$ in) long and fluffy clusters of tiny white and green flowers with a honied fragrance in early summer. Of the same family and similar but with more substantial leafage and larger clusters of creamy-white flowers is *Pileo-*

stegia viburnoides. Suitable for shady and sunny walls alike, this attractive climber is rather slow-growing during its early years and not as hardy as one could wish. It is another of Ernest Wilson's 1908 collections from south west China but also grows in the Khasia Hills of north India and on the Ryukyu Islands. The R.H.S. considered it worthy of an Award of Merit as long ago as 1914. China is also the home of *Euonymus fortunei*, *E.f. radicans* and its bright variegated forms which can clothe a wall very satisfyingly. Moving to Chile on the opposite side of the world we come to the home of *Hydrangea serratifolia (integerrima)*, a cousin of the more familiar deciduous climbing hydrangea, *H. anomala petiolaris*. It is a member of the southern temperate rain forest flora and elsewhere thrives best in mild, high rainfall areas, though it will stand a fair bit of frost. It is a striking sight in the wild and I well remember the excitement of seeing it soaring up into the tops of trees 24–30 m (80–100 ft) high on the island of Chiloe. This gives a clue to its most effective use in the garden but it also clothes a wall most effectively with its leathery, elliptic, dark, shiny leaves and fluffy masses of small creamy flowers. The leaves are in fact only rarely toothed and it is unfortunate that this rather unsuitable species' name has precedence over the more apt one (*integerrima* meaning with no teeth or lobes).

Chile trio

Growing cheek by jowl with the hydrangea is *Ercilla volubilis*, a vigorous but less high-flying self-clinger with oval, somewhat lustrous pale-veined leaves arranged in two parallel ranks. Grown on an old tree it will cascade off the higher branches displaying its dense axillary spikes of tiny whitish or greenish bells. A compatriot is the showy *Asteranthera ovata*, a slender creeper which roots into mossy logs and tree trunks and on which it can occasionally reach 3 m (10 ft) or so. One of my more vivid memories whilst plant collecting in the island of Chiloe is of a tall dead southern beech (*Nothofagus*) enveloped by ramifying strands of wiry stems set with small hairy leaves and huge hooded, flame-like red flowers. It is in fact a close ally of the greenhouse columneas and needs a sheltered, humid, shady site with no more than light frost. Another companion in the wild is *Mitraria coccinea*, a very attractive red-flowered plant which is a weak climber in mild wet climates (see p. 88).

Cissus striata (*Vitis s.* and *Ampelopsis s.*) is a little hardier and native to a wider variety of habitats, some of them drier. The fast-growing, slender zig-zag stems bear deep lustrous green leaves divided into three to five leaflets which can make a dense and distinctive clothing for a sheltered wall. It is common in South America and has been called the "ivy of Uruguay". Japan provides us with a final self-clinging evergreen in *Trachelospermum majus* (*T. japonicum*). This weaves a lustrous tapestry of elliptic leaves some of which redden strikingly in winter. Established plants produce fragrant white, rather jasmine-like flowers but generally in rather scant supply.

Twiners

Japan also provides us with a decorative example of a twining evergreen. *Stauntonia hexaphylla* is a vigorous climber to 10 m (33 ft) or more, with divided leaves composed of three to seven dark green oval leaflets each 7·5–13 cm (3–5 in) in length. The fragrant white, purple-tinted flowers are unisexual, the males and females in separate racemes on the same plant in spring. If the summers are warm, flowering may be followed by egg-shaped purplish fleshy fruits to 5 cm (2 in) long. Of the same family (*Lardizabalaceae*) is *Holboellia coriacea* from west China, a plant with bolder trifoliate leaves, duller greenish-white flowers and fleshy pod-like fruits to 7·5 cm (3 in) long. Pollination of the flowers by hand will aid the setting of fruit. *H. latifolia* (*Stauntonia latifolia*) is similar but more tender, with even larger leaflets.

Honeysuckle

Hardiness, fragrant flowers and evergreen leaves all come together in a very pleasing honeysuckle, *Lonicera japonica*. It is a vigorous twiner with ovate pointed leaves in pairs and very fragrant flowers which open white and age to yellow. In Britain at least it is generally represented by a number of forms: *L. j.* 'Aureoreticulata' with all the leaf veins picked out in gold, *L. j. repens* (*flexuosa*) which has dark red-purple stems, deep green leaves with red veins and purple-flushed flowers, while *L. j. halliana* has purplish stems and bright green leaves. Both are less hardy than the original wild type and all can lose some leaves in hard winters.

Mediterranean birthwort

Slender, wiry stems, varnished, heart-shaped leaves and quaint little yellowish or purplish flowers shaped rather like a Dutchman's pipe are the hallmarks of *Aristolochia sempervirens*. It needs a sheltered, sunny corner and is really a fun plant. In hard winters it can be killed back to ground level but usually grows again. In mild winters the foliage is cheerful and distinctive. It can be grown up a tripod of twiggy sticks or will make a shrub-like tangle on the ground.

Coral plant

If the aristolochia is a fun plant then the coral plant, *Berberidopsis corallina* is only for the serious and dedicated gardener. It needs shelter and shade, a fair amount of humidity and neutral to acid soil rich in humus. Given these factors it should thrive, throwing up strong, semi-scrambling, semi-twining stems to 4 m (13 ft) or more. The semi-lustrous, rather square-based oval leaves are variable in their degree of prickly toothing and ultimate size, well grown ones exceeding 13 cm (5 in) in length. The flowers are reminiscent of those of barberry, being bowl-shaped and pendent, but they are deep crimson and 12 mm ($\frac{1}{2}$ in) long, opening from summer to autumn. It is a very rare plant in its Chilean homeland.

Copihue

Chile's national flower copihue, *Lapageria rosea*, is happily not uncommon in its homeland and can be seen scrambling over shrubs and trees in several places, even by roadsides. Capable of attaining 3–4 m (10–13 ft) or more, this wiry-stemmed twiner has leathery, ovate to heart-shaped deep glossy-green leaves up to 10 cm (4 in) long. These make a fine foil for the superb, waxy-textured lily-like flowers which nod from the upper leaf axils in summer and autumn. Typically they are about 7·5 cm (3 in) long and rose-crimson, but clones exist with larger flowers in shades of pink and red. The only ones generally available are 'Albiflora', blush-white and 'Nash Court', soft pink. This beautiful climber needs the same conditions as those outlined for *Berberidopsis* with even less winter frost.

Clematis

Even the non-gardener or true beginner will know the Latin name *Clematis* and that it stands for a race of climbing plants with large, handsome flowers. He is less likely to know the few evergreen, smaller-flowered species and might well not recognize one when he sees it. Such a clematis is *C. cirrhosa*, a very slender-stemmed plant to 3 m (10 ft) high with dissected, almost fern-like foliage, which takes on purple-bronze tints. The nodding flowers are rather bell-shaped and of a modest creamy hue. Their primary value is their un-expected winter to spring opening time—providing there are sufficient mild spells. Rather more decorative and only margin-ally less hardy is *C. c. balearica* from the Balearic Islands, Corsica and other Medi-terranean islands, with beautifully cut foliage and flowers spotted red-purple within. When the temperature in the open garden dropped to − 18°C (0°F) in 1979, a young plant of this clematis which I raised from Majorca-collected seed, not only sur-vived on a west wall but retained every leaf unmarked, so it is not necessarily as tender as is sometimes suggested. More imposing and of a bolder mien is *C. armandii* from China. Another of Ernest Wilson's fine introductions, it has trifoliate, leathery lus-trous leaves, each lance-shaped leaflet up to 15 cm (6 in) long. In spring, axillary clus-ters of white or cream flowers open, each with six petals (sepals) and about 5 cm (2 in) wide. As the flowers age they may take on pink tints and in the cultivar 'Apple Blossom' this is a feature from the begin-ning. 'Snowdrift' is pure white throughout. Both of these clematis and indeed all mem-bers of the genus that climb, fasten to their supports in a unique way, the stalks of one or more leaflets of each leaf acting as a tendril.

Roses

'Everybody loves a rose', but unfortunately very few are evergreen or if they are, are damaged by hard winters. Such is the Macartney rose, *R. bracteata* from China, though if it does lose its shining leaflets, it can still redeem itself in summer with 7.5–10 cm (3–4 in) wide lemon-scented white flowers. Almost evergreen and hardy enough is *R. wichuraiana*, a trailer from Japan best suited as ground cover, but which can also be trained upwards. It has rather small, dark, polished leaves divided into seven or nine leaflets and in late summer produces small clusters of beauti-fully scented, 5 cm (2 in) wide white flowers followed by globular red hips.

R. luciae is similar and both it and *R. wichuraiana* have been used by hybrid-ists to create some lovely rambling roses with glossy more or less evergreen foliage. The best known of these is undoubtedly 'Alberic Barbier' with creamy-yellow buds opening to white flowers over a long season. It makes attractive and unusual ground cover where there is plenty of room. There are of course, several roses with semi-evergreen leaves. Particularly appealing is 'Madame Gregoire Staechelin' though in so glorious a flowering climber winter foliage is very much of a luxury bonus.

6 Non-woody plants

Whilst it is the evergreen trees and shrubs which make the greatest impact on the garden in winter, some of the more lowly perennial plants should not be neglected. Herbaceous borders or areas where perennials are grown are usually considered a write-off as far as providing interest in winter is concerned, but this need not be entirely so. Indeed a walk around a well-stocked garden will show that a wide variety of perennials have some sort of greenery to show. My pleasant task has been to pick out some of those that are worth growing for their foliage alone.

World-wide miscellany

Of foremost importance as we move through the genera in alphabetical order is *Asarum*, one of the few genera grown largely for its evergreen leaves and providing attractive ground cover. One of the finest hardy species is *A. hartwegii*, a wild ginger from north west North America with heart-shaped leaves to 13 cm (5 in) wide, veined and sometimes mottled whitish or greyish. *A. shuttleworthii* is an eastern North American version with smaller leaves. Having plain green leaves sometimes to 15 cm (6 in) wide is *A. caudatum*. One of the best ground-coverers of the genus it is also noteworthy for the three 5 cm (2 in) long tail-like calyx lobes on the hidden brownish-purple flowers. Despite the attractions of the species mentioned, my favourite is the European asarabacca, *A. europaeum*. This has the neatest kidney-shaped leaves with the brightest gloss—and the smallest brown flowers, but that hardly matters. Queen of the evergreen perennials is *Bergenia*, an Asiatic genus of the saxifrage family and formerly known as *Megasea*. The best sorts have massive oval to rounded leathery, lustrous leaves which look cheerfully fresh all the winter. *B. cordifolia*, with heart-shaped leaf bases, and *B. crassifolia* without, are the most common as are their hybrids. All these have green leaves but *B. purpurascens* takes on strong red-purple hues in winter and can be quite magnificent. The plant listed as *B. beesiana* is now included in *purpurascens* and has similar attractions. The modern hybrid cultivars, though raised mainly for their flowers, also have good leaves, notably 'Abendglut' ('Evening Glow'), shades of maroon; 'Ballawley', dark blood-red, and 'Sunningdale', bronze.

The wiry-stemmed compound leaves of *Epimedium* are always a delight, the individual leaflets often intriguingly lopsided. Best winter value is provided by *E. perralderanum* a surprisingly hardy Algerian with dark, lustrous trifoliate leaves, the individual leaflets like slightly waved glossy hearts. *E. pinnatum* is a good second best plant having less deeply hued leaves composed of three to nine leaflets, the outer

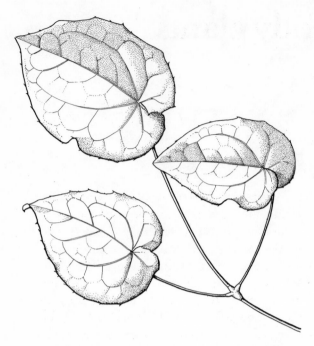

Epimedium perralderianum, the best species for winter foliage effect.

ones of which are angular at the base.

Many of the sea hollies (*Eryngium*) die away in winter or have little to show, but *E. variifolium* retains a rosette of dark green, prominently white- or pale-veined leaves which are particularly rewarding in the depths of winter. Some of the South American species are worth considering if grown in sheltered areas. *Agave*-like, *E. agavifolium* has rosettes of broad, slightly rumpled and spine-toothed rich green swords, while *E. eburneum*, confused with *E. bromeliifolium* in gardens has more graceful clumps of slimmer leaves.

A great contrast of foliage can be found among the spurges, *Euphorbia*. *E. characias* and *E. c. wulfenii* are semi-shrubby and erect to 1 m (3 ft) or more with dense, narrow, hairy, greenish-grey leaves. *E. robbiae* may top 30 cm (1 ft) before flowering, its deep, smooth green leaves forming

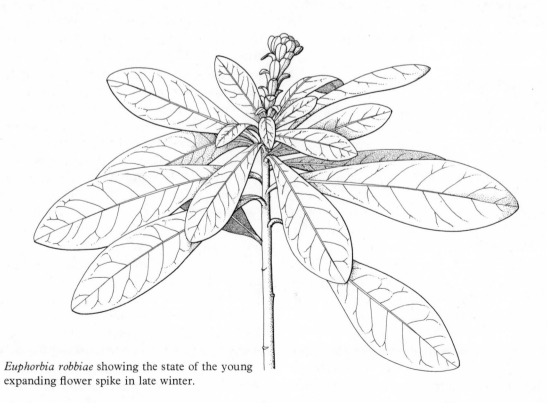

Euphorbia robbiae showing the state of the young expanding flower spike in late winter.

Leaf forms in *Helleborus lividus*: centre *H. lividus lividus*; left, *H. lividus corsicus* and right, *H. l.* 'Sternii', one of the hybrids between them.

terminal rosettes. The latter spreads with alarming speed in good moist soil but also tolerates dry shade and is then less rampant. Indian strawberry, *Fragaria (Duchesnea) indica*, is another good ground coverer which can get out of hand and looks good if the winter is not too snowy or fiercely cold. Wand flower and beetleweed are common names rather at odds with each other for the very hardy winter green perennial *Galax aphylla (G. urceolata)*. A native of open woods in east North America it forms dense, extensive patches of long-stalked rounded, firmly leathery and beautifully polished leaves 5–15 cm (2–6 in) wide; superb ground cover where the soil is neutral or acid.

The evergreen species of *Helleborus* are particularly rewarding often adding winter flowers to their handsome leaves. Somewhat shrubby-based is *H. lividus*, a less than hardy plant with trifoliate dark leaves having a marbled pattern of pale veins and reddish stalks. The green flowers also have a red-purple flush. More robust and hardier is *H. lividus corsicus* with larger, waved and pointed-tipped bright green leaves with bold marginal toothing. The flowers too are larger and bright yellow-green. Setterwort or stinking hellebore, *H. foetidus* has a similar habit of growth but the leaves are deeply fingered and of a marvellously sombre shade of near black-green. Christmas rose (*H. niger*) has lighter leaves divided into fewer, broader fingers and lacks the erect stem of the previous species. Its white, bowl-shaped flowers will be familiar to all.

The variegated form of yellow archangel or yellow dead-nettle, *Lamiastrum galeobdolon* 'Variegatum', with its silver-flushed heart-shaped leaves is undoubtedly superb in winter, but it is so outrageously rampant that it should never be planted in a garden less than an acre in extent! *Lamium maculatum* is vigorous enough but more easily kept under control. Silver-white striped leaves are the norm in gardens but there is now 'Beacon Silver' a form in which the whole upper leaf surface is solidly silvered. This is an eyecatching plant of the first order and is destined to travel far and wide. *Petasites fragrans*, the winter heliotrope is another very invasive plant which is probably best not planted at all in the garden proper. On a rough bank however, it gives excellent winter value with its round, heart-shaped leaves and honey-scented pinkish groundsel-like flower heads.

Japanese spurge
Popular as ground cover, *Pachysandra terminalis*, the Japanese spurge, also provides cheerful greenery all the year round. Ramifying underground it sends up erect stems bearing most of its boldly-toothed obovate leaves near the tips. Showing up particularly well in shade is *P. t.* 'Variegata', its leaves white-bordered.

Europeans
Common primrose, *Primula vulgaris* and its forms and hybrids, including the polyanthus, should not be overlooked purely as foliage plants. Providing the winters are not unduly severe they produce fresh green leaves that are a real foretaste of spring, more especially when the odd premature flower or two shows during mild spells. Several of the lungworts are evergreen and though the largish oval leaves are rather coarse they are welcome enough in winter. Especially good are *Pulmonaria officinalis* and *P. saccharata* with silvery-spotted foliage, while *P. rubra* has brighter unspotted ones. Lambs'-ears, *Stachys olympica*

(*S. lanata, S. byzantina*) is almost too familiar to mention but it does produce its silvery, woolly leaves all the year round and looks good during dry spells in winter.

A trio of Americans
Known as fringecups in its native west North America, *Tellima grandiflora* forms substantial ground-covering clumps that are pleasant to look at throughout the year. Cast in a similar mould and also a member of the saxifrage family is the pickaback plant, *Tolmiea menziesii* from the same part of North America. Its somewhat maple-like leaves are long-stalked and stay a fresh green all through the winter. Intriguing to all who see it is the way a plantlet forms in the centre of each mature leaf—hence the common name. Also a saxifrage ally is the foam flower, *Tiarella cordifolia* from east North America. Unlike the tellima it spreads by strawberry-like stolons, soon covering the ground with hairy maple-like bright green leaves that take on coppery tints in winter. The periwinkles (*Vinca*) have long graced our gardens but all too often their cheerful winter greenery is overlooked. Boldest and bushiest is *V. major* with lustrous ovate to almost heart-shaped leaves. *V. m.* 'Variegata' with yellow-cream leaf margins is particularly eye-catching. Flatter and neater with narrower leaves is *V. minor* the common periwinkle of which there are several cultivars varying in leaf and flower colour.

Winter rosettes
Although not evergreen in the perennial sense, several biennials and over-wintering annuals remain green through the winter and some are very handsome indeed. Pride of place must go to several species of *Meconopsis*, in particular *M. superba*,

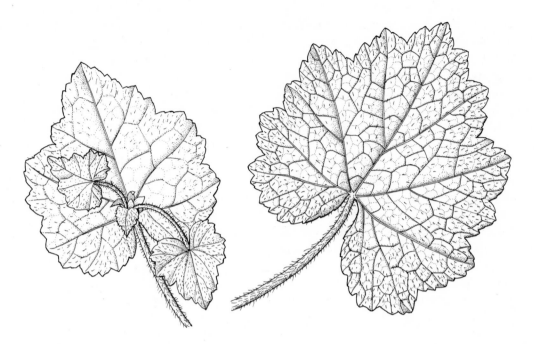

Tellima grandiflora (right) and *Tolmiea menziesii*,
two closely allied members of the saxifrage family.

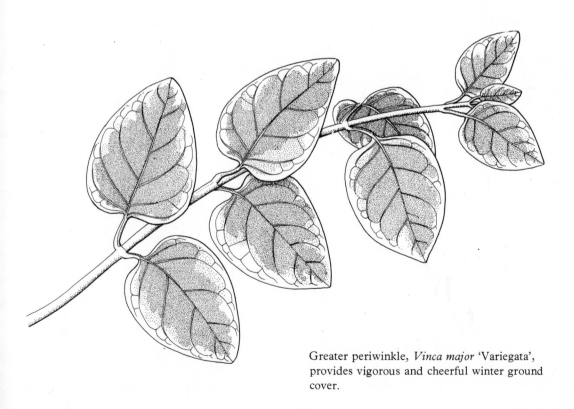

Greater periwinkle, *Vinca major* 'Variegata',
provides vigorous and cheerful winter ground
cover.

napaulensis and *regia* which form great ornate cartwheels of silver or golden hairy leaves. Scotch thistles (*Onopordum*) produce even larger but generally more arching grey or grey-white leaves with prickly margins. Similarly coloured but smaller and softly woolly are the rosettes of certain mulleins, notably *Verbascum bombyciferum* (*V. broussa* of gardens), silky grey-white; *V. olympicum*, white and woolly, and *thapsiforme* (*densiflorum*), yellow-white and woolly. Rich greens are easily provided by such familiar plants as Canterbury bells, *Campanula medium*, and common foxglove, *Digitalis purpurea*. Even the dense leafy clumps of the garden forget-me-not, *Myosotis sylvatica* and its cultivars are not to be despised.

Grassy-leaved perennials

Slender, arching or erect grassy leaves provide striking contrast to the broader leaves mentioned above and several such plants are reliable evergreens. Largest are the New Zealand flaxes, *Phormium tenax* and *P. cookianum* (*colensoi*). For some unknown reason they regularly find their way into nurserymen's catalogues under the tree and shrub heading, but are very definitely massive evergreen perennials. Largest is *P. tenax* with leathery, more or less erect, sword-shaped leaves often greyish beneath and with a fine orange line around the margins. There are now several cultivars with variegated or purple-flushed leaves which make striking specimen plants. Some of these are hybrids with *P. cookianum*, the mountain flax. This latter plant is generally smaller with laxer leaves and is readily identified by its slender, twisted pendent pods (those of *P. tenax* are shorter, fatter and erect). Next in size but still a lot smaller is *Iris foetidissima*, named

gladwin, or more unfortunately, stinking iris. Most satisfactory is the variegated form with each dark green leaf bearing a cream band on the inner edge. Similar variegation occurs in the grey-green-leaved *Sisyrinchium striatum*, a distinctive clump-former but not very hardy.

Almost as broad-leaved is *Luzula sylvatica* (*L. maxima*) the greater woodrush, but in this plant they arch outwards with the flat side uppermost. *L. s.* 'Marginata' is the form generally grown, distinguished by the yellow-cream line around each leaf margin. Several sedges (*Carex*) provide elegant grassy tufts. Particularly handsome is the Japanese sedge or 'grass', *C. morrowii* 'Variegata', having glossy dark leaves striped with white. Lily-turf (*Liriope*) is a member of the lily family, but has grassy though leathery-textured leaves and makes interesting ground cover. Among the true grasses the majestic clumps of pampas *Cortaderia selloana* stay green unless the winter temperatures drop disastrously. The same can be said of *Helictotrichon sempervirens* (*Avena candida*, *A. sempervirens*), a tight clump-former with grey-green, very narrow arching leaves to 60 cm (2 ft) long.

Ferns

As is the case with the grassy-leaved plants the ferns too provide a contrast of form and texture so important when leaves only are relied upon for garden decoration. The following small selection should be in every garden. One hardly expects to have the delicately and intricately divided fronds of maidenhair fern in a northern temperate garden, but the Himalayan *Adiantum venustum* provides them. In mild winters it stays green although hard frosts turn the fronds a pleasing rusty-brown leaving them otherwise unchanged. Very different are the undivided strap-shaped fronds of the hart's tongue fern, *Asplenium scolopendrium* (*Phyllitis scolopendrium*). It is a good beginner's fern being indifferent to soil if not too wet, and thriving in sun or shade. The bright green 30 cm (1 ft) tall fronds stay cheerful all the year round. Several hard ferns (*Blechnum*) are worthy of consideration, notably the small *B. pennamarina* from the cooler parts of the Southern Hemisphere and its usually longer-fronded Northern equivalent *B. spicant*. Both have a spreading habit and make interesting ground cover; *penna-marina* in particular also takes on bronze tones in winter. They have spreading, pinnate fronds from 7·5–30 cm (3–12 in) long, and erect, much narrower spore-bearing fronds which turn dark brown in late summer.

The handsome shuttlecocks of male ferns (*Dryopteris*) are well known, but the most truly evergreen and hardy, *D. pseudomas* (*D. borreri*), is strangely neglected in gardens. Even rarer and well worth seeking out is *D. erythrosora*, the spore cases (sporangia) on the leaf undersides being bright red. Common polypody, *Polypodium vulgare*, is another easy fern. It produces broad, pinnate fronds up to 30 cm (1 ft) long from creeping rhizomes and can eventually form large colonies. In areas of high rainfall it will grow epiphytically on mossy tree branches. More decorative is *P. v.* 'Cornubiense' with almost lacily divided fronds. Also lacily-cut are the forms of soft-shield fern, *Polystichum setiferum*. My favourite is *P. s.* 'Acutilobum' (*proliferum*), with dense clumps of low, arching fronds to 45 cm (1½ ft) or more long. In addition it has the intriguing habit of producing plantlets on the leaf mid-rib. Marginally more elegant is 'Divisilobum', but it is not easy to come by nowadays.

Rock and alpine plants

Most of the small perennials suitable for rock gardens or raised beds are evergreen or partially so, and as the majority are grown for their flowers, the enthusiast for these little plants gets the best of both worlds. Naturally enough, however, some rock plants have more winter foliage value than others and the following notes endeavour briefly to cover some of the best genera to concentrate upon. Although not at their best in the depths of winter, all the New Zealand burs or bidibidis are attractive, especially the hairy blue-grey *Acaena caesiiglauca*, the bronze *A. microphylla* and green *A. novae-zelandiae*. Also bronze-purple, green or variegated are the smooth leaves of the bugle, *Ajuga*. Grey is the primary attraction of *Alyssum saxatile* and *A. wulfenianum*, while the familiar *Arabis* and *Aubrieta* are hoary. *Arenaria balearica* maintains its film of bright green unless winters are very frosty. The many pinks (*Dianthus*) have mostly short, stiff, grassy grey leaves though a few, e.g. *D. alpina* are green. *Dryas*, the mountain avens, has small, dark, glossy oak-like leaves that are white-downy beneath. The mountain daisies of New Zealand (*Celmisia*) have splendid leathery leaves in shades of dark green (e.g. *C. spectabilis*) and grey (e.g. *C. coriacea*) but none are totally hardy and need cool, acid soil conditions. *Epigaea* needs the same conditions but is much hardier, forming, when happy, satisfying mats of lustrous oval leaves. Sea heath, *Frankenia laevis* is much overlooked and makes very pleasing mossy mats in the driest and poorest soils. Some of the *Globularia* species are good, notably *G. punctata* (*willkomii*) with dark spoon-shaped leaves. The corrugated dark rosettes of *Haberlea* and *Ramonda* give life to vertical crevices,

Three rock plants which provide decorative
ground cover: left, *Acaena caesii-glauca*; centre,
Waldsteinia ternata; and right, *Dryas drummondii*.

as do the fleshy, smooth ones of *Lewisia
cotyledon* and its allies. The African mountain species *Haplocarpha ruepellii* usually
retains interest in winter with smaller dark
glossy leaves that are white and hairy
beneath and rather like those of dandelion
but shorter and broader.

Iberis sempervirens, candytuft, makes a
low dark bushlet, and *I. semperflorens* will
even add glistening white flowers during
mild spells. *Luetkia pectinata* from western
North America is like a refined mossy
saxifrage and the eastern American part-
ridge berry, *Mitchella repens*, forms mats
of small, rounded, dark leaves often with
a pale vein pattern; these grow best in

shade. *Mitella breweri* forms dense, low
hummocks or mats of bright green maple-
like leaves. Most species of *Parahebe* and
Penstemon are winter green, though they
may look a bit jaded after hard weather.
Pimelea prostrata forms charming mats of
tiny grey leaves and though different, the
same could be said of its New Zealand
compatriot *Raoulia australis*; *R. glabra* is
bright green.

Polygala chamaebuxus 'Grandiflora' is a
tiny hummock-forming shrub with glossy
oval leaves which, in mild winters may
shelter a few quaint rosy-purple and yellow
flowers. Mossy and cheerfully golden green
all the year round is *Sagina subulata*
'Aurea'; it it sometimes listed as *S. glabra* or
S. pilifera. Many saxifrages have winter
interest; the mosses providing rich green
cut leaves and the encrusted sorts having
the leaves margined with silvery encrus-

tations of lime, e.g. *S. callosa* (*lingulata*), *cochlearis*, *cotyledon* and *paniculata* (*aizoon*). Very different is London pride, *S. ×urbium*, and its parents and allies, e.g. *spathularis*, *umbrosa* and *hirsuta*, with rosettes of rounded, toothed, spoon-shaped leaves. Tight, smooth hummock-forming plants are the joy and sorrow of alpine gardens. Strange then that the perfect and easy *Scleranthus biflorus* is so neglected. Its bright yellow green 'buns' are a joy all the year round. Many stonecrops (*Sedum*) and all houseleeks (*Sempervivum*) are musts, providing interest and colour in winter and summer alike. The much less easy to please

The lush primrose-like foliage of *Wulfenia carinthiaca*.

Soldanella and *Shortia* also have attractive leaves but they are not beginners' plants. Mats and hummocks are the speciality of the thymes (*Thymus*) and practically all are garden worthy. Most of the pansy-type *Viola* species and cultivars are cheerfully wintergreen as are the substantial primula-like leaves of *Wulfenia*. Lastly there is *Waldsteinia ternata*, a strawberry ally with pleasing trifoliate leaves which make fine ground cover.

7 Cultivation, propagation, pests and diseases

Cultivation

Site and aspect

Very few people are able to select the locality and exact position of their house and garden. If a choice is possible then a sloping site is best, preferably inclined towards the south or south-west with some sort of wind shelter from the north. The soil should be neutral to acid, fairly deep and well drained but moisture retentive. Do not despair if none of these advantages is yours. Many evergreens are very tolerant of exposure and there is virtually no soil that cannot be made suitable with the addition of humus and fertilizers.

Wind shelter

Wind shelter is a prime requisite if a garden is to be enjoyed throughout the year. If it does not exist already then the provision of a hedge or taller wind-break should be a priority job. Evergreens of course, are the ideal choice, and none better than some of the conifers. Lawson, Leyland, and Monterey cypresses and yew are effective and popular but there is much to be said for being a bit more adventurous, and trying western hemlock, incense cedar and Serbian spruce, etc.

Soil and fertility

Humus is the key to the fertility of all soils and unless the ground is really rich it should be added to the planting holes at least and then used as a mulch. Peat is a clean and readily available source of humus and if bought in the largest possible bales is not too expensive. Farmyard or stable manure is ideal but not always easy to come by and needs stacking for a few months before use. Compost made from garden and kitchen waste, e.g. non-seeding weeds, soft prunings, grass mowings, vegetable parings etc, is a very good second best and there are several systems available commercially for producing it quickly. In some areas spent hops—a biproduct of the brewing industry—are available. It can be used directly but is best stacked for a few months. If there is ready access to fallen autumn leaves, leaf mould can be made and this is a splendid source of humus for trees and shrubs. A simple way of dealing with garden and kitchen waste, spent hops, leaves etc, is to make an enclosure at least 1·2–5·5 m (4–5 ft) square with metal stakes and chicken wire. Put the material to be rotted down in layers and add one or two spadefuls of garden soil and a handful of sulphate of ammonia once each layer is about 15–20 cm (6–8 in) deep. Bacteria are needed for the decaying process and the soil readily supplies these. In turn, the bacteria need nitrogen, hence the sulphate of ammonia. Ideally the enclosure or bin should be filled with rottable material, at one go, or within a week or two of starting. It will then break down rapidly and evenly and soon be fit for use. An alternative is to make two or more smaller enclosures each of which can be filled quickly. Turning large amounts of material with a fork also aids the rotting process. Whatever means is used, make sure the material never gets dry, or rotting will cease. Depending on time of year, size of enclosure and material used, good compost should be ready to use in three to six months from the time the last lot of raw material is added.

Preparation of the site

Unless one is lucky enough to have a new garden on a former smallholding or arable farmland, some preparation of the area to be planted with evergreens will be needed. A new garden in the suburbs may have been partially stripped of its top soil and/or may contain lots of builders' rubble. The worst of the latter should be removed and if possible, more topsoil brought in. If the latter is not feasible and providing the subsoil is not raw clay, then the planting holes should be dug and the soil removed mixed roughly with equal parts of the humus sources mentioned above. It may be that the site is covered with rough orchard grass or a lawn, in which case the planting hole should be marked out and the turf skimmed off. Dig out the hole a little deeper than required, place the turf in the bottom and chop up roughly. Apply a sprinkling of general fertilizer, cover with enough soil to make it right for planting. Quite often the soil will be a former flower bed and then the task is a similar one, that of digging out the hole to the required size.

In all these examples, drainage should be considered. The average garden soil usually drains well enough for most evergreens but few will thrive in waterlogged sites. Providing drainage is not always easy.

Firstly there must be an outlet for drainage water or failing that, a sump hole must be dug. This should be 1·2–2 m (4–6 ft) deep at the lowest point and be filled with rubble, stones, etc. Tile drains can now be laid radiating away from the sump and under the area to be planted. Where only a few choice evergreens are to be planted, drainage pipes can be run from the bottom of each planting hole to the sump. An alternative is to make raised beds. When preparing a site for any permanent planting, particularly trees and shrubs, attention must be paid to the removal of all perennial weeds, particularly such strangling climbers as bindweed which are almost impossible to remove efficiently once they colonize the root system of a favourite shrub. One of the modern herbicides can be used to clean up the site well beforehand. Then, as each planting hole is dug, any residual weed roots can be picked out by hand. I have, as yet, made no mention of cultivating the whole site to be planted; of course if time/energy or mechanical aids are available, this can be done. Generally however, if good planting holes are made cultivation in between is not necessary unless the ground is full of perennial weeds.

Buying evergreens

If containerized plants are chosen at a garden centre there are a few points to watch out for before the purchase is made. Make sure that the leaves are a healthy green and firm and that growth is vigorous. Yellowish leaves could denote starvation or a faulty root system. Starvation is curable with feeding and prompt planting-out. A poor or rotting root system is not easy to deal with and the plant may never recover to full vigour, or may die. The tree or shrub should feel firm in its container, denoting it has a well established root system which will not fall apart, with subsequent root damage at planting-out time. If the plant feels loose and the potting soil is soft, this could mean it has been recently potted-on from a smaller container or lifted from the open ground and containerized. Although the plant may be perfectly alright, to sell it in this newly-moved state is a form of sharp practice. Ideally, a containerized tree or shrub should have made strong new roots and be in a state to plant out without further disturbance.

Planting

The ideal time to plant an evergreen varies with the area and the season. Where winters are comparatively mild, early autumn is best, allowing new roots to grow rapidly and the plant to become well established before winter. In areas where the ground stays frozen for much of the winter, spring or early summer is favoured. Added to this is the rainfall factor. Where dry springs are the norm, planting evergreens can be somewhat risky unless watering is conscientiously carried out. The distance apart at which to set out any plant, tree or shrub, let alone evergreens, is a constant problem for the beginner. So much depends on the sort of effect required and the growth habit of the chosen plants. As a broad generalization, shrubs should be planted the same distance apart as their average ultimate height. Narrow or columnar species can be planted closer together, while spreading sorts which are ultimately wider than high can be put in one and a half to twice as far apart as high. This may leave large areas of ground around young plants, and to provide interest in the early years, the spaces can be planted with fillers; cheap, quick-growing—usually deciduous—shrubs that can be discarded once the permanent occupants are big enough. These recom-

mended distances refer of course to the shrub-bed or border. Plants that are grown as specimens or for their attractive outlines must be given plenty of room, being placed at least three to four times their heights apart.

Evergreens are generally sold in containers, or are lifted from the open ground with a ball of roots and soil which is wrapped in plastic sheeting or hessian (burlap). Planting is then a very straightforward procedure. A hole is dug larger than the root ball, ideally half as large again and if hard subsoil is encountered at the bottom this should be loosened with a fork and a little decayed manure, compost, peat, etc, worked in. The plant is placed in the hole so that the top of the root ball of a containerized plant, or the soil mark on the stem of a wrapped specimen is about 3 cm ($1\frac{1}{4}$ in) below the surrounding soil surface. This is so that when filled in a saucer-shaped depression can be left for watering. Once the plant is satisfactorily in position in the hole, remove the container or wrapping and fill in with a mixture of soil and humus plus a handful of general fertilizer, firming at intervals. If the plant is a tree or seems top-heavy a stake may be necessary and this should be knocked or pushed into the bottom of the hole before the plant is finally set in place. Some evergreens can be lifted and planted bare root, i.e. when the root system has little or no soil adhering to it. This is alright for young conifers and some older ones, but the roots must not dry out and replanting must take place immediately. Larger specimens should have the roots spread out as evenly as possible in the hole and the plant should be gently shaken up and down once they are covered with soil to make sure it filters in between the finer roots. The soil should be well firmed with the heel at least twice during the filling operation. Larger bare-root plants often need a stake or some other form of support.

Supporting

Small or even larger container-grown shrubs seldom need supporting, their heavy root ball is anchor enough. Taller conifers and larger broad-leaved evergreen trees will almost certainly need steadying against strong winds and this can be done in a variety of ways. A single strong cane or stake is usually adequate, and for larger specimens, 2 m ($6\frac{1}{2}$ ft) or more high, this is best inserted into the bottom of the hole before planting. Quite often the tree has a strong stem needing support only to prevent wind rocking at the base. In this case the stake can be inserted after planting, at an angle of 45° pointing into the prevailing wind. The tree stems then forms one side of a triangle with a single tie at the apex. It is unlikely that large, heavy-headed evergreen trees will be planted, but if so, then there are two alternatives. The first is the use of two erect stakes, one on either side of and about 15 cm (6 in) from the main stem. A cross bar is then nailed to the top of the two stakes and the tree tied to it. An alternative is to have straining ropes or wires from tree stem to stakes. The second method is to use three guy ropes or wires, secured just below the head of the tree or at least two-thirds of the way up the main stem or trunk. These straining members should radiate downwards at an angle of about 50° and be secured to strong wood or metal pegs driven well into the soil. The actual material and method used for securing stakes, ropes or wires to a tree is important as the bark and living tissues must not be severely chafed or cut into. Where applicable it is best to use proprietary tree-ties; those employing a strap

and rubber or plastic buffer can be recommended. Less expensive and at one time regular practice in nurseries, is the use of strips of hessian or burlap. This is wound two or three times round the tree stem and secured with raffia or plastic tape. Next, soft string is wound several times around this protection and the stake in a figure of eight formation and tied in the middle. For smaller trees, sections of old hose pipes can be split down the sides and placed around the stem instead of the hessian. Old hose piping is very useful for the guy rope method, being threaded on the wire which goes round the tree stem.

Climbers

The supporting of young trees and shrubs is a temporary thing and need not last more than two years. With climbers and trained wall shrubs however, the supports must last the lifetime of the plants. Wooden stakes, posts and trellis work should be thoroughly treated with a preservative before erecting. Galvanized wire and eye bolts (vine eyes) though less aesthetically pleasing are ideal for training wall shrubs and are soon covered with verdure. The wires may be set 30 cm (1 ft) apart horizontally—the most useful—or vertically for stem twiners. Pergola poles should always be set in a concrete base, for when covered with foliage they carry a considerable weight and this also creates a wind-barrier. Useful semi-permanent support for climbers is a tripod of stakes or rustic pole. A good method for adding height and interest to a planting of shrubs or other low-growing plants. The most natural support for climbers is an old tree or tall dead tree stump. *Clematis, Decumaria, Pileostegia* and the ivies look particularly well grown in this way. If the tree is living and of rather dense growth it should first be thinned. Old, neglected or poorly-fruiting apple trees are ideal as they have a fairly open habit and a deep root system. Trees with a dense surface web of roots present problems of watering and feeding to get the climber vigorously established. Where this is the case the climber should be planted just outside the canopy of branches, and a rope, wire or long stake led up and secured to a strong branch.

After-care

However well the site and planting hole are prepared and the actual operation is carried out, this is not enough for the plant's continuing welfare. Watering is important, particularly if the plant is set out in spring and dry spells are expected. Watering must be thorough, hence the reason for a depression around each plant at least 2·5 cm (1 in) deep in the middle. Fill this depression at least twice in succession, three times would be better, then repeat at weekly intervals as long as the dry weather continues. If dry cold or dry warm winds are a seasonal feature then the foliage is best sprayed with one of the anti-dessicant or plastic sprays which stop or cut down water loss from the leaves. If freezing winds occur after planting, then some sort of barricade should be provided. Plastic sheeting, hessian or burlap secured to a tent of stakes is effective and easily erected. Alternatively, self-supporting collars can be made of two sheets of chicken wire sandwiching a filling of dry bracken or straw. A lid can be made in the same way. Mulching helps to conserve the moisture of the soil and keep it cool during prolonged warm spells. Any of the forms of raw humus already mentioned are ideal, with the addition of pulverized bark or wood chips. A ground-cover of low plants too is useful, uniting the trees and shrubs with the soil in the most natural way

and cutting down weeding to a bare minimum. Where a bed or border is concerned, mulching or ground-cover planting should be carried out as soon as all the shrubs are in position and certainly before annual weed seeds have time to germinate. By carrying out one of these alternatives weeding will never become a chore and even less so as the individual shrubs grow and finally touch each other.

Feeding

Providing the soil is fertile, or made so to begin with, regular feeding is not essential. Nevertheless there is no denying that a light application of a general fertilizer each spring can make a wonderful difference to speed and vigour of growth. If pulverized bark or wood chips are used as a mulch, the application of a nitrogen fertilizer is necessary in the following spring. If this is not carried out, poor growth often results owing to the drain on the soil's nitrogen reserves by the bacteria of decay working on the wood tissue. It is also worth noting that wood and bark mulches of this kind have an acidifying effect on the soil and are excellent where rhododendrons and other members of the *Erica* family are grown. They are especially useful where the soil conditions are neutral in reaction (around 7 on the pH scale).

Pruning

Setting aside the essential curtailment of growth and shaping of formal hedges, it is fair to say that no evergreen tree or shrub needs pruning to thrive and/or flower well. During the early life of some broad-leaved evergreens, however, particularly if propagated by cuttings, judicious pruning will result in a more shapely bush. A good example of this occurs in *Daphne odora*. Rooted cuttings tend to grow straight up to

30 cm (1 ft) or more before branching naturally, and as a result form rather leggy plants. Cutting or pinching out the growing tip when half this height, initiates branching sooner and a more shapely shrub develops. This shortening back of the current season's growth should be the essence of the pruning of evergreens. By its means, growth can be curtailed if too exuberant and be made bushier if rather thin or leggy. It can also increase flower production in certain cases. Despite these advantages, continuous pruning of this nature can alter or destroy the natural habit of a species and thus spoil the effect. Should this pruning be deemed necessary, late summer is the best time for broad-leaved trees and shrubs, late spring or early summer for conifers. A pair of sharp secateurs is the best tool for this job, though the nurseryman would probably prefer a sharp knife. If the shrub is exceeding its allotted space then all the young leading stems can be cut back by half to two-thirds.

Shrubs or trees with large prominent buds, particularly rhododendrons, can be dealt with in spring or even late winter. It is very important to be able to distinguish between flowering and growth buds. By late winter and often before, the buds which will later produce flowers can be seen to be at least twice as large as the growth or shoot buds. The latter can be gently snapped out with a sideways motion of the fingers. Their removal will result in more shoots arising lower down on each stem thus curtailing spread, making bushier plants and potentially increasing flower production the following year, all in one operation. This pruning of young growth can be used on certain conifers, notably pines, though firs and spruces can also be so treated. In this case the young shoots or 'candles' are allowed to extend until the needles begin to develop and are snapped in half. The needles will then grow to full size and mask the snapped ends, but no further extension growth will occur until the following year. This is a good method for the dwarfer species and cultivars with a normally compact shape, e.g. *Pinus mugo*. If continuously carried out in the larger species of *Picea*, *Abies*, *Pinus*, etc. it soon destroys their naturally graceful outline. Conifers with more slender, wiry growth, e.g. *Cupressus*, *Chamaecyparis*, *Thuja*, can be pruned in the same way as broad-leaved species, removing the tips of branchlets. Never cut back to leafless stems for these will not break into new growth as those of broad-leaved trees and shrubs usually do. This shaping and curtailing is not the only type of pruning that may be needed; sometimes, generally after a gale, a branch or branchlet may stick out and spoil the outline of a tree or shrub. If it cannot be tied back in neatly it is best removed, cutting back within the mass of branches either to a shorter lateral or to its base. In the same way any dead twigs, branches or branchlets must be removed.

Hedges
Evergreen shrubs used for hedging require more and regular pruning. Initially the young plants should be tipped in late summer or the following spring, removing about one third of the current or previous season's growth. This will initiate branching low down ensuring that the ultimate hedge is dense from ground level upwards. Failure to do this may well result in a loose or open-bottomed hedge, a situation well-nigh impossible to rectify. Once full width and height are reached, pruning consists of an annual shearing in late summer or, if growth is very vigorous, two such clippings, the other around mid-summer.

Although hand or mechanical shearing is quick and efficient the result can be unsightly where large-leaved evergreens are concerned. A newly trimmed hedge of cherry laurel with all its fine large leaves variously chopped in half is a far from satisfying sight. In such cases the secateurs are the only answer. Whether sheared or pruned with secateurs the outline of a hedge should be that of a narrow decapitated pyramid, i.e. broader at the base than the top, with flat, sloping sides. This practice ensures that a fair amount of the plant's energy goes into keeping the base well supplied with young growth. Flowering hedges should never be sheared, the flowering stems and others of equal length being pruned with secateurs immediately the last bloom fades. If sheared over in the formal way, curtailment or loss of floral display will result.

PROPAGATION

From time to time, most gardeners want to increase a particular evergreen either to replace a too large or aging specimen, to create a larger planting of a favourite, or simply to give away to friends. Many evergreens, in all categories, are comparatively easy to propagate with a minimum of specialized knowledge and equipment. The main methods of propagating the plants described in this book are by seeds, cuttings, layering, suckers, division and grafting. Those applicable to woody stemmed plants will be discussed first.

Cuttings
Cuttings are lengths of stem, in various stages of development, which should be inserted in a suitable rooting medium and in conditions of warmth and humidity conducive to rooting. There are three categories of cuttings based upon maturity. Softwood refers to soft, recently-formed stems generally with the growing tips left on. Semi-hardwood are those which are becoming firm and woody and hardwood are fully woody stems at the end of the growing season. In addition there are two types of cuttings based upon the way they are trimmed ready for insertion. Nodal cuttings are lengths of stem cut cleanly below a leaf. Heel cuttings are lateral or side stems of the current season's growth carefully pulled or cut from the parent stem and carrying a wedge or sliver of it at the base. Cuttings of either sort must be trimmed to an optimum length and this varies with the vigour of the tree or shrub and robustness of the stems. For example, wiry-stemmed plants such as heathers are best at 2·5–5 cm (1–2 in), common holly and its cultivars 7·5–10 cm (3–4 in) and cherry laurel 13–15 cm (5–6 in) or more in length. When trimming semi-hard and hardwood cuttings it is the softer tip which is removed. When the cutting has been reduced to the right length, the leaves from the bottom third to a half are removed, though for many conifers, heaths and heathers this is not necessary. If the remaining leaves are large or long, certainly if more than about 7·5 cm (3 in), then the top half should be cut away with sharp scissors or a razor blade. This will prevent undue water loss from the cuttings before they root. Softwood cuttings are taken in late spring or early summer, semi-hardwood in late summer or early autumn and hardwood late autumn to early winter. Hardwood cuttings are placed in a cold frame or outside in the open ground in a sheltered, shady site. Soft and semi-hard types are placed in a propagating frame. Preferably the frame should have bottom heat in the range 18–24°C (65–70°F).

Most evergreen trees and shrubs are best

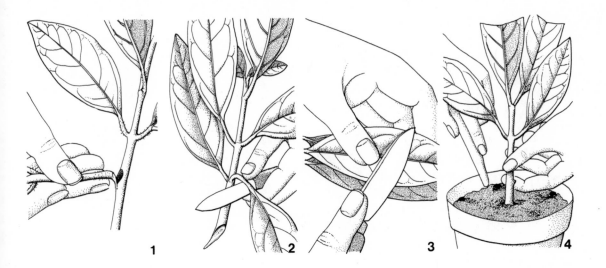

1   2   3   4

as semi-hardwood heel cuttings in a propagating frame with bottom heat, though many root without it. Many conifers root well though slowly in autumn as heel-cuttings in a shaded cold frame. The use of a hormone rooting powder, though not always essential, is recommended. Choosing a suitable rooting medium can be a problem for the beginner. I strongly recommend a mixture of equal parts really coarse sand and moss peat passed through a 6 mm ($\frac{1}{4}$ in) mesh sieve. The distance apart each way the cuttings are inserted in the rooting medium should be proportional to the length of the cuttings. As a rule of thumb guide, the leaves of each cutting should just overlap those of its neighbour. Once a batch of cuttings is inserted it is advisable to spray with a fungicide such as Captan or Benlate to prevent grey-mould disease (*Botrytis*) attacking leaves and stems. One of the fairly cheap rigid, transparent plastic-topped propagating cases are best, or one can be made of a wooden box with clear or milky plastic sheeting or glass as a cover. Light shading from direct sunlight is essential if clear plastic or glass is

Propagation: taking cuttings with a heel:
1 Carefully pulling off a firm based shoot with a heel of parent stem. 2 Removing the lower leaves. 3 Reducing the leaf area to prevent undue transpiration. 4 Inserting the cuttings prior to placing in the propagator.

used. If the expense is deemed worthwhile, a properly installed mist propagating unit gives excellent results though care must be taken in weaning the rooted cuttings to normal conditions. If small numbers of cuttings are being taken it is best to put each species or cultivar in a small pot of its own. This also aids inspection when rooting takes place three to six weeks or more later. The pot full of cuttings is inverted and gently tapped out to see the extent or lack of roots. Once the cuttings have roots 2·5–5 cm (1–2 in) or so long they should be carefully separated and potted in one of the standard potting soils and kept out of direct sunlight for a week or so until established. Cuttings rooted in rows in a cold frame can be either potted or lined out in nursery rows in a plot of land set aside for such purposes, or at the edge of a kitchen garden.

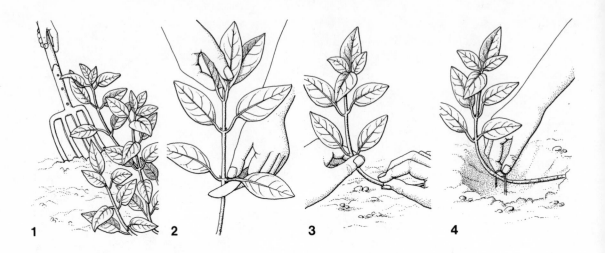

1   **2**   **3**   **4**

Propagation by layering: **1** Loosening the soil close to the shrub to be layered. **2** Removing the leaves from that area of the stem to be buried. **3** Positioning the stem to determine where the hole must be made. **4** Placing the stem in position in the hole and securing it with a layering pin. The final stage is to fill in the hole level with the surrounding soil surface.

Layering

Layering is a practice whereby the stem of a plant is induced to root while still attached to the mother plant, then severed and either treated as a young plant or a rooted cutting. Almost any plant can be layered, particularly evergreen shrubs such as rhododendrons, pieris, viburnum and all the climbers. To do this a flexible stem is chosen which will touch the ground with 15–20 cm (6–8 in) to spare. The soil at that point is loosened, coarse sand and peat forked in, then a shallow hole about 5 cm (2 in) deep is made. The end of the stem is bent into a U-shape and to induce the formation of roots the bottom of the U is deeply nicked, or sliced obliquely halfway through and the wound treated with hormone rooting powder. The U is then pegged to the bottom of the hole and covered with some of the peat, sand and soil mixture. If the tip of the layer is slender, support with a short cane. Approximately one year needs to elapse before the rooted layer can be severed. It is best to do the severing in two operations, first cutting halfway through, then two to three weeks later completing the operation. Leave *in situ* for a further month before transplanting. Trees or stiff-stemmed shrubs that cannot be bent down to ground level can be air layered. This was done formerly with balls of clay and moss or with flower pots split in half, but the advent of plastic sleeving has simplified the operation. A healthy one-year old stem is selected and nicked or sliced as for ground layering about 15–20 cm (6–8 in) from the tip. A section of plastic sleeving 20–25 cm (8–10 in) wide is slipped over the stem and secured at the bottom with insulating tape so that the nicked part of the stem is about halfway up. The sleeve is now filled with a mixture of one part potting or seed-sowing soil and two parts sphagnum or wood moss. If necessary, the stem bearing the sleeve can be supported with a long cane or tied to a nearby branch. Subsequent treatment is as for ground layering.

Suckers

Some shrubs, notably such *Berberis* species as *B. verruculosa* produce shoots from ground level at varying distances from the parent plant. These shoots are suckers and if carefully dug around and severed from the parent plant afford an easy means of increase. Poorly rooted suckers are best grown on in a reserve bed but well rooted ones can be put into a permanent site. Autumn or the following spring are the best times to remove suckers.

Seeds

In the wild, the natural means of increase by all flowering plants is by seeds. Quite a number of evergreens produce seeds in cultivation and these can provide an interesting and rewarding method of propagation among popular genera. Fairly easily raised from seeds are *Aucuba, Berberis, Camellia, Cotoneaster, Daphne, Fatsia, Ilex, Mahonia, Nothofagus, Pittosporum, Pyracantha, Prunus, Skimmia, Stranvaesia, Viburnum*. The essential requirements for seeds to germinate are water, oxygen from the air, and a suitable temperature. The last factor is a variable one, depending largely on the provenance of the parent species. For example, some alpine plants will germinate at just above $0°C$ ($32°F$), while few palms will respond below $21°C$ ($70°F$). Unless a large quantity of evergreens needs to be raised, seeds are best sown in small pots or pans 6–10 cm ($2\frac{1}{4}$–4 in) in diameter. Any of the proprietary seed-sowing composts are suitable or mixtures of equal parts peat, loam and coarse sand; or simply moss peat. Sand and peat-based mixtures should be watered with half-strength liquid feed as soon as the seed is sown and then again when seedlings appear. If pricking off is delayed then full strength liquid feed should be used at 10–14 day intervals.

Home-saved seeds are best sown as soon as ripe; those purchased as soon as received. In either case they should then be placed in a cold frame. The primary exceptions to this are the very small seeds, particularly of members of the *Erica* family, e.g. *Calluna, Erica, Daboecia, Rhododendron*, etc., which often seem to germinate more successfully if placed in a greenhouse or propagating frame with gentle heat, say $13–18°C$ ($55–65°F$). Very small seeds like these are best sown on the surface of the seed compost with perhaps just a light sugaring of sand to hold them in place. Watering must then take place from beneath, the pots or pans placed in a bowl of water and left until the soil surface glistens with imbibed moisture. Thereafter the seeds should be kept humid in a plastic container or bag or closed propagator.

Seeds in berries or similar fleshy fruits should be extracted, if possible, washed in clean water then sown. Large quantities of fleshy fruits are 'stratified' by nurserymen. This means mixing with equal parts sand and soil, or placing layers of fruit and soil alternately in a pot or similar receptacle and keeping outside over winter. The fruits are best bruised first to facilitate rotting. In late winter the mixture is rubbed through a sieve and sown. Seeds from fleshy fruits rarely germinate before the following spring and in some cases a further twelve months will elapse. Delayed germination or dormancy of this sort is not uncommon in hardy plants of all kinds and it pays to keep a seed-pan for at least eighteen months after sowing. Several factors are responsible for seed dormancy including imperviousness to water and chemical inhibitors in the seed coat. Winter rains and the gradual rotting of the seed coat remove these factors. For this reason it is often best to leave the seed pots outside plunged in a soil or sand bed to protect the container from frost. If this is done, a layer of fine gravel or chippings should be placed on the seed-sowing medium to prevent compaction from heavy rain. Temperature also plays a part and the seeds of many hardy plants germinate well only after several weeks or months of low temperatures—0–3°C (32–37°F) is usually adequate—followed by warmer conditions.

Once the seedlings have well-developed seed leaves and the first true leaf is showing they are best pricked off either singly into small pots or spaced out in larger containers. Tiny slow-growing seedlings such as rhododendrons, however, are usually best left until they have several true leaves and this can mean leaving them in the seed-sowing containers for almost a year. Young trees and shrubs can be either potted on into larger containers when the present ones are full of roots or planted out in rows in a nursery or reserve bed to grow on. Either way there is much to be said for planting out into permanent sites as soon as possible. The less the roots are disturbed (and this will inevitably occur each time the plant is moved) the more vigorous and rapid growth will be.

Propagating perennials and alpines

The advice given above on growing from seed applies equally well to perennials and alpines. The general comments on cuttings also apply though the cuttings themselves will usually be shoots or single rosettes from the bases of the plants. More often a method of increase known as division will be easiest or more convenient.

Division

Clump-forming plants such as *Epimedium, Iris, Pulmonaria, Tellima*, etc., can easily be divided. This involves digging up the plant and carefully prizing it apart into two or more pieces. If a clump is big and tough, two forks can be thrust back to back into the centre of it and levered apart. Each division should have several shoots or stems and plenty of root and should be planted immediately.

Other methods

A few evergreen perennials and rock plants have alternative modes of increase. Houseleeks (*Sempervivum*) rosettes produce smaller versions from among the outer leaves. These are known as offsets and may be detached when well grown and either planted direct or potted singly. The soft shield fern, *Polystichum setiferum* 'Acutilobum' produces buds along the midrib of each frond which later develop into plantlets. At this stage the leaf can be either pegged flat *in situ* with forked twigs or hairpins, or detached at the base and similarly pegged into a box of potting soil and kept humid. Once the plantlets have roots of their own they can be cut from the frond and potted singly.

PESTS AND DISEASES

Happily, most evergreens are remarkably free of pests and diseases. The following list outlines the symptoms of the most common problems and suggests controls. When using insecticides and fungicides it is important to follow exactly the makers' instructions; an underdose will probably leave the pest or disease unscathed, and an overdose may damage the plant.

Leaves

Deformed leaves

Slightly or severely deformed leaves are usually the result of damage by aphids (green and blackfly). Aphids are tiny, soft, oval-bodied creatures usually in some shade of green but they can also be yellowish, pinkish or greyish. There are winged and wingless forms. Derris and malathion are effective insecticides to use. If young leaves look somewhat tattered or have irregular holes in addition to being puckered or distorted, capsid bugs are likely to be the culprits. These are fast-moving, small, flattened, greenish, oval, shield-shaped insects which suck the sap and then move on. Where damage is a frequent and regular occurrence spraying at intervals during the period of active growth with HCH (BHC) or fenitrothion is recommended.

Discoloured leaves

Holly, particularly *Ilex aquifolium* is frequently attacked by the holly leaf miner, the maggots of a tiny fly which tunnels within the leaf tissue causing whitish, brown marked, irregular blotches. This seldom affects the vigour of the tree unless very young, but looks unsightly. To reduce attack in future years spray with HCH (BHC) at intervals from late spring to summer.

Dense clusters of tiny soft insects

Young leaves and the undersides of older ones may be infested with aphids; see the entry 'Deformed' above.

Eaten leaves

Pieces eaten out of leaves denotes that a caterpillar or earwig is feeding. If damage is slight, search for the caterpillar and destroy in an approved manner. Earwigs feed only at night but can be trapped in rolls of corrugated cardboard or small containers filled with straw. These must be checked daily and the earwigs killed. Alternatively spray at intervals with HCH (BHC). An irregular but continuous notching of leaf margins, particularly those of rhododendrons is due to the feeding of adult vine and clay-coloured weevils. If damage is severe spray with HCH (BHC).

Mottled leaves

Climbers and shrubs grown on warm, sheltered walls may suffer attacks of red spider mites, minute allies of the spiders which cause a fine, lightish mottling of the upper leaf surface often followed by yellowing and premature falling. At first signs of attack spray with malathion, dimethoate or formothion. If a similar mottling on rhododendron leaves is accompanied by rusty or brown marks on the undersides this is caused by rhododendron bug. If attacks are severe spray with HCH (BHC) in early and mid-summer.

Leaves with scales

Undersides of leaves may be infested with glossy humpback or smaller, flatter, pale brown scale insects; see the entry 'Stems with scales'.

Leaves with sooty film

Sometimes a puzzling blackish film appears on leaves with no obvious cause. Invariably the plants in question are growing beneath trees, in Britain often lime (*Tilia*), which are suffering a severe attack of aphids (see entry 'Deformed', above). Aphids excrete a sugary liquid known as honey dew which gently rains down on the leaves beneath. The sticky layer so formed is then colonized by a minute fungus known as sooty mould. The only cure is to spray the tree above—or to remove the spoiled plant, whichever is easiest! If the sooty patches have a brownish or olive tint and occur on pyracanthas, see 'Fruits with blackish or brownish scales' below.

Leaves spun together

Several leaves may be spun together or individually rolled or folded. In each case a small, usually very wriggly green caterpillar of a tortrix moth will be found. Chemical control is not easy and hand picking and destroying is the most effective control. Forceful spraying with HCH (BHC) or pirimiphos–methyl can be tried.

Withered leaves

If flower and leaf clusters of *Pyracantha* or *Cotoneaster* wither and turn brown, the bacterial disease fireblight can be suspected. This is primarily a disease of apples and pears and in Britain its presence must be reported to a local officer of the Ministry of Agriculture. There is no chemical cure and all infected branches must be cut out and burnt. If the leaves of a branch or branchlet wilt, wither and dry up rather suddenly, then honey fungus is likely to be the cause. See entry below, 'Whole plant'.

Yellowing leaves

The leaves of evergreens do not last for ever—in most cases only from one to a few years. In autumn or late spring as the new leaves grow out, the old ones yellow and fall. If however, the young current season's leaves yellow then the possibility of red spider mite (see the entry 'Mottled' above) or dryness at the roots should be investigated; both troubles are more likely to occur on wall plants.

Stems

Deformed stems

Crippled or deformed stems are often the aftermath of a severe aphid attack; see entry 'Deformed leaves', above. On conifers, particularly the firs, spruces, and pines, crippling is caused by adelgids, close allies

of the aphids but covered by waxy white wool. Some adelgids cause galls, the best-known being pineapple gall on *Picea abies*. This shows in early summer as an ovoid, somewhat pineapple-shaped swelling at the base of the shoot. Later, the individual 'cells' of which the gall is composed open up and the insects emerge. The leaves on the gall turn brown and the damage is then more obvious. If damage is severe spray with HCH (BHC) or malathion on a mild day in early spring.

The so-called artichoke gall of common yew is similar but smaller and more leafy occurring at the tips of the shoots. It is formed by the minute reddish maggots of a gall midge. Young yews may be hand picked and the galls burnt. Large yews can be sprayed at mid-summer and again two weeks later using HCH (BHC).

Dense clusters of tiny soft insects

Shoot and stem tips may be infested with aphids; see entry 'Deformed leaves'.

Seedlings collapsing

Crowded seedlings, particularly those that are thin and drawn are liable to damping-off disease. This withers the base of each seedling stem and it topples over. Water remaining seedlings with captan, zineb or Cheshunt compound. In future, sow seeds more thinly.

Flowers

Dormant flowering buds failing to expand

The plump flowering buds of rhododendron which are formed in autumn and are prominent throughout the winter at the tips of the shoots, may fail to open in spring. If closely examined, the bud is found to be studded with tiny, black, knob-tipped bristles, the spore-bearing bodies of bud blast disease. This fungus can only attack buds via the wounds made by the small, slim, green and red rhododendron leaf hopper and to control the fungus the hoppers must be eliminated. Spray about three times during the late summer or early autumn period with HCH (BHC) or fenitrothion.

Withered flower clusters
Pyracantha and *Cotoneaster* flower clusters and adjacent leaves may wither and turn brown. See the entry 'Withered leaves'.

Fruits

Fruits with brownish or blackish scabs
Pyracanthas are sometimes attacked by pyracantha scab. This shows as dark, or dirty olive-brown or blackish scabby patches on fruits and leaves, rendering them unsightly. At the first signs of this spray at 10–14 day intervals with captan.

Whole plant: sudden death

Occasionally a well grown shrub or small tree dies comparatively suddenly, the leaves withering and wilting without falling. If left, clusters of honey-coloured toadstools appear at the base of the plant giving the disease its name of honey fungus. When dug up the fungus itself is seen as blackish bootlace-like strands which gives the alternative name of bootlace fungus. To prevent these bootlace growths spreading to other plants nearby, the root area of the dead plant should be soaked with a preparation known as Armillotox, or a 2% solution of formalin. If the dead shrub is a *Daphne* the cause of death is less certain. The so-called die-back or sudden death of daphnes appears to be due to a variety of combinative factors, the main ones being: bad drainage, too deep planting, dryness at the root, virus infection and grey mould (*Botrytis*).

Appendix:

Lists of evergreens for particular purposes or with special attributes

1 Leaves with clearly defined silver/white/cream variegation.

2 Leaves with golden-yellow variegation.

3 Leaves with an overall silver, white or cream effect.

4 Coloured leaves: red, purple, pink.

5 Coloured leaves with an overall gold effect

6 Columnar/fastigiate plants.

7 Plants of pendulous habit.

8 Plants with fragrant flowers.

9 Plants with aromatic foliage.

10 Plants which do not thrive in alkaline soils.

11 Plants suitable for limy soils.

12 Plants suitable for heavy shade.

13 Plants suitable for hedge or wind-break.

14 Plants suitable for ground cover.

15 Plants suitable for coastal sites.

1. Leaves with clearly defined silver/ white/ cream variegation

Azara microphylla 'Variegata'
Daphne cneorum 'Variegata'
D. odora 'Aureomarginata'
Euonymus fortunei 'Silver Pillar'
E. f. 'Silver Queen'
E. japonicus macrophyllus 'Albus'
× *Fatshedera lizei* 'Variegata'
Fatsia japonica 'Variegata'
Griselinia littoralis 'Dixon's Cream'
G. l. 'Variegata'
Hebe × *andersonii* 'Variegata'
H. glaucophylla 'Variegata'
Hedera canariensis 'Variegata'
H. colchica 'Variegata'
H. helix 'Glacier'
Hoheria populnea 'Alba Variegata'
Ilex aquifolium 'Argenteomarginata'
I. a. 'Ferox Argentea'
I. a. 'Handsworth New Silver'
I. a. 'Silver Milkboy'
Iris foetidissima 'Variegata'
Lamium maculatum
Osmanthus heterophyllus 'Variegatus'
Pachysandra terminalis 'Variegata'
Phormium tenax 'Variegatum'
Pieris japonica 'Variegata'
Pittosporum tenuifolium 'Garnettii'
Prunus lusitanica 'Variegata'
Rhamnus alaternus 'Argenteo-
  Variegatus'
Ruta graveolens 'Variegata'
Salvia officinalis 'Tricolor'
Sisyrinchium striatum 'Variegatum'
Thujopsis dolabrata 'Variegata'
Viburnum tinus 'Variegatum'

2. Leaves with golden-yellow variegation

Aucuba japonica 'Crotonifolia'
Elaeagnus pungens 'Dicksonii'
E. p. 'Gilt Edge'
E. p. 'Maculata'
Euonymus japonicus 'Aureo Pictus'
E. j. 'Ovatus Aureus'
Hedera helix 'Goldheart'
Ilex × *altaclarensis* 'Golden King'
I. × *a.* 'Lawsoniana'
I. aquifolium 'Aureomarginata'
I. a. 'Ferox Aurea'
I. a. 'Golden Milkboy'
I. a. 'Golden Queen'

I. a. 'Pinto'
Lonicera japonica 'Aureo reticulata'
Phormium tenax 'Veitchii'
Salvia officinalis 'Icterina'
Thuja plicata 'Zebrina'
Vinca major 'Variegata'

3. Leaves with an overall grey, white or cream effect

Abies concolor 'Violacea'
A. pinsapo 'Glauca'
Calluna vulgaris 'Silver Queen'
C. v. 'Sister Ann'
Cassinia vauvillersii albida
Cedrus atlantica 'Glauca'
C. a. 'Pendula Glauca'
Chamaecyparis lawsoniana 'Allumii'
C. l. 'Blue Jacket'
C. l. 'Ellwoodii'
C. l. 'Forsteckensis'
C. l. 'Glauca'
C. nootkatensis 'Glauca'
C. pisifera 'Boulevard'
C. p. 'Squarrosa'
Convolvulus cneorum
Cupressus glabra
C. g. 'Pyramidalis'
Erica tetralix 'Alba Mollis'
Eryngium variifolium
Eucalyptus, several
Hebe albicans
H. allenii
H. glaucophylla 'Variegata'
H. 'Pagei'
H. pimelioides
Helichrysum splendidum
Juniperus chinensis
J. 'Grey Owl'
J. horizontalis 'Bar Harbor'
J. h. 'Douglasii'
J. scopulorum 'Hill's Silver'
J. s. 'Pathfinder'
J. squamata 'Meyeri'
J. virginiana 'Burkii'
J. v. glauca
J. v. 'Skyrocket'
Lamiastrum galeobdolon 'Variegatum'
Lamium maculatum 'Beacon Silver'
Olearia × *mollis*
O. moschata
O. × *scilloniensis*
Phlomis fruticosa
Picea pungens glauca
P. p. 'Hoopsii'

P. p. 'Koster'
Pimelia prostrata
Pinus ayacahuite
P. montezumae
P. pumila
P. wallichiana
Pittosporum tenuifolium 'Silver
  Queen'
Pseudotsuga menziesii 'Glauca'
Santolina
Senecio greyii
S. laxifolius
S. 'Sunshine'
Saxifraga, many encrusted species
Sempervivum arachnoideum
Stachys olympica
Teucrium fruticans
T. polium
Verbascum bombyciferum
V. olympicum
V. thapsiforme

4. Coloured leaves: red, purple, pink

Hoheria populnea 'Purpurea'
Phormium tenax 'Purpureum'
Photinia × *fraseri* 'Birmingham'
P. × *f.* 'Robusta'
P. glabra
P. g. 'Rubens'
P. serrulata
Pieris formosa 'Forrestii'
P. f. 'Jermyns'
P. f. 'Wakehurst'
Pittosporum tenuifolium 'Purpureum'
Pseudowintera colorata
Salvia officinalis 'Purpurea'
Viburnum tinus 'Purpureum'

5. Coloured leaves, with an overall gold effect

Calluna vulgaris 'Gold Haze'
C. v. 'Sunset'
Cedrus deodara 'Aurea'
Chamaecyparis lawsoniana 'Lanei'
C. l. 'Hillieri'
C. l. 'Stewartii'
C. l. 'Winston Churchill'
C. nootkatensis 'Lutea'
C. obtusa 'Crippsii'

*young leaves, chiefly in spring.

C. o. 'Tetragona Aurea'
C. pisifera 'Squarrosa Sulphurea'
Cupressus macrocarpa 'Donard Gold'
C. m. 'Goldcrest'
Euonymus japonicus 'Ovatus Aureus'
Hebe ochracea
Hedera helix 'Buttercup'
Ilex aquifolium 'Flavescens'
I. crenata 'Aureo-Variegata'
I. c. 'Golden Gem'
Juniperus chinensis 'Aurea'
Lonicera nitida 'Baggesen's Gold'
Laurus nobilis 'Aurea'
Pinus sylvestris 'Aurea'
Pittosporum tenuifolium 'Warnham
  Gold'
Taxus baccata 'Dovastonii Aurea'
T. b. 'Elegantissima'
T. b. 'Fastigiata Aurea-marginata'
T. b. 'Standishii'
Thuja occidentalis 'Rheingold'
T. orientalis 'Aurea Nana'
T. plicata 'Stoneham Gold'
Thujopsis dolabrata 'Aurea'

6. Columnar/fastigiate plants

Calocedrus decurrens
Cedrus atlantica 'Fastigiata'
Cephalotaxus harringtonia 'Fastigiata'
Chamaecyparis lawsoniana 'Allumii'
C. l. 'Columnaris'
C. l. 'Ellwoodii'
C. l. 'Fraseri'
C. l. 'Kilmacurragh'
  × Cupressocyparis leylandii
  'Haggerston Grey'
  × C. l. 'Leighton'
  × C. l. 'Naylor's Blue'
Cupressus glabra 'Pyramidalis'
C. sempervirens 'Fastigiata'
C. s. 'Gracilis'
C. s. 'Stricta'
C. s. 'Swaine's Gold'
Juniperus scopulorum 'Hill's Silver'
J. s. 'Pathfinder'
J. virginiana 'Canaertii'
J. v. 'Skyrocket'
Picea omorika
P. pungens 'Koster'
Taxus baccata 'Fastigiata'
T. b. 'Standishii'
T. × media 'Sargentii'

7. Plants of pendulous habit

Cedrus atlantica 'Pendula'
C. a. 'Pendula Glauca'
Chamaecyparis lawsoniana
  'Intertexta'
Ilex aquifolium 'Pendula'
Picea brewerana
P. smithiana
Sequoiadendron giganteum 'Pendulum'
Taxus baccata 'Dovastoniana'

8. Plants with fragrant flowers

Azara lanceolata
A. microphylla
A. petiolaris
Berberis sargentiana
Buxus microphylla
B. suffruticosa
Camellia sasanqua
Choisya ternata
Cistus
Clematis armandii
C. cirrhosa
C. c. balearica
Clethra
Daphne
Decumaria sinensis
Drimys lanceolata
D. winteri
Elaeagnus macrophylla
Holboellia latifolia
Ligustrum
Magnolia delavayi
M. grandiflora
Mahonia japonica
M. × media
Myrtus lechleriana
M. luma
Olearia avicennifolia
O. × haastii
O. ilicifolia
O. macrodonta
O. moschata
O. nummularifolia
Osmanthus
Phillyrea
Prunus lusitinica
Pyracantha
Rosa bracteata
R. wichuraiana
Sarcococca
Skimmia japonica 'Fragrans'
S. j. 'Rubella'

S. laureola
Trachelospermum majus
Viburnum × burkwoodii
V. carlesii
V. utile
Yucca

9. Plants with aromatic foliage

Abies
Chamaecyparis
Calocedrus decurrens
Cistus × cyprius
C. ladanifer
Clethra arborea
Cupressus
Drimys
Escallonia macrantha
E. rubra
Eucalyptus
Gaultheria procumbens
Juniperus
Lavandula spica
Laurus nobilis
Myrtus communis
Olearia ilicifolia
O. × mollis
O. moschata
Picea
Pseudotsuga
Rhododendron, some
Rosmarinus
Ruta
Salvia
Santolina
Skimmia
Thuja plicata
Umbellularia

10. Plants which do not thrive in alkaline soils

Abies balsamea
A. magnifica
A. procera
A. veitchii
Arbutus menziesii
Arcterica nana
Arctostaphylos
Asteranthera ovata
Berberis empetrifolia
B. hypokerina
Blechnum penna-marina
B. spicant
Calluna

Camellia
Cassiope
Chamaecyparis thyoides
Clethra arborea
Crinodendron hookerianum
Daboecia
Desfontainea spinosa
Embothrium coccineum
Epigaea asiatica
Erica (except those on list 11)
Eucryphia
Gaultheria
Ilex glabra
I. opaca
I. pedunculosa
Leucothoe
Mitraria
Pernettya
× Philageria veitchii
Philesia magellanica
Phyllodoce
Pieris
Pinus densiflora
P. pumila
P. radiata
Podocarpus macrophyllum
Pseudotsuga menziesii
Rhododendron (almost all)
Rubus parvus
Sciadopitys verticillata
Trochodendron aralioides
Tsuga heterophylla
Vaccinium

Hebe (most)
Helichrysum
Helleborus
Hypericum calycinum
Iberis
Ilex aquifolium
Juniperus communis
J. × media
Lamiastrum
Lamium
Lavandula
Lonicera
Mahonia aquifolium
Olearia
Phillyrea
Photinia
Pinus mugo
P. nigra
P. sylvestris
Rosmarinus
Rubus tricolor
Salvia
Sarcoccoca
Senecio
Taxus baccata
Teucrium
Thuja occidentalis
T. plicata
Thujopsis dolabrata
Thymus
Viburnum × rhytidophylloides
V. rhytidophyllum

Gaultheria
Hedera
Helleborus
Hypericum calycinum
Ilex × altaclarensis
I. aquifolium
Iris foetidissima
Lamiastrum galeobdolon 'Variegatun
Leucothoe fontanesiana
Ligustrum henryi
L. japonicum
Lonicera pileata
Luzula sylvatica
Mahonia aquifolium
Mitchella repens
Pachysandra
Pachystima
Pileostegia
Polypodium
Polystichum
Prunus laurocerasus
Pseudowintera
Pulmonaria
Rubus tricolor
Ruscus
Sarcococca
Skimmia
Taxus
Tellima
Tiarella
Tolmiea
Viburnum × pragense
V. utile
Vinca
Viola

11. Plants suitable for limy soils

Abutilon vitifolium
Alyssum
Arabis
Aubrieta
Berberis (except empetrifolia and hypokerina)
Buxus sempervirens
Ceanothus
Cistus
Cotoneaster
Epimedium
Erica carnea
E. × darleyensis
E. erigena
E. terminalis
Euonymus
Euphorbia characias
E. c. wulfenii
Globularia

12. Plants suitable for deep shade

Asarum
Asplenium
Aucuba japonica
Berberidopsis
Bergenia
Blechnum
Buxus sempervirens
Camellia japonica
C. × williamsii
Cephalotaxus
Danae racemosa
Daphne laureola
D. pontica
Decumaria
Dryopteris
Elaeagnus
Epigaea
Euonymus fortunei
Euphorbia robbiae
Galax

13. Plants suitable for hedge or wind-break

Berberis × bristolensis
B. darwinii
B. julianae
B. × stenophylla
Buxus microphylla
B. sempervirens
Chamaecyparis lawsoniana
Cotoneaster lacteus
× Cupressocyparis leylandii
Elaeagnus (most)
Escallonia (most)
Ilex × altaclarensis
I. aquifolium
I. cornuta 'Burfordii'
I. crenata
I. c. 'Convexa'
Laurus nobilis

Lavandula spica
Ligustrum ovalifolium
Lonicera nitida
Olearia avicenniifolia
O. × haastii
Osmanthus heterophyllus
Phillyrea, all
Pittosporum crassifolium
P. tenuifolium
Prunus laurocerasus
P. lusitanicus
Quercus ilex
Rhamnus alaternus
Taxus baccata
T. × media
Thuja plicata
Tsuga heterophylla
Viburnum × rhytidophylloides
V. tinus

14. Plants suitable for ground cover

Acaena
Ajuga
Alyssum
Arabis
Arctostaphylos
Asarum
Aubrieta
Bergenia
Calluna
Ceanothus thyrsiflorus repens
Cephalotaxus harringtonia 'Prostrata'
Cotoneaster congestus
C. conspicuus 'Decorus'
C. dammeri
C. d. radicans
C. microphyllus
C. m. cochleatus
C. salicifolius 'Parkteppich'
C. s. 'Repens'
C. 'Skogholm'
Daboecia
Danae racemosa
Erica
Euonymus fortunei
E. f. 'Kewensis'

E. f. 'Minimus'
E. f. radicans
E. f. 'Vegetus'
Euphorbia robbiae
Fragaria indica
Galax
Gaultheria
Hebe
Hedera
Juniperus communis 'Hornibrookii'
J. c. 'Depressa'
J. c. 'Repanda'
J. conferta
J. horizontalis
J. h. 'Bar Harbor'
J. h. 'Douglasii'
J. sabina tamariscifolia
J. scopulorum repens
Lamiastrum galeobdolon
Lamium maculatum
Leucothoe fontanesiana
Lonicera pileata
Mahonia aquifolium
M. repens
Mitchella repens
Pachistima canbyi
P. myrsinites
Pachysandra terminalis
Pernettya prostrata
Petasites fragrans
Prunus laurocerasus 'Otto Luyken'
P. l. 'Schipkaensis'
P. l. 'Zabeliana'
Pulmonaria
Rubus calycinoides
R. tricolor
Ruscus
Sequoia sempervirens 'Prostrata'
Stachys olympica
Stranvaesia davidiana 'Prostrata'
Tellima
Thymus
Tiarella
Tolmiea
Vaccinium
Viburnum davidii
Vinca
Waldsteinia ternata

15. Plants suitable for coastal sites

Arbutus unedo
Bupleurum fruticosum
Cassinia fulvida
C. vauvilliersii
Chamaerops humilis
Choisya ternata
× Cupressocyparis leylandii
Cupressus macrocarpa
Elaeagnus, all
Escallonia, all
Eucalyptus, most
Euonymus fortunei
E. japonica
× Fatshedera lizei
Fatsia japonica
Garrya elliptica
Griselinia littoralis
Hebe, all
Helichrysum
Ilex × altaclarensis
I. aquifolium
Juniperus communis
J. horizontalis
Laurus nobilis
Lavandula spica
Lonicera pileata
Olearia, all
Phillyrea, all
Phlomis, all
Phormium
Pinus mugo
P. pinea
P. radiata
Pittosporum
Pyracantha
Quercus ilex
Q. suber
Rhamnus alaternus
Rosmarinus
Santolina
Senecio
Viburnum tinus
Yucca filamentosa
Y. flaccida

Index

Prefatory note

The numbers in parentheses that follow plant names denote the amount of cold they can stand. Each number relates to a zone of the Earth where the average absolute minimum temperatures* (given in the zone table) can be expected in winter. This zonation and its numbering was first worked out in the U.S.A. and has been followed through to include Europe. It can only be considered to give an approximate hardiness rating. Although low temperatures are of great importance, ancillary factors also must be considered, such as the duration of a cold spell, whether conditions are still or windy and whether cold was experienced gradually to allow acclimatization, or suddenly. The amount of summer sun and general warmth a plant received prior to winter must also be taken into account, as well as the degree of shelter afforded to the plants by larger plants, walls, fences and the general lie of the land.

* This is an average of the single lowest temperature for each winter over a period of about 20 years. Britain falls largely into zone 8.

Table of Zone Numbers

Zone No.	Temperature
1	below $-46°C$ (below $-50°F$)
2	-46 to $-40°C$ (-50 to $-40°F$)
3	-40 to $-34°C$ (-40 to $-30°F$)
4	-34 to $-29°C$ (-30 to $-20°F$)
5	-29 to $-23°C$ (-20 to $-10°F$)
6	-23 to $-18°C$ (-10 to $0°F$)
7	-18 to $-12°C$ (0 to $10°F$)
8	-12 to $-7°C$ (10 to $20°F$)
9	-7 to $-1°C$ (20 to $30°F$)
10	-1 to $4°C$ (30 to $40°F$)

Page numbers in italic denote line drawings; page numbers in bold denote colour photographs.